Political Socialization
of Chicano Children

F. Chris Garcia

The Praeger Special Studies program—utilizing the most modern and efficient book production techniques and a selective worldwide distribution network—makes available to the academic, government, and business communities significant, timely research in U.S. and international economic, social, and political development.

Political Socialization of Chicano Children
A Comparative Study with Anglos in California Schools

Praeger Publishers   New York   Washington   London

PRAEGER SPECIAL STUDIES IN U.S. ECONOMIC, SOCIAL, AND POLITICAL ISSUES

Library of Congress Cataloging in Publication Data

Garcia, F   Chris
    Political socialization of Chicano children.

    (Praeger special studies in U. S. economic,
social, and political issues)
    Bibliography: p.
    1. Mexican Americans—California.
2. Children and politics.   I.   Title.
F870. M5G37   301. 5'92   72-12973

PRAEGER PUBLISHERS
111 Fourth Avenue, New York, N.Y. 10003, U.S.A.
5, Cromwell Place, London SW7 2JL, England

Published in the United States of America in 1973
by Praeger Publishers, Inc.

Printed in the United States of America

ACKNOWLEDGMENTS

The successful conclusion of a survey research project such as this requires the cooperation, diligence, and goodwill of many. Of much assistance to me throughout this undertaking were four individuals. Edmond Costantini, Alvin Sokolow, and Lou Weschler offered their expert knowledge and guidance from the initial conception and design of this project through the final revision of the manuscript. Any shortcomings in the final product may be due to not following their advice more closely and are wholly the responsibility of the author. Most of all I am indebted to my wife Sandra, not only for her tolerance, understanding, and encouragement in her role as a writer's wife but also for her meticulous technical assistance as illustrator, typist, and proofreader.

Several education officials considered this study sufficiently worthwhile to offer their support. Fred Gunsky of the Bureau of Intergroup Relations, California State Department of Education, and his fine secretary, Dorothy Fisher, went out of their way to make available to me some much needed data. Public school principals Royden Cartwright, Richard Pulice, Ted Restovich, and Lorenzo Sandoval kindly offered their time and assistance in administering the survey in their east Los Angeles County schools, as did the principals of sample schools in northern California, especially Clarence Depew. A special note of gratitude must be extended to Robert Derania, superintendent of schools in a northern California district, for his unwavering backing through sometimes difficult circumstances in his community.

One of the keys to the success of survey research lies with the "front line" personnel--the interviewers--and I was very fortunate in securing some highly competent and motivated people including Diedere Butler, Jane Gonzales, Isabel Hansen, Beverly Johnson, Sara Krauthamer, Gloria Leyva, and Connie Walker.

The considerable expense associated with this investigation was defrayed by a stipend from the Chancellor's Patent Fund, University of California at Davis, and by a grant from the Ford Foundation.

Most of the computer manipulation and analysis of data was accomplished at the Computing Center, University of New

Mexico. The patience and perseverance of program application personnel Ken Friedenbach, Roberto Duffy, and Fred Springer were greatly appreciated. And a more skilled and conscientious typing of the final draft than that produced by Donna Hines would be impossible.

The encouragement of Richard Rowson and the expert editorial advice of John Gedeist, both of Praeger Publishers, ultimately were the key factors in making the production of this book possible.

Finally, I must gratefully acknowledge the subject-participants of this study--the schoolchildren whose sincerity, openness, and enthusiasm were a continual source of delight and inspiration.

CONTENTS

LIST OF TABLES

LIST OF FIGURES

Political Socialization
of Chicano Children

POLITICAL SOCIALIZATION, SYSTEM SUPPORT, AND CHICANOS

INTRODUCTION

Has the turbulent history of ethnic group relations in the United States had a significant effect on the political attitudes of Americans of Mexican-Spanish ancestry? Does the Chicano child have a fundamentally different orientation toward the political system than does his "Anglo" counterpart?* If so, what implications might this distinctive socialization have for the functioning of the American political system? This study will suggest some answers to these questions through examination of the political orientations of Mexican-American children and comparison with the attitudes of their "core culture" peers. However, not all political attitudes will be investigated; this research is concerned only with those political orientations germane to support of the American political system.[1]

Research into the political orientations of these minority group children not only will indicate the degree of their induction into the American political culture[2] but also may provide some clues as to the future stability

---

*Although there continues to be a debate over the proper label for the American of Mexican-Spanish ancestry, with much significance attached to the connotations of each name, we will use most of the names--Chicano, Mexican American, Raza, and others--interchangeably. "Anglo" is the term used in the American Southwest to refer to all who are not Chicano, not Indian, and not black.

and viability of the American political system.* That
this is so will be clarified by the following discussion
of the major concepts involved in a study of the political
socialization of Mexican-American children with regard to
their support of this political system.

THE IMPORTANCE OF ETHNICITY
AS A POLITICAL VARIABLE

One of the most formidable problems that has confronted
the United States throughout its history has been the task
of creating a cohesive national entity from the conglomer-
ation of various ethnic groups within its boundaries.**
While immigrants from European countries have been accepted,
with varying degrees of difficulty, into the American mainstream, "colored" peoples of non-European ancestry have
largely been rejected. Discrimination against Americans of
African, Oriental, Mexican, and American Indian ancestry
has been the historical rule, even to the extent of its
codification in statutes. This "American Dilemma"[3] between
the democratic value of equality and the reality of discriminatory practices was a major cause of the greatest
political conflict yet to occur in American history, the
Civil War, and recent civil disturbances suggest that the
end of conflict over this situation is not yet in sight.
Where ethnic-based conflicts have not been manifested in
physical violence, they often have taken the form of more
ostensibly political activities ranging from participation
in electoral politics to boycotts, marches, and demonstrations.

Political activity by groups based on ethnicity is
nothing new in the United States. Ethnicity has been a
major and persistent factor in American politics from at
least the writing of the Declaration of Independence to
the present.[4] People tend to see themselves and are seen
by others as members of social groups. Social group mem-
berships become politically important when they affect the
political orientation of the individuals identified with
them. Since racial and ethnic divisions are among the
most salient in American society, ethnicity is an attribute with important political consequences.[5]

---

*Stability is taken to mean the absence of drastic, and
particularly violent, change.
**The word "ethnic" is used to mean race, religion,
and/or national origin.

4

Historically, ethnic political activities have largely taken the form of local electoral politics. Various national-origin groups have had a fair measure of success working within the established political system.[6] Many areas of the United States have come to be dominated by ethnic blocs wielding substantial political power at the state or local level.[7] Except for the inroads made during the Reconstruction period, however, nonwhite minority groups have wielded very little power. Recently, blacks have been able to capture a few political offices.[8] These successes have only come after, and perhaps as a result of, great turmoil, including urban riots that resulted in substantial destruction of life and property.

Fortunately, these kinds of disturbance are an exception rather than the standard method of representing a group's needs and demands to those whose decisions result in the authoritative allocation of resources in a polity. However, some degree of conflict is inevitable in the political decision-making process. In fact, conflict may be the essence of the political process. While some persons see conflict as not only unavoidable but actually beneficial to a society,[9] almost everyone would agree that it is undesirable to have a high level of conflict involving large proportions of the population and resulting in extensive human casualties. Many would hold that conflict should not be so severe as to destroy the political system; in fact order and stability* probably are valued by most of the American public.[10] The stress on the political system produced by ethnic group demands has drawn mainly unfavorable reaction from the American citizenry.

An interest in the stability of the American political system leads one to inquire as to what variables are related to the condition.

David Easton's formulation of diffuse support provides a theoretical concept that can be utilized to examine the

---

*Although one concern of this study is the future stability of the American political system, this should not be interpreted to mean that the author deems stability to be of overarching importance. Indeed, given the existence of great gaps between the promise and the accomplishments of American democracy, particularly in the area of minority civil rights, the author feels that a view of stability as an ultimate goal can obstruct the attainment of ethnic equality.

conditions of stability and change.* This study will seek
to make some statements about conflict and consensus in
America by comparing the patterns of diffuse support for
the political system exhibited by Mexican- and Anglo-American children. It may be that the high level of ethnic
conflict in this country is based partially on a major
disagreement between ethnic and racial groups over the
very nature of the political foundations of society and
not merely on their differential reactions, within a basic
consensus, to the allocation of goods. An examination of
Easton's theoretical conceptualization of the political
system is thus in order. Only a brief discussion of this
theory will be presented here; a complete and complex
presentation of his ideas may be found in several of his
works.[11]

THE POLITICAL SYSTEM

Easton sees the political system basically as a relationship between three major components: inputs, outputs,
and the conversion process. Any system must maintain an
equilibrium among its related parts and its environment if
it is to survive over time. Although at times the system
may be in a state of disequilibrium, it eventually must ad-
just to the stresses causing imbalance; continued stress,
unsuccessfully countered, will lead to the disintegration
of a system. Inputs are of two major types: (1) demands
that members may make upon the political system and (2)
support, such as taxes, that members must contribute in order that the system be maintained. The system's political
structures convert the demands into binding decisions, or
policy outcomes.

Stress may stem from several sources. For example,
output stress may result from the failure of the politically
relevant members of a system to accept the policy outcomes
as authoritative and binding. Unless the decisions of the
political authorities are considered legitimate, a society
quickly may be reduced to chaos. Socialization can be one
mechanism to prepare a system's new members to accept the

---

*Briefly defined, diffuse support is the unconditional
backing of a political system by its members irrespective
of specific system performance.

rulings of political officials.* On the input side of the
model, stress could be the result of excessive demands by
the populace that would overload the communications and
processing structures. Here, "proper" socialization might
lead to a sense of self-restraint on members that would
limit the quantity and shape the quality of these wants.
Stress also may arise from the inability of a system to
keep the input of support at some minimal level. Support
may be defined as "feelings of trust, confidence, or affection, and their opposites, that persons may direct to some
object."[12] Both positive and negative aspects of support
are important. If positive, a person favors an object;
if negative, his favor is replaced by feelings of hostility.
Feelings of support for a system usually are selective or
differentiated and not directed at all aspects of the system.

Major Structural Components

In order to analyze more carefully the objects of
support, the political system may be broken into three components: (1) the political community, (2) the regime, and
(3) the authorities. Major sources of system stress may
result from the lessening of support toward any one of
these objects. The political community is seen as "that
aspect of a political system that we can identify as a
collection of persons who share a division of political
labor."[13] Any individual may be only minimally active in
this labor to the extent of only cooperating with others
with whom he identifies in accepting binding decisions.
Such a political community, then, is any group of persons
who share mutual ties that give them a sense of identification with one another and a feeling of distinctiveness
along some common dimension. In speaking of political communities, we generally refer to the nation-state as the
highest order of this genus. Thus a citizen of a territory
called Mexico will feel that he is a Mexican and not an
American or Britisher. Since this is of such an elemental
nature, it is not surprising that a high priority is given
to socializing the child to feel a part of a particular
nation, distinct from others. In this country, the United
States is held forth as the highest entity with which one

---

*Briefly, socialization is the learning of a society's
values; the concept is discussed at length below.

7

may be associated, and "un-American" objects are to be eschewed. Obviously if a person feels estranged from his political community, i.e., feels closer to another nation or subculture, his positive feelings of support toward the former probably will be correspondingly reduced.

The regime is described as follows:

> That part of the political system that we call its constitutional order in the very broadest sense of the term. It refers to the underlying goals that the members of the system pursue, the norms or rules of the game through which they conduct their political business, and the formal and informal structures of authority that arrange who is to do what in the system.[14]

Easton's regime is equated with the entire constitutional system, including the structure of government and the values and norms guiding its conduct. Support for the regime can be equated with a sense of its legitimacy. A feeling of legitimacy among its members is perhaps the most basic means a regime has in assuring that its decisions are accepted. Coercion and intimidation also can be used, but the political costs would be quite high and difficult to sustain over a long period of time in the face of widespread opposition. Voluntary and willing compliance is more efficient. For this reason, all governments attempt to inculcate among their younger members attitudes supportive of their regimes, i.e., to socialize them toward believing the regime is legitimate.

The political authorities constitute the third component of input support. These are the "members of a system in whom the primary responsibility is lodged for taking care of the daily routines of a political system."[15] These, then, are the actual occupants of the seats of political authority, the elected office-holders, appointed officials, or public bureaucrats. System members must be willing to accept these positions and also to serve in good faith, or else must be at least neutrally disposed toward those who do fill these positions. When support for any or all of these three major components drops below a certain level, the system will experience stress. If stress is not alleviated through system adjustments, the ultimate result could be the system's failure or, minimally, a major modification of one component's functioning.

Thus it is necessary that any system seeking persistence attempt to instill feelings of support among its mem-

bers. In addition to those physical resources necessary
for a system's continuation--e.g., taxes--the system must
contain members possessing at least a minimal level of
trust, affection, or confidence in the system, or part of
the system. Such support may be classified conveniently
into two types: specific and diffuse.

Specific and Diffuse Support

Members of the system vary in their satisfaction with
its performance outputs. As long as their satisfaction
with system performance balances out the costs of maintaining membership in that system, specific support will be extended to it. However, if disaffection or dissatisfaction
with policy outputs increases due to performance falling
below a certain level of citizen expectation, stress on
the system could result. Although at first criticism would
most likely be leveled against particular public authorities or policies, continued dissatisfaction and grievances
might spill over to the regime in general. If changes in
the regime fail to alleviate the negative support directed
toward it, the result could be disaffection toward the political community.[16] Individuals might feel no attachment
to other persons in the system, and this could lead to serious alienation and division within the community. When
this lack of solidarity becomes strong enough, dissatisfied
groups or individuals will disclaim membership in the system and claim allegiance to another existing system or
even create a separatist movement.

Such stressful negative sentiments need not inevitably
lead to the system's destruction. Discontented members
may not have the resources or the will to activate their
feelings. Also, many other compensating mechanisms may be
brought into play to alleviate the stress of increasing
dissatisfaction. Yet if sufficient numbers of politically
relevant or significant members of a system lose confidence
in its basic components, stress inevitably will be manifested in some form. Then the system might persist only
because of an additional kind of support--diffuse support.

Diffuse support serves as a second line of defense
against stress in a system. Diffuse support is defined as
"the generalized trust and confidence that members invest
in the various objects of the system as ends in themselves."[17] This support is not based on any particular ex-
change of system performance for individual member support.
It is offered unconditionally--independent of system per-

formance. This reservoir of goodwill toward the general
system allows it to survive in times of dissatisfaction
and even in the face of a lack of specific support. Thus
a great addition is made to the system side of the individual's calculus when balancing the hardships and depriva-
tions he may be called upon to undergo against the benefits
deriving from membership. In addition, diffuse support
may provide a common bond between various constituent
groups who are competing fiercely over the allocation of
goods within a polity. Groups may moderate their demands
in order to preserve the system they have been conditioned
to accept through the mechanism of diffuse support.

It is not necessary that all members have equally high
levels of diffuse support for systems to continue. But
for some kind of system to persist even though its com-
ponents--authorities, regime, or community--may change,
most of the politically relevant members must possess a
minimal level of diffuse support for the political system.
This allows the system to hedge against breakdown because
of its failure in obtaining support through satisfaction
of specific demands and needs. Of course, when both specific and diffuse support fall below some minimal level,
the system is in serious trouble.

Support Through Socialization

The importance of the existence of supportive attitudes
among a system's membership means that the formation of
these orientations cannot be left to chance. All societies
seeking to ensure their stability and survival must make a
determined effort to convince their citizens that their
political systems are legitimate, i.e., that constituted
authority should be obeyed.

One universal means of creating this loyalty to and
acceptance of the political system is through socialization
processes. Through various agencies the political system
inculcates supportive consensual attitudes in its members.
We know that totalitarian systems "indoctrinate" their
young into the "party line," as has occurred in the party-
controlled schools of Nazi Germany and Communist Russia.
And in the United States much is made of the school's role
in "citizenship training" and civic education so that the
individual will be able to function appropriately in a
democracy. Although these socializing processes are seen
as indoctrination through propaganda when carried out by
inimical foreign nations and simply as the instilling of

patriotism through education in America, functionally all serve the same purpose of bolstering citizen support for the system.

Richard Dawson and Kenneth Prewitt state that "most nations do not really permit the citizen's sense of obligation to be contingent. . . . political socialization mechanisms replace fear or purchase as a way of maintaining citizenship loyalty."[18] Socialization is seen as particularly important in fragmented societies where many diverse groupings may tend to weaken the bonds between the individual and the larger society. In fact, Dawson and Prewitt state that the extent to which a society is consensual rather than having a fragmented political culture greatly affects its political functioning and stability. Since the United States is foremost a nation of immigrants from many diverse cultures, this observation may be particularly applicable. People of varying cultures are bound to transmit differing attitudes, beliefs, and behavioral norms congruent with the unique mores and customs of each group. And subgroups that maintain or represent significant subcultural variations are most likely to impress their differences in childhood.[19] As Richard M. Merelman has observed:

It is a mistake to believe that the levels of legitimacy which a government enjoys are equally distributed throughout a society. We would expect that the response to symbols of legitimacy will be lower the more deprived the subgroup.[20]

And Dawson and Prewitt caution that the "tendency for emotional attachments to subgroups to overlap nascent political awareness is one factor that makes for explosive political conflict in the adult political world."[21] Thus a severely fragmented political culture may result, a situation that would significantly affect political functioning and stability.

This is not to say that the American polity must force a consensus on all political orientations and cultural assumptions by every member of the system in order that a common regime be supported. It is neither probable nor desirable that all individual and group variations be submerged in one melting pot, social or political. Variety in customs, perceptions, and behavior is conducive to individual self-development as well as necessary for the system flexibility needed to cope with change. What is required, however, is a basic consensus among politically significant members over a society's fundamental political arrangements. Most essential from a system viewpoint would be the inculcation of general supportive orientations toward the political community, the regime, and, to a lesser extent, its authorities. Socialization is one of the major methods through which this building of diffuse support is attempted. In fact, it may be the system's major attempt to generate positive support for those basic political objects without which a system could not operate.

SOCIALIZATION: DEFINITIONS
AND LITERATURE

Although the general ideal of what constitutes socialization is easy to grasp, every writer on the subject seems to favor creating his own definition of this universal social process.[22]

And the great variety in definitions of the general socialization process has been matched by scholars concerned with its specifically political applications. For example, Gerald Bender has relayed ten definitions of the term and added one of his own: "a process through which the individual internalizes politically relevant attitudes, beliefs, cognitions and values."[23] Each writer on political socialization in turn has added his own definitive modification.

Fred Greenstein has attempted to divert this nonproductive trend through two steps. First, he offers a thorough and encyclopedic definition that leaves little room for addition:

> All political learning, formal and informal, deliberate and unplanned, at every stage of the life cycle, including not only explicitly political learning but also nominally non-political learning of politically relevant social attitudes and the acquisition of politically relevant personality characteristics.[24]

Second, Greenstein advocates another objective:

> There is little to be said for attempting to establish an orthodox usage of the term [political socialization]: the main thing is to be clear about one's meaning in particular contexts and to get on with the task of enunciating theoretically interesting hypotheses and testing them.[25]

12

Since Easton's theoretical framework is employed in this study, his succinct definition--"those developmental processes through which persons acquire political orientations and patterns of behavior"[26]--will suffice for the purposes of our presentation. It is particularly appropriate for use in research on the socialization of a subculture whose values are hypothesized to vary from those of the core culture since it implies neither the existence of only a single socialization process nor a set of acceptable norms and behavior.

Studies of socialization per se have developed within the last 40 years and have been primarily the domain of psychologists, sociologists, and anthropologists.[27] Even though the term political socialization is of quite recent vintage--Greenstein tells us the phrase first appeared in print in 1954[28]--students of politics have long been interested in citizen acquisition of orientations toward political authority. For example, Plato was greatly concerned with the political education of citizens toward the good of his Republic. But political scientists renewed their interest in the political aspects of socialization only a little over a decade ago. The major stimulus for this revival was the publication in 1959 of Political Socialization by the sociologist Herbert Hyman.[29] The work is essentially a synthesis of various findings in fields other than political science about political activity as learned behavior. Although from today's viewpoint Hyman's work can be criticized as lacking a conceptual framework, it served the important function of calling attention to an important problem in political inquiry and reviewing the rather limited research in this area up to that time.

The first book based on empirical field research by a political scientist was Greenstein's study of over 600 fourth- through eighth-grade children in New Haven, Connecticut.[30] He discovered that political learning begins surprisingly early and that this informal education is strongly supportive of the political system. The child begins his entrance into the political world through his awareness of a few outstanding governmental authorities, particularly the President. The affective responses to political authorities were warm and positive.

Four years later, the first of two books based on a nationwide sample of 12,000 schoolchildren largely supported and expanded Greenstein's findings.[31] However, Robert D. Hess and Judith V. Torney contend that the school, rather than the family, is the most influential determinant of children's political attitudes. Kenneth P. Langton's

13

research, focusing mainly on the effects of various socializing agents on the orientations of American and Ja-
maican high school students, contends that the family is
the most important political influence on children but that
such other factors as inter-familial relationships, various
school situations, and peer group pressures substantially
modify the family's overall impact.[32]

Just ten years after Hyman's effort at synthesizing
the then existing resource on political socialization,
Dawson and Prewitt attempted "to draw together divergent
and still inconclusive data about political socialization."[33]
After reviewing the findings on the content, processes,
and agents of political socialization, the authors stated
that although it was still premature to suggest a theory
of political socialization they could propose an "ideal-
type summary statement" that seeks to link the product of
political socialization--political orientations--with processes, chronological patterns of political maturation,
and socializing agents. The result is their developmental
cycle or profile, which the authors term "the most significant point we offer in this essay." This pattern pro-
gresses from an initial situation in which the child learns
his most basic attitudes while in the role of a subordinate
recipient of values; next he adds specific content and
more information while maturing toward an equal social
status; finally the individual "tests reality" by means of
his more direct experiences with the political world.

Perhaps the most theoretically and analytically sophisticated contribution yet to emerge from the explosion
of recent research on political socialization is the second book based on the comprehensive University of Chicago
survey of the early 1960s.[34] Whereas Hess and Torney analyzed the nationwide data primarily from a psychologist's
interest in child development, Dennis and Easton focus on
its relevance to the functioning of political systems. In
developing their "political theory of political socialization," the authors hypothesize that stress, which may
threaten the persistence of a political system, is amelio-
rated by that system's support among citizens who feel
trust, confidence, and affection for it.

The combination of a general political theory--that
of system politics--and exhaustive empirical research provides perhaps the most thorough product of political socialization research to date. The bulk of the research
shows how the child first develops political awareness
through "personalization," the attribution of human characteristics to institutions, and how this early positive sup-

port for particular persons, or "idealization," develops
into a more diffuse support for governmental institutions,
or "institutionalization." This positive orientation
toward the American governmental system (or at least its
authorities and institutions) is seen as a major reason
for the stability (or persistence) of this system.

Subcultural Variations

One striking feature of published research on American
political socialization is the dearth of studies dealing
with subcultural variation within the United States. Many
researchers have been cognizant of this state of affairs,
but until recently little or no work was done to fill this
gap.[35] Hyman's inventory includes no research on minority
group socialization; Greenstein, while classifying the
ethnic composition of his research sample, does not employ
ethnicity in analyzing his data.[36] While confirming the
desirability of cross-national research and varying "social
and political contexts," he mentions particularly divergent
political subsystem characteristics (such as state legislative system characteristics and party strength), rather
than ethnicity, as major "independent" variables. Langton
is concerned with cross-national comparisons between Ja-
maican and U.S. secondary school students and fails to concern himself much with subcultural variations within one
polity. However, he does discuss the differential effect
of the civics curriculum on blacks vis-à-vis whites.[37]
Concerned with the relationship of political socialization
to the political culture, Dawson and Prewitt do hint that
"geographic isolates," such as American Indians and blacks,
are likely to develop a political culture quite unlike the
dominant one, and even remark that "the problem associated
with distinct subcultures . . . [is] well illustrated by
the urban riots in the United States."[38] But not much
more is said of U.S. subcultural variations. After reviewing the literature of the last decade, Dawson and Prewitt
list "some little understood aspects" of political socialization, one of which is the "considerable variation among
cultural groups within the same nation." They continue:

> Patterns of political learning are not alike for
> all population groups (within one nation). Some
> groups experience political socialization in
> forms quite different from others. It is not
> possible to list, or even suggest, all these sub-

group variations. The reader should be aware
that examples or statements pertaining to any
given nation often overlook considerable variation among population subgrouping. . . . A
comprehensive theory of political socialization
must be sensitive to such variations.[39]

Nor has the University of Chicago group done much
with ethnicity as a major socialization factor. In their
first report's chapter on "Method of Study," a paragraph
on ethnicity as an independent variable explains that the
project was designed to "establish a base line of socialization" by examining the "most characteristic" forms of
political socialization in the United States. Therefore,
"it was decided to defer consideration of subcultural
groups in which political socialization might differ from
the dominant culture."[40] City neighborhoods lacking large
ethnic minority populations were purposely selected. A
footnote explains that data from 269 Mexican, Oriental, and
black children were collected as part of the larger sample
but that analysis of this data would be deferred to a later
time.[41]

In the later book, Easton and Dennis report that they
have analyzed but will not report the effects of race and
nationality as independent variables. Stressing the limited and atypical nature of their ethnic sample (274 non-
whites from mostly white neighborhoods in large cities),
they find "only a few, very small and nonsystematic differences between such children and our white or native-born
children."[42] It is admitted that greater subcultural
variety might produce greater divergences.[43] Data is lacking on "some groups in which political socialization might
be proceeding at a very different pace and in which less
awareness of and less positive affect for the political
authorities might be present."[44] Minority group children
were excluded due to economy and feasibility: "Black or
other major distinctive ethnic groups, such as the Spanish-
American, would have required special instruments and different testers."[45]

Although missing from the larger studies, there have
been a few articles and unpublished works concerned with
race or ethnicity as important socialization variables, although a small but rapidly growing body of research on the
political socialization of American blacks does exist.[46]
In general, surveys of African-American children have demonstrated that initially they have quite positive attitudes
toward the American political system, but, as they mature

16

and experience the effects of racial discrimination, they become increasingly alienated psychologically. Highly idealized images of political authorities undergo severe deterioration; feelings of cynicism and low political efficiency are more predominant than among whites.

Although the results of black and white socialization experiences exhibit significant differences, the specific mechanisms involved in the differential socializing process are not yet understood. It is apparent that the subordinate status of this ethnic subculture is a powerful factor in shaping its political orientations.

CHICANOS AND THE POLITICAL SYSTEM

If there exists only a relatively small number of socialization studies on American blacks--this country's largest and most visible minority--it could be deduced that other nonwhite minority groups have received even less attention. In fact, as of 1972 there existed no published studies of the political socialization of Mexican Americans,* native American Indians, or Asian Americans in the United States. As mentioned, this is a serious gap in knowledge in the area of political socialization.

Moreover, there is a severe shortage of published works on any aspect of the politics of Spanish-speaking people in the United States, although at present several studies are in progress. A new period of interest in the nation's second largest minority and its political activities seems to have been ushered in, largely because of the activities of Mexican Americans in several areas of the West and Southwest.

Although Mexican Americans have participated to some degree in system politics, they have not done so in proportion to their numbers for several reasons. Largely due to their economic subordination, Chicanos are disproportionately in the lower socioeconomic classes of American society.[47] In California, the site of this study, the median family income is $8,791 for Chicanos compared to $10,969 for whites. Fourteen percent of Spanish-speaking families in the state have incomes below the poverty level,

---

*Although members of this group technically are classified as Caucasian (white), their generally darker skin color has evoked a nonwhite designation from many Anglo Americans.

17

while 7.5 percent of white families fall below that line. The median number of school years completed by white Californians is 12.5; Chicanos average 10.6 years of formal education.[48] Of course, persons of low income and educational level are in general less active in politics than those in higher socioeconomic positions.

Chicanos also speak a language that generally has not been accepted in American politics. In fact, with the exception of New Mexico, which is officially bilingual, all American legal and political documents including the ballot are published in English only. In addition, some investigators have attributed to the Mexican American cultural characteristics--such as a respect for authority as evidenced in the traditional family or a "fatalistic" view of life--that, if valid, would tend to favor a more passive membership in the dominant political culture.[49]

Perhaps most importantly, the American of Mexican ancentry has historically been forced by the dominant white majority into a passive, nonparticipant status, in several ways paralleling the black experience. While the experience of slavery was not formally institutionalized with respect to Mexican Americans, existentially the relationship between them and their white "superiors" have been quite similar.[50]

By conquest, the white, Anglo-Saxon American has imposed his legal and political system upon the previously existing Indo-Hispanic culture in many parts of the West and Southwest, extinguishing many of the traditional forms of social and political organization.[51] In many areas, the Mexican American has been treated as a vanquished person of inferior status possessing few or no legal rights and subject to the whims of the conqueror. In fact, the superior-subordinate "colonial" relationship between the Chicano residents of the Southwest and the Anglo-American "victors" in the Mexican American War is perhaps the single best key to understanding the political, as well as social and economic, status of the Chicano.[52] Anglos historically have attempted to vitiate any political activity or movement among Mexican Americans through various discriminatory practices. In California, this political racism has taken the form of voting tests based on English language literacy, threats of deportation, gerrymandering, and outright intimidation.[53] These factors all have worked against the Mexican American playing an active role in the politics of the American system.

Thus it is more than coincidental that in a state whose Chicano population is some 15 percent of the total, less than 2 percent of the state's elective officers in the U.S. Congress and state legislature are Chicanos. Of 15,650 elected and appointed officials at the local, state, and federal levels in California, only 310 (1.98 percent) are Mexican American. Los Angeles County numbers over 1.1 million Chicanos among its inhabitants, with half of them clustered in the Greater East Los Angeles area; yet not one Chicano serves on the Los Angeles City Council or County Board of Supervisors.

However, in recent years several political movements have sprung up in various parts of the West and Southwest, and Mexican Americans are warming to the possibility of wielding political power commensurate with their population size and individual ability. Mexican Americans are becoming increasingly discontented with their status as politically inferior persons, and some recent activities have hinted that much more dissatisfaction will boil to the surface.

The major stimulus for the contemporary "brown paper" movement came from the activities of Cesar Chavez and the United Farm Workers' Organizing Committee (UFWOC) in the Central Valley of California.[54] Cries of "Huelga" (strike) have served to promote a new sense of unity, cultural as well as political, among Chicanos in the United States. In New Mexico the zealous efforts of Reies Lopez Tijerina and his Alianza have catalyzed new political movements.[55] Rudolfo "Corky" Gonzales and his Crusade for Justice are becoming increasingly important to the politics of Colorado. And in Texas the formation of the La Raza Unida party has been a major development in American politics, at least regionally, and national effects are likely.

It seems that the traditional forms of political accommodation will not suffice for the "colored" minorities now flexing their political muscle. Nonelectoral forms of political activism—such as demonstrations and boycotts, used effectively by Afro-Americans—also are being employed by Mexican American groups.[56] Violence, in the form of civil disturbances, also has broken out in the barrios of American cities, such as Los Angeles.* A quickening of the pace of political activity is expected.

---

*From January 1970 to January 1971 five civil disturbances erupted in the barrio of east Los Angeles, resulting in many injuries, much destruction of property, and the loss of several lives.

A PREVIEW

In light of the continuing and perhaps increasing political conflicts between Chicanos and the dominant society,
one might be curious as to the attitudinal foundations of
the situation. Are the signs of political unrest simply
dissatisfaction with the present distribution of goods by
our political system? Or are they symptomatic of a deeper
and more basic disaffection with the American political
system in general? If the basis for legitimacy of the system is weak among some of the important groups agitating
for political change in this country, might there not ensue
serious consequences for its future stability? And, from
the viewpoint of those desiring change, what strategies
and tactics would be most congruent with the orientation
of Chicanos toward the political system and consequently
might be most effective?

Certainly an investigation into the socialization patterns of Mexican-American children will suggest some answers
to these questions.

It is hypothesized that there does exist a substantial
difference in the political orientation toward (and level
of support of) the American political system by Chicano,
compared to Anglo, children, as evidenced by their expressed
attitudes toward the three major analytical levels of the
system: the political community, the regime, and the political authorities. Three major "ideal-type" patterns of
socialization toward the political system can emerge as
Chicano children become adults (see Figure 1.1). They
might initially contact the political system in a much different manner or at a significantly different level than
do Anglo children, reflecting culturally different familial
influences. As, with age, they increasingly experience direct political socialization with nonfamilial agents, this
original differentiation may continue (Type I) or it may
diminish, as one group leads or lags in their perceptions,
but finally come together (Type II). Or growing up in an
ethnically discriminatory society may provide experiences
that increasingly will divide the orientations of the
minority group children as they mature (Type III).

RESEARCH PROCEDURE AND
CONSIDERATIONS

During the spring of 1970 and January of the following
year, over 1,500 questionnaires designed to sample the

20

FIGURE 1.1

Ideal Models of Differential Socialization Patterns

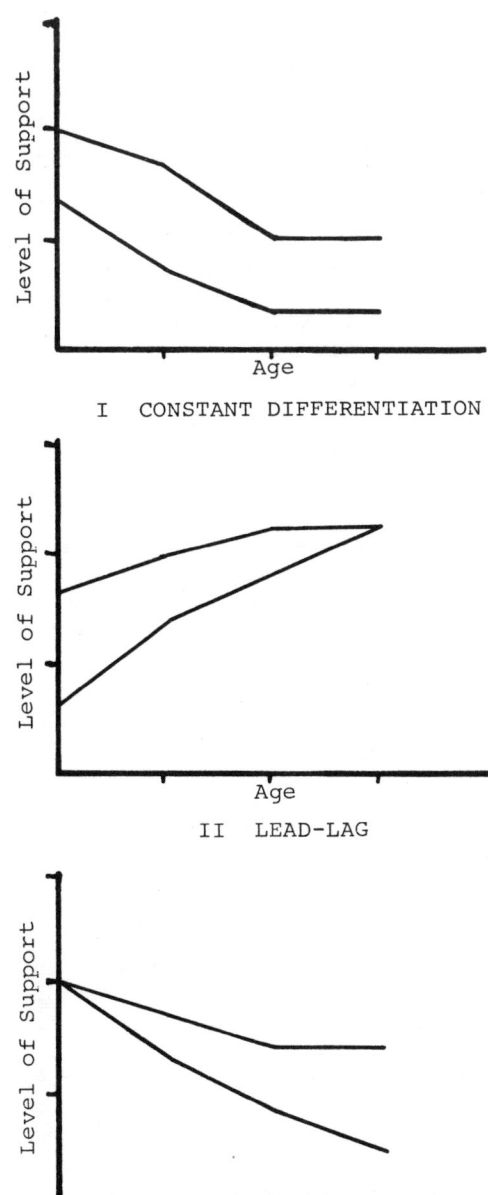

I   CONSTANT DIFFERENTIATION

II   LEAD-LAG

III   INCREASING DIVERGENCE

political orientations of American schoolchildren were distributed in eight California public schools (a more detailed presentation of methodology is contained in Appendix A). Since a major objective of the survey was to compare the responses of Mexican American and Anglo children, the schools were located in two geographic areas of substantial Mexican American population—the Central Valley of California and east Los Angeles County. Moreover, it was felt that each region was politically significant to recent Mexican American political activities. The valley has been the locale of the Huelga movement initiated by Cesar Chavez and the UFWOC, and the barrios of east Los Angeles have spawned several Chicano activist political organizations and have been the scene of several walkouts, demonstrations, and "civil disturbances." Therefore, it was thought that children residing in these areas were likely to be particularly "politicized," i.e., politically aware.

Due to the great difficulty in securing access to schoolchildren for the purposes of social survey research, it was not possible to draw a random sample from the schools in these areas. Rather than abandon the project due to potential criticism about the unrepresentativeness of the sample, it was decided to proceed with an availability sample. No claim is made that these findings accurately reflect the attitudes of Mexican American children throughout the Southwest; indeed, because of the great variety of Mexican American experiences in such states as Texas, New Mexico, and California, such a position would be untenable. We do feel, however, that the results are typical of Mexican American children in the areas sampled and most likely quite indicative of a much larger number of young California Chicanos.

In addition to the difficulty in securing access, two other major problems were foreseen: (1) accurately identifying children of Mexican-Spanish heritage and (2) bridging any cultural gap that might seriously threaten the validity of the results. Since ethnicity was the prime control variable, great care and discretion was used in determining cultural identification. A combination of techniques were used, including visual identification, consultation with teachers and principals, language usage, and self-identification (the latter two derived from responses to items placed at the end of the questionnaire to avoid prematurely raising ethnic consciousness). After excluding the questionnaires of Mexican nationals, Asian Americans, and Afro-Americans, the responses of 683 Mexican Americans and 544 Anglos (total N = 1,227) were included in the final tabulation. Cultural differences were minimized through the use of idiomatic Spanish-language questionnaires administered by local Spanish-speaking interviewers experienced in working with school-age Mexican American children.

Several other variables were considered to possibly have a significant effect on the political attitudes of these children, and therefore information was gathered on sex, socioeconomic class, parental birthplaces, and length of residence in the United States. In the presentation of the findings, only those independent variables that were found to have the greatest effect on a particular response are presented, with the exception of socioeconomic class. Since the socioeconomic status of an individual more often than not has very significant effects on his political attitudes, the effects of this control variable on almost every opinion are presented.[57]

Since data were desired covering the developmental pattern of political orientations from early childhood into adolescence, a quasi-longitudinal research design was employed. Students at the third, fifth, seventh, and ninth grade levels were given the same questionnaire.

Dependent variables are the political attitudes of Mexican and Anglo-American children as measured by their responses to the questionnaire.

In Chapters 2 through 6 we will examine the attitudinal attachments of Chicano children (and their Anglo peers) to the American polity. More specifically, our purpose is to delineate the cognitive and affective orientations of these children to the three major components of the American political system: the political community, the regime, and the political authorities. We shall determine the degree of attachment to and support for the major system elements by Chicano children in comparison to that of other ethnic groups, primarily the core Anglo culture. Implications of these findings for the future political behavior of Chicanos and the resultant effect on system stability also will be discussed.

Since this project is an attempt to map out previously unexplored territory, we decided to cover as much terrain as feasible rather than do a microscopic, detailed analysis of one small area. Consequently the results should be considered as exploratory and descriptive in nature; while some attempts are made at explanation, these are sometimes subjective and even speculative. We hope that these findings will provide some direction or at least a stimulus to further research in this neglected area.

CHAPTER

2

ORIENTATION TOWARD
THE AMERICAN
POLITICAL COMMUNITY:
MEXICAN OR AMERICAN?

Perhaps the most basic feeling of goodwill toward the
political system, and a prerequisite for other attachments,
is the feeling of belonging to some particular political
group or community, in this case the American nation-state.
For a child to feel any kind of emotion toward the political system, he must first be aware of "we-they" differences,
i.e., recognize that he is a member of a collectivity of
people who share attachments with each other and to a common set of institutions, the American polity. Moreover,
he must recognize that other people and countries are "foreign" and not part of his community.

Although some persons question the desirability of
high degrees of ethnocentrism or nationalism, some minimal
degree of preference for, not to say awareness of, one's
own political community is certainly the most fundamental
foundation for diffuse system support.

Developmental psychologists have discovered that a
child aged four to six has very little conception of the
idea of nationality or the existence of any kind of community larger than the family;[1] he is said by Piaget to be
very "egocentric." As his cognitive abilities develop the
child enters a "sociocentric" stage, becoming more aware
of external collectivities. At this stage, seven to ten
years of age, a child first becomes aware of the closest
political community--the city--and only later does the

Some of the material in this chapter appears, in re-
vised form, in "Orientations of Mexican American and Anglo
Children Toward the American Political Community," Social
Science Quarterly, LIII, 3 (March 1973).

idea of the larger national entity develop. During the eleventh through thirteenth years, a distinction is made between one's own nation and other national communities, and the concepts of citizen and foreigner--"reciprocity"-- emerge. By age 15, a level of cognitive maturity is reached.

Almost all the literature on the attachment of young children to their nation evidences a very early, warm and diffuse orientation.[2] Hess and Torney sum up the findings on this subject of researchers whose sample population in each case has been white, urban and middle class:

> The young child's involvement with the political system begins with a strong positive attachment to the country; the United States is seen as ideal and as superior to other countries. This attachment to the country is stable and shows almost no change through elementary school years. This bond is possibly the most basic and essential aspect of socialization into involvement with the political life of the nation. Essentially an emotional tie, it apparently grows from complex psychological and social needs and is exceedingly resistant to change or argument.[3]

Greenberg has found that young black children manifest this same positive attachment.[4] Do Mexican American youngsters also share these attitudes?

Because of their unique position in American society, Mexican Americans may be expected to exhibit certain peculiarities with respect to awareness of and feeling of belonging to the American community. Even their typically hyphenated designation implies some kind of nonacceptance or separateness. Many Chicanos, because of geographical proximity to their country of origin, remain very close psychologically to Mexico, often visiting relatives and friends. This is probably more true for Mexican Americans in California than in states like New Mexico, where some Chicanos had settled before the 13 British colonies won their indepencence.[5] Census figures reveal that, of California Mexican Americans, 25.2 percent either were born in Mexico or had at least one parent who was.[6] Adult Mexican Americans are thus much closer--geographically, chronologically, and culturally--to their original homeland than are, for example, Afro-Americans, who in most ways are remote from their African origins.

Might not this closeness to two national communities affect Mexican-American children's socialization in and orientations toward the U.S. community? Perhaps their perceptions of the distinctiveness between nations would be affected in such a manner that their cognition of these differences would be blurred, and consequently their affect toward the American political community might be diminished, at least relative to what they feel for Mexico.

COGNITION OF POLITICAL COMMUNITIES

The measurement of attitudes toward our political community is accomplished in the present study by ascertaining responses to political symbols. Leonard W. Doob has suggested that the most prominent symbol evoking response from citizens is the name of their country.[7] When the children in our sample were asked to name their country, 71.9 percent of the Mexican Americans named the United States while 86.6 percent of the Anglos did. Over the years Mexican American children show a rather even incremental increase in their ability to name this country while the Anglo pattern is a rapid climb to a 90 percent level at the fifth grade after which it gradually increases (see Figure 2.1).* A small percentage of Chicano children at the third grade level gave a Mexican name--"Mexico" or a subdivision thereof--for their response, reflecting their familiarity with a Mexican political unit. While the fifth and seventh graders did not respond in this manner, 1.7 percent of the ninth graders again responded with the name of a Mexican political unit, usually Mexico. This may show a disinclination to write down the name of a country that attaches a hyphenated prefix to this group of people before designating them "American," or it may evidence a greater cultural pride in the ancestral homeland.

---

*The reader is reminded that quasi-longitudinal research necessarily assumes a lack of discontinuity over the age span of the subjects, i.e., the third graders of this study will have views similar to those of the current ninth graders if they are surveyed six years later. Thus we shall speak of individual changes over this age span even though the time series data to verify such developmental patterns are lacking. All similar political socialization research employs this research design and necessarily makes this same assumption (see Appendix A).

FIGURE 2.1

Percent, By Grade and Ethnicity, Correctly Answering
"What Is the Name of Our Country?"

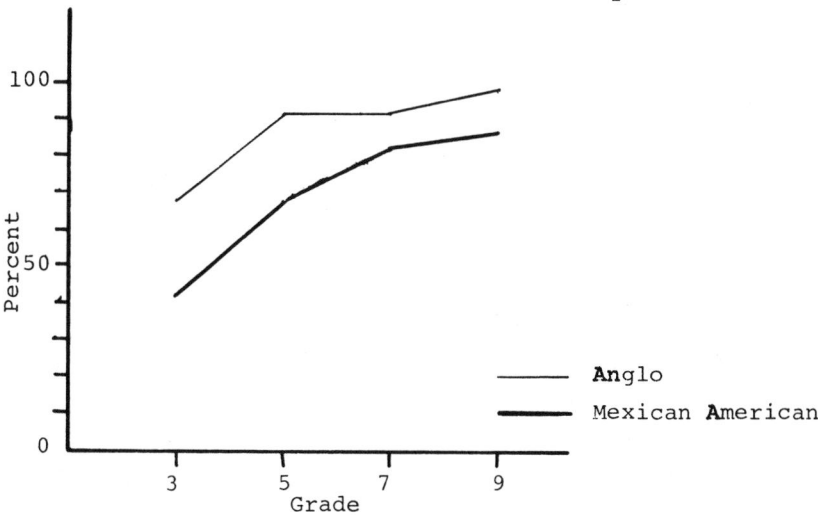

FIGURE 2.2

Percent, By Grade and Ethnicity, Correctly Answering
"What Is the Name of Our Country?",
Controlling for Social Class

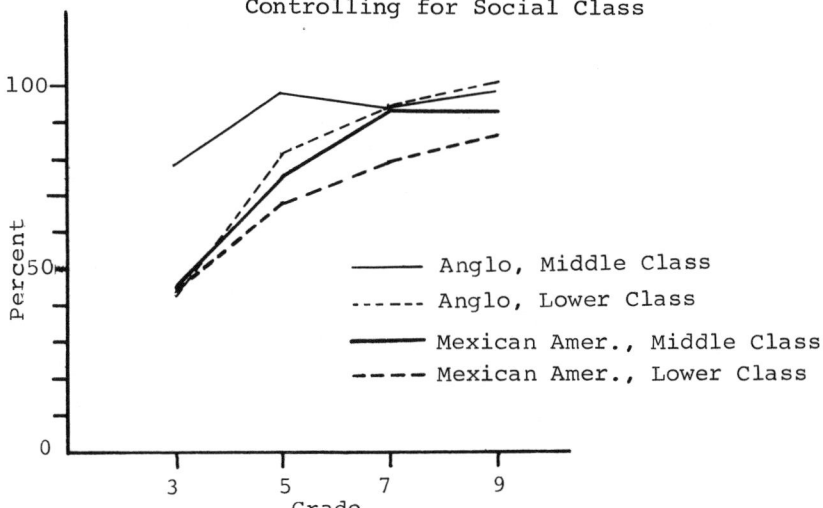

When controlled for socioeconomic status (see Figure 2.2), the picture does not change much. The responses of the Mexican American middle class and Anglo working class are most similar over the school years, while the Mexican-American working class lags behind all others. But ethnic differences remain for each class. Multivariate analyses confirm that, after grade level, ethnicity is the best predictor of responses to the question (beta = 0.11) when all other independent variables are held constant. This is followed by the amount of Spanish spoken (beta = 0.10) and length of residence in the United States (beta = 0.10), lending some substance to our earlier speculation about the possible effect of Mexico's closeness on the accuracy of the children's perceptions. The early high level of correct responses by the total Anglo group is seen to be largely the result of the initially high level of knowledge by its middle-class members. Of note is the unexpected decrease in correct responses by ninth-grade middle-class Chicanos, perhaps the result of the previously suggested diminution of affect for the United States and increased appreciation of Mexico, since it is highly unlikely that ninth graders would be less able to identify the United States than students two years their juniors.

Developmental and educational psychologists have long debated the developmental pattern of the child's awareness of the surrounding community. Some have argued that the child proceeds in his awareness from the geographically closest area to the most distant, i.e., in ever-expanding vistas from the family to the neighborhood through the city, state, national, and international levels. Many schools have arranged their social science curricula around this "concentric circle" theory, making it even more likely that younger children will be most familiar with their local political community and gradually become aware of the larger national community. On the other hand, some learning psychologists also have theorized that the young child is now exposed to greater contacts with the national community because of modern developments in technology, especially the mass media, which are nationally oriented. This cognitive world of the child, according to their theory, although largely vicarious, is more real than the local community, with which he now has few contacts, especially in a political context. Survey after survey has shown that the adult American is more familiar with the institutions, processes, and policies of the national government than with those at the state or local level. This parental knowledge certainly could reinforce the child's greater knowledge of the national political system.

These children gave an 86 percent correct response
when asked to name their state compared to a 78.3 percent
correct response on the "nation" item. Chicano children
responded correctly at the 81.8 percent level, Anglos at
the 92.1 percent level. Both groups are more familiar
with the name of their state than that of their country,
adding support to the concentric circle theory. Familiarity
increases for both groups over the four grades, although
the Anglos begin at a higher level and show subsequently
smaller incremental increases (see Figure 2.3). Controlling for social class (see Figure 2.4) makes some difference although both classes of Chicano children lag behind
both Anglo classes in cognitive development.

Actually, after age (grade), the use of the Spanish
language is most highly related to cognition of the state
(beta = 0.15), followed by the child's length of residence
in the United States (beta = 0.14), socioeconomic class
(beta = 0.08), and ethnicity (beta = 0.06). This suggests
that the apparent lower level of cognition by Chicanos
most likely is the result of a shorter length of association with the state of California. By the ninth grade,
100 percent of all but the lower-class Mexican Americans
correctly name the state. It might be noted that for the
Chicano group there is no drop-off after the seventh grade
as there was on the national question. Perhaps the theorized pride in Mexico does not compete with adolescent attachment to the state political community.

This increasing familiarity with decreasing levels of
government continues as we consider local government, as
92.8 percent of the total sample knew the name of the city
in which they resided. Ninety percent of the Mexican-
American students answered correctly as did 96.1 percent
of the Anglos. The developmental patterns of the groups
bear the same relationship as did knowledge of the state
and nation, with both groups exhibiting the biggest jump
in knowledge between the third and fifth grades. Chicanos
again "began" at a lower level of knowledge (see Figure
2.5). The typical pattern emerges when controls for socioeconomic status are introduced. The pattern of cognitive development for middle-class Chicanos is closer to
that of the Anglo group than to working-class Mexican Americans (see Figure 2.6).

However, next to grade, by far the best predictor of
knowledge of the city's name is the amount of Spanish used
by the respondent, which is inversely related to correct
response. Since the use of Spanish is substantially associated with socioeconomic level (gamma = 0.21), this may

FIGURE 2.3

Percent, By Grade and Ethnicity, Correctly Answering
"What Is the Name of This State?"

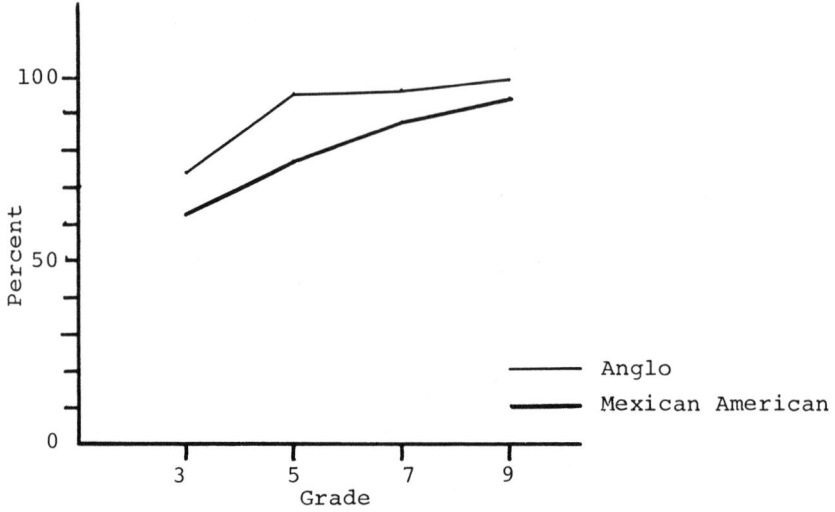

FIGURE 2.4

Percent, By Grade and Ethnicity, Correctly Answering
"What Is the Name of Our State?",
Controlling for Social Class

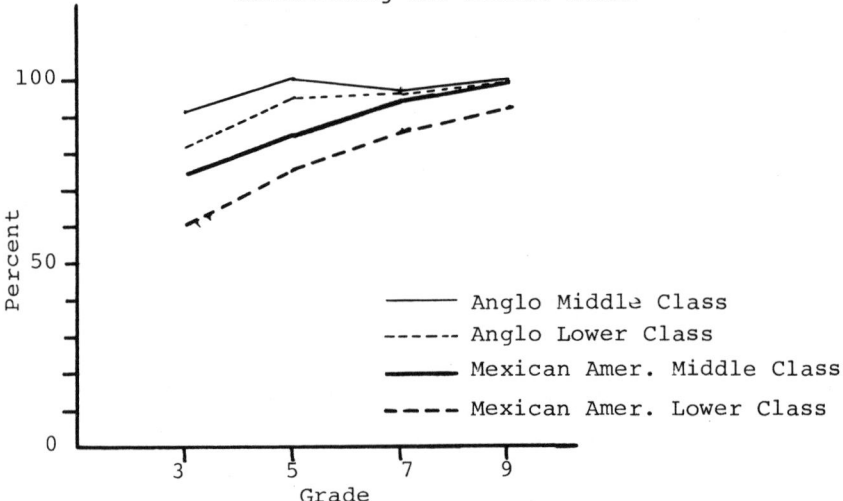

FIGURE 2.5

Percent, By Grade and Ethnicity, Correctly Answering
"What Is the Name of This City?"

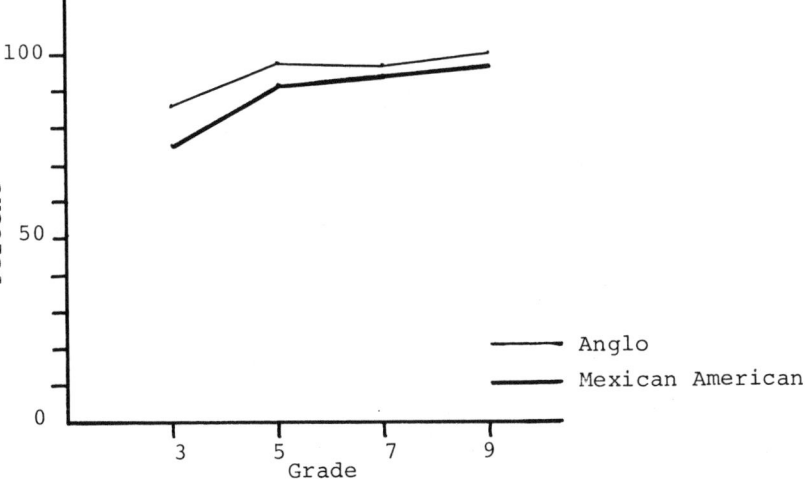

FIGURE 2.6

Percent, By Grade and Ethnicity, Correctly Answering
"What Is the Name of This City?",
Controlling for Social Class

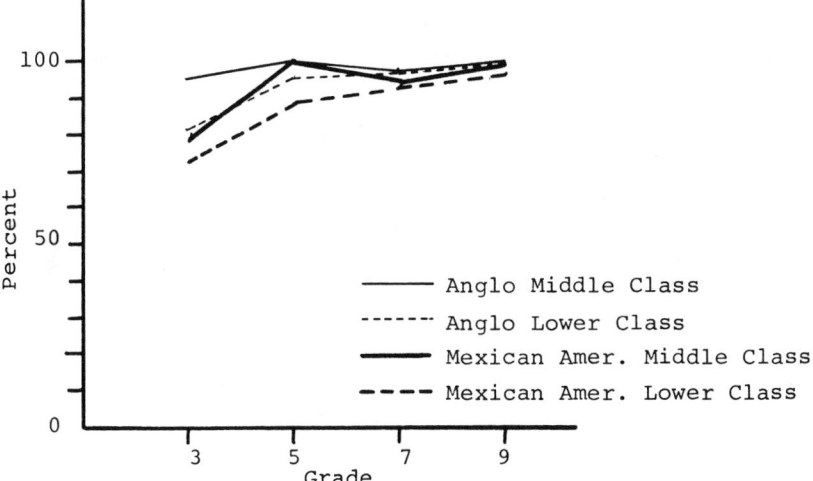

31

account in part for the difference in socioeconomic patterns. When all other variables are controlled, socioeconomic status produced a relatively low beta coefficient of 0.05.

Apparently, the concentric circle theory of learning comes closest to explaining both the Anglo and Mexican-American children's pattern of learning about the various levels of government in the United States. The cognition of the Mexican American children parallels that of the Anglo group at all levels. Although beginning at a lower level of awareness, the gap decreases with age.

This lower level of cognition seems to be the result of a shorter period of residence either by the child or his parents before him (as reflected by the language used in the home; the correlation between Spanish usage in the home and length of U.S. residence is substantial, gamma = 0.53). Length of residence has less effect on cognition of country than on cognition of the lower levels of government. Certainly even people residing in another country could much more easily identify the United States than any of its political subdivisions.

The youngest Chicanos are most familiar with the name of their city and least with that of the nation. However, at no level does the Mexican American show greater cognition of a political community than his Anglo counterpart does. While black third graders in Greenberg's study demonstrated greater awareness of the local community than their white classmates,[8] this peculiar phenomenon is not found among Chicano youngsters.

A small number of Mexican-American children responded with the names of Mexican political communities when asked to identify the local, state, and national polities in which they lived. No meaningful pattern of such responses emerged across the various grades. Not one Anglo student incorrectly responded to any of these items with a Mexican name.

Many would consider a country's flag the most important symbol of the national political community. This may be especially true for the United States, which seems to be greatly concerned about the use and abuse of the flag. Some scholars have suggested that since the United States lacks any ceremonial state leaders analogous to, for example, Great Britain's crown the flag has become its surrogate for the national polity. Thus the flag should loom large on the cognitive horizon of the child as the symbolic representation of his political community.

Several studies have used the recognition of national flags to provide evidence concerning the degree and distri-

bution of ethnocentrism among American children. A 1936
study by Eugene L. Horowitz revealed that young people's
appreciation of the U.S. flag increased from 27.3 percent
in the first grade to 100 percent by grade seven.[9] In a
more recent look at the phenomenon, Edward D. Lawson found
a different pattern--a high and consistent appreciation of
the U.S. flag by American students in kindergarten through
senior high school.[10] Greenberg found that both the black
and the white children in his sample had a near perfect
recognition of the American flag.[11]

When the Anglo children in this study were asked to
select "the flag of this country," they easily chose the
appropriate flag. Even the third graders selected the
Stars and Stripes at a 99.2 percent rate. Only at this
grade level did another flag (Mexican) receive a few (0.8
percent) responses from Anglo children. The pattern of
the Chicano students' selection is quite varied. Third
graders picked the U.S. flag 95.0 percent of the time;
this increased to 98.8 percent at the fifth grade. Yet
the seventh and ninth graders selected the U.S. flag at a
declining rate (94.3 and 93.2 percent, respectively).

This lower response exactly parallels the increase in
their choice of the flag of Mexico (see Table 2.1). It
should be noted that this phenomenon is almost entirely a
result of working-class responses (see Table 2.2). The
other two flag selections also were chosen by a few members
of this group. It is likely that a strict recognition
ability is emphasized in the lower grades where the smaller

TABLE 2.1

Correct Responses to the Question, "Which Is the Flag
of This Country?"
(in percentages; number of responses in parentheses)

Grade	Mexican Americans				Anglos			
	U.S. Flag		Mexican Flag		U.S. Flag		Mexican Flag	
3	95.0	(133)	0.7	(1)	99.2	(124)	0.8	(1)
5	98.8	(170)	0.6	(1)	100.0	(123)	0.0	(0)
7	94.3	(182)	3.1	(6)	98.5	(133)	0.0	(0)
9	93.2	(165)	5.1	(9)	99.4	(159)	0.0	(0)
Total	95.3	(651)	2.5	(17)	99.3	(540)	0.2	(1)

TABLE 2.2

Responses by Mexican American Lower- and Middle-Class Children to the Question,
"Which Is the Flag of This Country?"
(in percentages; number of responses in parentheses)

Grade	United Nations		Mexico		Star		United States		Don't Know/No Answer	
Mexican American Lower Class										
3	0.0	(0)	0.9	(1)	1.7	(2)	93.9	(108)	3.5	(4)
5	0.0	(0)	0.0	(0)	0.0	(0)	99.2	(123)	.8	(1)
7	0.7	(1)	3.7	(5)	1.5	(2)	94.1	(128)	0.0	(0)
9	0.0	(0)	7.2	(9)	0.0	(0)	91.2	(114)	1.6	(2)
Total	0.2	(1)	3.0	(15)	0.8	(4)	94.6	(473)	1.4	(7)
Mexican American Middle Class										
3	0.0	(0)	0.0	(0)	0.0	(0)	100.0	(20)	0.0	(0)
5	0.0	(0)	0.0	(0)	0.0	(0)	100.0	(40)	0.0	(0)
7	0.0	(0)	2.1	(1)	0.0	(0)	95.8	(46)	2.1	(1)
9	0.0	(0)	0.0	(0)	2.4	(1)	97.6	(40)	0.0	(0)
Total	0.0	(0)	0.7	(1)	0.7	(1)	98.0	(147)	0.7	(1)

children seriously attempt to discern their flag. At the higher grades, a strong element of effect probably comes into play since it is very unlikely that fewer seventh and ninth graders than primary students would know the flag. The Anglos show disaffection by not answering; the Mexican American children instead select the flag of Mexico.

An item designed to allow the children to pick the nonflag symbol--star, cross, the United Farm Workers' aguila (eagle), or the Statue of Liberty--best representing this country revealed no differences between the ethnic groups (see Table 2.3). It was thought that Cesar Chavez's eagle would particularly attract the Chicano children, but it had no special attracting power for most of them, as almost as many Anglo children selected it. An exception to the trend occurred among working-class Chicanos in the ninth grade, who were almost three times as likely to select the UFWOC eagle as best representing this country (see Table 2.4). Stepwise regression revealed that, for Chicanos, geographical location was the best predictor of response on this item; understandably enough, a larger percentage of the rural students selected the UFWOC eagle than did those residing in the Los Angeles area. The overwhelming majority of both groups (73.4 percent Chicano, 76.8 percent Anglo) selected the Statue of Liberty. Contrary to the results of similar studies,[12] there was no preference for the cross over the star by either group or by the total sample. This study provided no support for earlier contentions that the young child has a religious attachment to the nation, confusing religious and community symbols.

One of the manifestations of Americans' special reverence for the flag is the pledge of allegiance that millions of children recite daily in the classrooms of the United States. The pledge is made to both the flag and "the Republic for which it stands," although the symbol is emphasized over the reality it represents.* This is affirmed by the fact that 57.6 percent of the sample said the pledge is made to the flag, while one-half that number (28.0 percent) said they pledged their loyalty to the country. Only slightly fewer Chicanos than Anglos selected each of these options. The inclusion of the phrase "under God" by the Eisenhower administration seems to have con-

---

*The pledge of allegiance is also called the pledge to the flag; children are directed to look at the flag while reciting the pledge; and in the pledge the flag is mentioned before the nation that it represents.

TABLE 2.3

Percentage of Children Preferring Various Symbolic
Representations of the United States
(number of responses in parentheses)

Grade	Star		Cross		UFWOC Eagle		Statue of Liberty		Don't Know/No Answer	
				Mexican American						
3	10.0	(14)	5.7	(8)	19.3	(27)	63.6	(89)	1.4	(2)
5	4.7	(8)	8.1	(14)	16.3	(28)	69.2	(119)	1.7	(3)
7	4.1	(8)	3.6	(7)	9.3	(18)	79.8	(154)	3.1	(6)
9	2.8	(5)	3.4	(6)	11.3	(20)	78.0	(138)	4.0	(7)
Total	5.1	(35)	5.1	(35)	13.6	(93)	73.4	(501)	2.6	(18)
				Anglo						
3	5.6	(7)	7.2	(9)	19.2	(24)	68.0	(85)	0.0	(0)
5	2.4	(3)	4.9	(6)	14.6	(18)	77.2	(95)	0.8	(1)
7	3.7	(5)	2.2	(3)	12.6	(17)	78.5	(106)	3.0	(4)
9	3.1	(5)	4.4	(7)	8.1	(13)	81.9	(131)	2.5	(4)
Total	3.7	(20)	4.6	(25)	13.2	(72)	76.8	(418)	0.0	(0)

TABLE 2.4

Percentage of Chicano Children Preferring Various Symbolic
Representations of the United States, By Class
(number of responses in parentheses)

Grade	Star		Cross		UFWOC Eagle		Statue of Liberty		Don't Know/No Answer	
			Mexican American Lower Class							
3	11.3	(13)	6.1	(7)	13.0	(15)	67.8	(78)	1.7	(2)
5	5.6	(7)	7.3	(9)	16.1	(20)	68.5	(85)	2.4	(3)
7	4.4	(6)	2.9	(4)	9.6	(13)	80.1	(109)	2.9	(4)
9	2.4	(3)	4.0	(5)	13.6	(17)	74.4	(93)	5.6	(7)
Total	5.8	(29)	5.0	(25)	13.0	(65)	73.0	(365)	3.7	(16)
			Mexican American Middle Class							
3	5.0	(1)	5.0	(1)	40.0	(8)	50.0	(10)	0.0	(0)
5	2.5	(1)	10.0	(4)	15.0	(6)	72.5	(29)	0.0	(0)
7	4.2	(2)	6.3	(3)	8.3	(4)	77.1	(37)	4.2	(2)
9	0.0	(0)	2.4	(1)	4.9	(2)	90.2	(37)	2.4	(1)
Total	2.7	(4)	6.0	(9)	13.3	(20)	76.0	(114)	2.0	(3)

vinced 7.3 percent of the Mexican American children and
6.6 percent of the Anglos that their ritualistic fealty is
directed toward a divinity. In fact, among Chicano third
graders the "god" option ranked above all choices but the
flag (the other choices were the country and the President).
The same was not true for their young Anglo counterparts,
but 12.8 percent of the Anglos also thought they were participating in a religious ritual. These percentages
quickly shrink to third choice by the fifth year in school.
The President is thought to be the object of the pledge
by some Mexican American children at every grade level,
especially the third (5.7 percent), but only 0.8 percent
of the third-grade Anglos have the same feeling; and it
does not recur after the third grade (see Table 2.5).

COGNITIVE DIMENSION OF
COMMUNITY ATTACHMENT

The importance of visual symbols, especially the flag,
in developing a sense of identity with the American political community is emphasized by these findings. While less
than half the Mexican American third graders can name their
country, almost all can identify its flag. Apparently,
there exists an early realization that these stars and
stripes represent "us" even though the proper name of the
collectivity cannot yet be mustered.

The Mexican American, as well as the Anglo, children
first see themselves as members of the closest political
community, the city in which they live, and subsequently
become aware of membership in their state and country.
However, on all items Mexican American students lag behind
Anglos in cognitive awareness of U.S. community symbols,
approximating the Type II lead-lag developmental pattern
hypothesized in Chapter 1. Working-class Chicanos usually
trail behind the others.

While research has indicated that a lag in the cognitive
ability is common among students from lower socioeconomic
families, ethnicity remains a distinguishing factor among
our respondents even when socioeconomic status is controlled. It accounts for about the same variation in the
responses to items on the national, state, and local levels.
However, when other variables are controlled, the predictive power of ethnicity diminishes tremendously for the
subnational communities; the degree of Spanish usage and
the length of residence in the country become the most significant factors in the recognition of state and local

TABLE 2.5

Children's Perceptions of Object of Pledge of Allegiance
(in percentages; number of responses in parentheses)

Grade	Country		God		President		Flag		Don't Know/No Answer	
Mexican American										
3	18.6	(26)	23.6	(33)	5.7	(8)	45.0	(63)	7.2	(10)
5	24.4	(42)	5.2	(9)	1.7	(3)	64.0	(110)	4.6	(8)
7	32.6	(63)	2.6	(5)	0.5	(1)	56.5	(109)	7.8	(15)
9	32.2	(57)	1.7	(3)	1.1	(2)	55.9	(99)	9.0	(16)
Total	27.5	(188)	7.3	(50)	2.0	(14)	55.9	(382)	7.2	(49)
Anglo										
3	23.2	(29)	12.8	(16)	0.8	(1)	59.2	(74)	4.0	(5)
5	37.4	(46)	7.3	(9)	0.0	(0)	53.7	(66)	1.6	(2)
7	23.0	(31)	3.7	(5)	0.0	(0)	70.4	(95)	3.0	(4)
9	33.1	(53)	3.8	(6)	0.0	(0)	53.8	(86)	9.4	(15)
Total	29.2	(159)	6.6	(36)	0.2	(1)	59.2	(322)	4.8	(26)

names. Since both these variables are indicative of a
relatively shorter period of residence in the area by the
child and/or his parents, it is not surprising that this
is reflected in a lower level of cognition.

The working-class, Spanish-speaking, recent immigrant
from Mexico is least likely to be "a part of" and more
likely to be "apart from" the American polity. His experiences with American society are primarily those within
the barrio, with its heavily "Mexican" atmosphere. Even
the mass media, which could be expected to socialize the
Chicano toward greater awareness of the American political
community, are largely Spanish language and/or produced in
Mexico.[13] Thus the socializing agents of media and family,
which are less "Americanized" than those of the Anglo culture, provide the Chicano child with less exposure to the
American political communities.

Although the Anglo/Chicano gap in cognition of verbal
symbols decreases slightly through the school years, the
change is slight through the middle years in which the
schools should have the greatest effect. Even though both
ethnic groups attend the same schools, it is probable that
Mexican-American students undergo a subjectively different
educational experience than do their Anglo classmates.[14]
Almost all the teachers of these children were Anglo, and
all classes were conducted entirely in English. The lack
of Chicano perspective and bilingual instruction is bound
to restrict, or at best neglect, the cognitive development
of Mexican-American children. This also might explain
the gap in performance between selection of a visual symbol
and verbalization of a symbolic label (the community's
name).

AFFECT FOR THE AMERICAN POLITICAL
COMMUNITY

Although realization of the fact that his own political community is an entity distinct from others is a sine
qua non of an individual's support for this component of
the system, the crux of the matter is whether the citizen
sees his nation in a favorable light. If this positive
affect for one's nation is learned early in life, it can
provide a firm foundation of patriotism that should have
a substantial effect on adult orientation toward national
affairs.[15]

In the present study, flags again were employed as
one of the symbols best representing the national political

39

community, this time to measure affect rather than cognition. The children were asked to select the "best" flag
from the four presented.* The results lend weight to the
earlier speculation regarding the strong affective component attached to national banners. Mexican-American children, particularly those who use more Spanish than English,
liked the American flag less than did the Anglos; both
groups showed decreasing affection for the flag through
their school years (see Figure 2.7).

Of special note is the reaction to the Mexican flag.
Only 2.4 percent of the Anglos selected it as the preferred banner, the lowest number for any flag, while it was
the second choice of the Chicano group (16.7 percent).
The Chicano pattern is one of increasing preference for
the Mexican flag until it is the choice of almost one-
quarter of the ninth-grade Mexican-American sample. Even
the third-grade children show a 10 percent preference for
this flag. Thus as some Chicanos become older they are
socialized away from the symbol of America and toward that
of their ancestral nation. This may be evidence of the
fact that "cultural nationalism" is on the rise in the
Mexican-American community.** Indeed, increasingly the
flag of Mexico is flown proudly at Chicano gatherings and
displayed in the homes of many families.

There also is a corresponding decrease in Anglo support
for the American flag, especially between the seventh and
ninth grades. However, their support goes toward the UN
flag (12.5 percent in the ninth grade) or toward no flag
(13.1 percent). This latter figure may demonstrate decreasing ethnocentrism and increased preference for the
principle of one world since by the age of 15 students
have a good idea of the intrinsic meaning of the flag symbols.[16]

Since affect for one's political community is a multi-
dimensional phenomenon,[17] several other items were included
in an attempt to measure such things as pride in the nation,
the distinctiveness of one's own nation, and the comparative

---

*The flags were that of the United Nations, the United
States, the United Kingdom, and Mexico.
**The opposite also could be true if the differences
between the older and younger Chicano students were attributed to generational differences, e.g., if the older students as a group were of more recent immigration backgrounds. However, our data provide no basis for replacing
our quasi-longitudinal assumptions with this interpretation.

40

FIGURE 2.7

Percent, By Grade and Ethnicity, Selecting the American
or Mexican Flag as "the Best Flag"

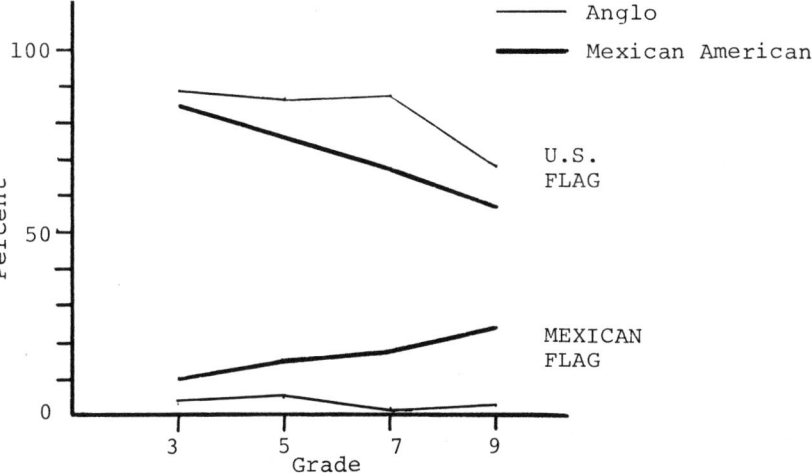

rating of other nations.[18] When asked whether they agreed
that "just about everybody in the world would like to live
in the United States of America," half of the Anglos and
35.4 percent of the Chicanos answered negatively. Over
one-half (56.2 percent) of the Mexican-American children
agreed with this. The trend over the years (parallel for
both groups) is one of initial high support diminishing
to 48.6 percent of the Chicanos and 38.1 percent of the
Anglos. A higher level of support for the statement by
the Chicanos continues throughout the years (see Figure
2.8).

When broken down by socioeconomic levels, three of
the four groups demonstrate parallel patterns of response
through the years (see Figure 2.9). For some reason, perhaps the differential influence of their social science
studies, all the Anglo students plus the middle-class Mexican Americans show a rise in agreement in the seventh
grade before continuing their downward trend; however, the
lower-class Chicanos show no upswing. By the ninth grade,
the middle-class students, particularly the Anglos, are
least likely to think that most foreigners would like to
emigrate to the United States.

When asked in two separate items whether people who
live in other countries--England and Mexico--are as proud

FIGURE 2.8

Percent, By Grade and Ethnicity, Agreeing that
"Just About Everybody in the World Would Like to Live in
the United States of America"

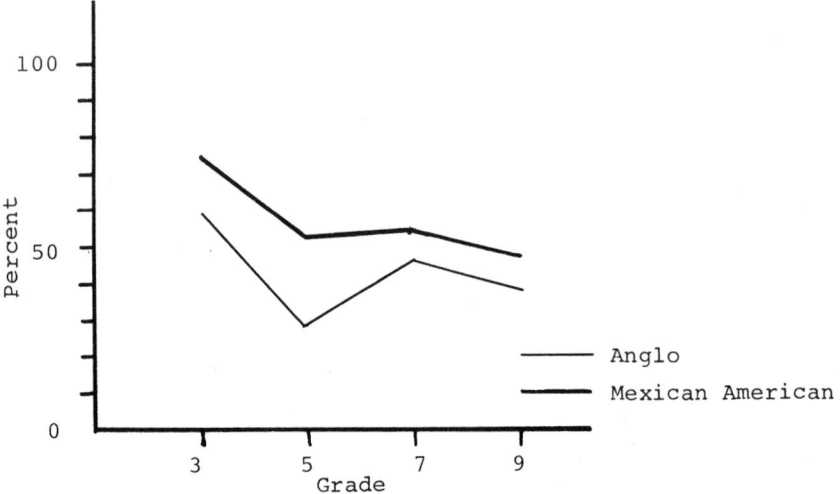

FIGURE 2.9

Percent, By Grade and Ethnicity, Responding that
"Almost Everyone Would Like to Live in the U.S.,"
Controlling for Social Class

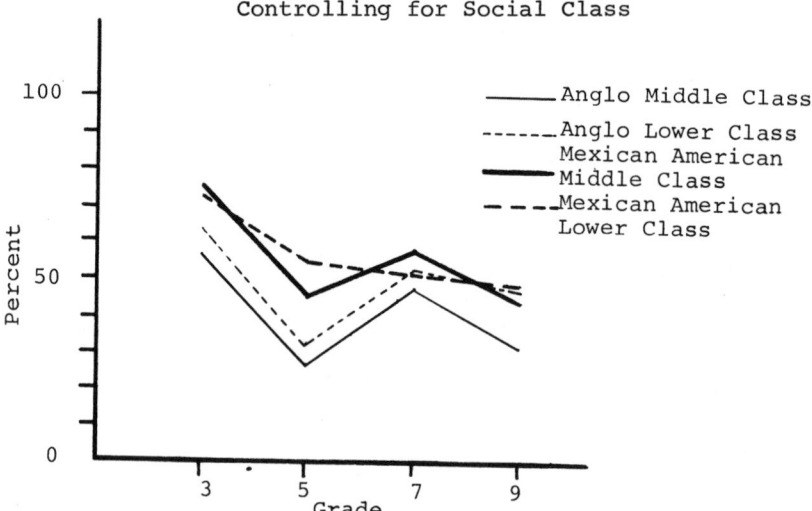

of their country as Americans are of theirs, the responses
show a marked similarity for both ethnic and grade categories (see Figure 2.10). Agreement with these propositions
is initially high and remains constant through the years.
The Chicano children are slightly less apt to think foreigners in either country are as proud as Americans, distinguishing little between those in England and Mexico.
The Anglos are slightly more inclined to think people in
other countries are just as proud, more so the English
than the Mexicans.

The Anglo children's opinion that the English are
more proud of England than the Mexican people are of Mexico
perhaps reflects the historical derogation and unfavorable
stereotyping of Mexico and its people in the United States.[19]
No such distinction is made by the Mexican-American students.
Controls for social class changed the picture very little.

At this point it is not certain whether in comparing
their feelings with those of foreigners the children are
weighing most heavily the foreigner's pride or their own
(American) pride. An examination of their agreement and
disagreement with the statement "Sometimes I'm not very
proud to be an American" is helpful. While a comparison
of the overall response of each group demonstrates marked
similarities--a majority of both groups disagree with the
statement--a closer look at the developmental pattern of
each ethnic category is more revealing (see Figure 2.11).
For the Anglos the classic pattern emerges: initially,
pride in membership in the American political community is
quite high, with less than a third stating they sometimes
were not proud to be Americans. A growing dissatisfaction
with their Americanism quickly develops and intensifies
until a majority of the oldest children admit they sometimes are not proud to be an American. Chicano children
in the third grade are not as socialized to being proud,
but during the next two years of experience their pride
in America increases. Over the next few years the Chicanos
show a development parallel to that of their Anglo counterparts. A growing disaffection is evident even though among
Chicanos the level of pride in being American remains
slightly higher than among Anglos.

Analysis by social class shows that the Mexican-American middle-class child is most proud to be American,
while the Anglo middle-class child is least proud.

Multivariate analysis reveals that social class is
a relatively weak predictor compared to most other variables.
The highest predictive value is a beta of 0.17 for Spanish
language usage. Betas of 0.10 are computed for the respon-

FIGURE 2.10

Percent, By Grade and Ethnicity, Affirming Britishers'
and Mexicans' Pride in Their Countries

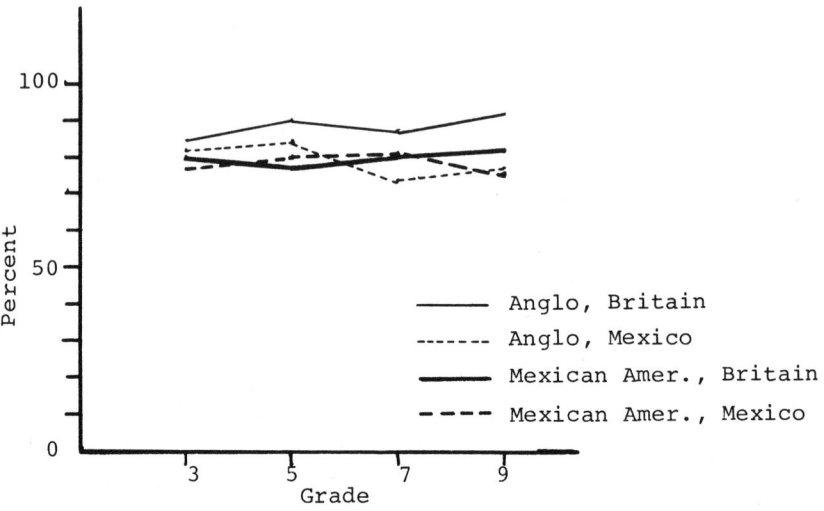

FIGURE 2.11

Percent, By Grade and Ethnicity, Agreeing that They Are
"Sometimes Not Very Proud to Be an American"

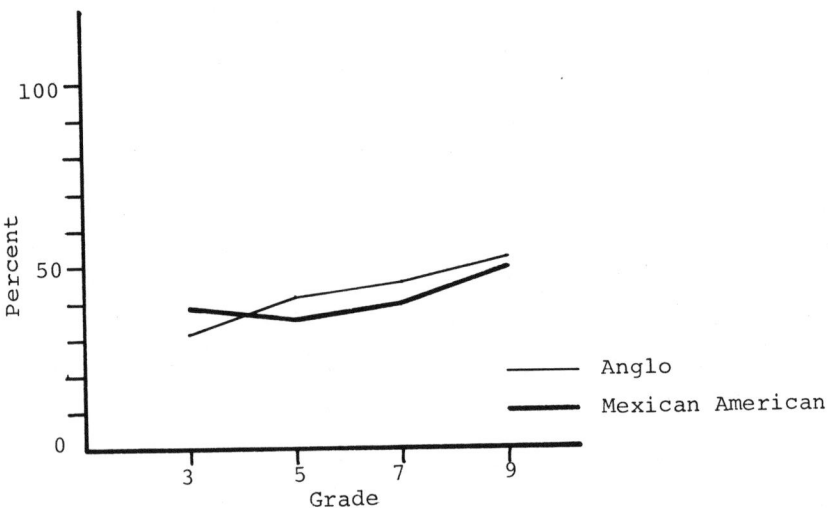

dents' perception of ethnic discrimination and region of residence in California, north-rural or south-urban. That perception of ethnic discrimination in the United States is significantly correlated (gamma = 0.27) with a lack of pride in being American is not surprising. Of those Chicanos feeling discrimination, 46 percent state they sometimes lack pride in being American, while only 32 percent of those not perceiving discrimination feel that way. By the ninth grade over half the Chicanos seeing discrimination sometimes do not feel proud.

Area of residence is highly correlated (gamma = 0.43) with pride in being American. The northern, rural California Chicanos felt less proud (63.2 percent) than did those living in Los Angeles (40.5 percent). Figure 2.12 shows that this negative feeling begins high (it is higher among third graders than among the urban ninth graders) and increases steadily until it is shared by almost two-thirds of the rural residents by age 15 or so. In addition, those who are most Mexican as measured by language usage, and therefore most likely to be discriminated against, tend to feel the least proud of America.

What is the source of this early strong pride in being American? Given five choices, young Americans overwhelmingly selected the phrase that "Americans have freedom" (62.6 percent) as the characteristic making them "most proud to be an American." Of the Chicanos, 58.6 percent find this the most important source of pride while 69.5 percent of the Anglos do. The pride in freedom remains relatively unchanged throughout the child's school years (see Table 2.6). Coming in a distant second place is the phrase "Americans can vote for their own leaders," which 14.3 percent of Mexican Americans and 14.0 percent of Anglos selected. Both ethnic groups show an increasing appreciation of suffrage with age. This is a specific example of the well-established progression of learning patterns from the concrete to the abstract. The vote becomes more significant as it is better understood by the maturing child. The vote is the least-picked option among the youngest Chicanos, but by the ninth grade more Chicanos selected this option than did the Anglos. The remaining choices were selected infrequently by both groups, and each diminished in importance greatly from third to ninth grade.

Finally we turn to an item encompassing the most direct approach to measuring the children's affection for the American political community. They were asked straightforwardly to agree or disagree with the statement, "The United States of America is the best country in the world."

FIGURE 2.12

Percent of Chicanos, By Grade and Area of Residence,
Agreeing that They Are "Sometimes Not Proud to Be an
American"

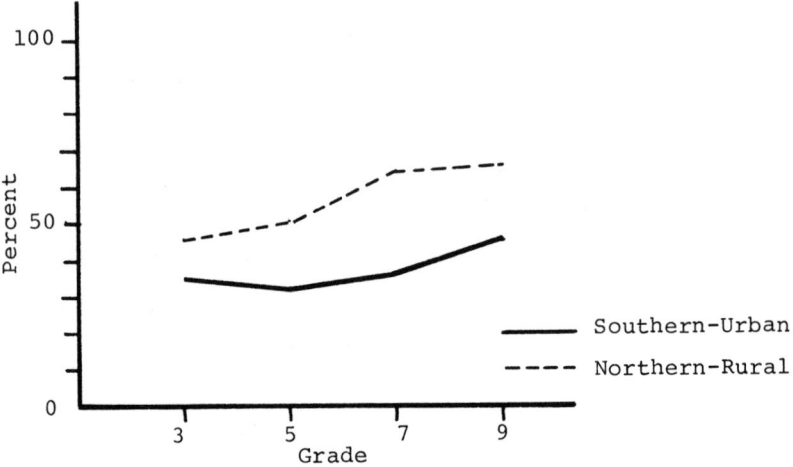

FIGURE 2.13

Percent, By Grade and Ethnicity, Agreeing that
"The United States of America Is the Best Country in
the World"

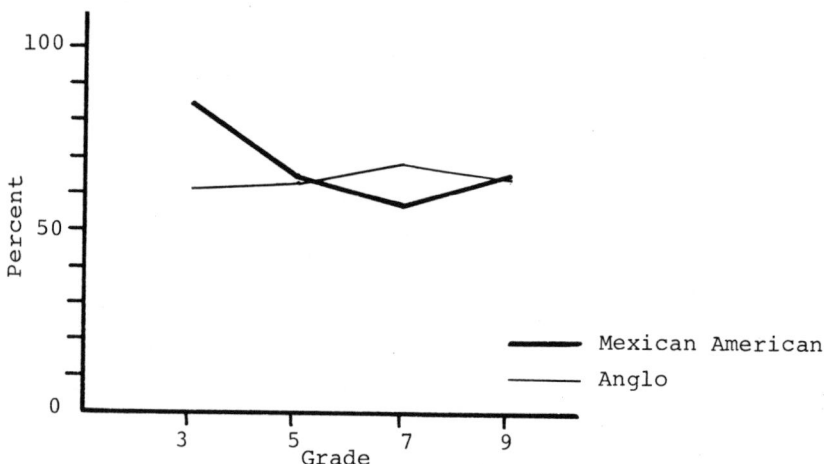

TABLE 2.6

Mexican American and Anglo Children's Responses to the Question, "What Makes You Most Proud To Be an American?"
(in percentages)

Grade	People's Generosity	Beauty of Country	Election of Leaders	Freedom	President	Don't Know/No Answer	Total N
			Mexican Americans				
3	16.4	13.6	12.1	40.0	17.1	0.7	140
5	8.1	12.8	12.8	58.7	5.8	1.7	172
7	4.1	5.2	13.0	67.9	5.2	3.6	193
9	2.3	5.6	19.2	62.7	1.1	8.5	178
Total	7.2	8.9	14.3	58.6	6.7	4.2	683
			Anglos				
3	12.8	8.0	8.8	63.2	5.6	1.6	125
5	5.7	2.4	8.9	77.2	4.1	1.6	123
7	5.9	2.2	17.8	69.6	0.7	3.0	135
9	1.3	1.9	18.8	68.1	0.6	9.4	161
Total	6.1	3.5	14.0	69.5	2.6	4.2	544

A total of 67.5 percent of the Chicanos and 64.7 percent of the Anglos agreed that this is the case. Although by the ninth grade the agreement for both groups was very similar (Mexican American, 65.5 percent: Anglo, 64.4 percent), each followed a different path in arriving at that point (see Figure 2.13).

The Mexican American child in the third grade thinks very highly of his country vis-à-vis others (84.3 percent), but this high opinion erodes rapidly until it reaches a low point of 58.5 percent at the seventh grade level, after which it again ascends. The Anglo third grader expresses more doubt initially, then his opinion rises gradually toward a seventh-grade apex, after which it descends slowly. At the ninth grade level both groups' opinions seem to level off at an average 65 percent support. The descent in the graph line for Chicanos from the third to the seventh grade may indicate a reaction to their experience as a minority group in the United States with all the consequent hardships. The rise after age 13 remains an unexplained change in the direction of opinion, although those Chicano adolescents most dissatisfied with the system may have dropped out of school.

Controlling for social class shows slightly different patterns for three categories, with the pattern of Chicano middle-class responses noteworthy for its range, from 90 percent to 40 percent. Again the use of Spanish accounted for more variation in the response than did any other control variable. A majority (56 percent) of those students using more English than Spanish answered in the affirmative, while only 21.9 percent of the more Spanish-oriented agreed. Whether Chicanos reside in the northern rural area or the southern urban location also makes a difference in attitude, with the urbanite more likely to agree that the United States is the best country (79 percent versus 68 percent). While some disillusionment occurs among the urban children as they mature, that of the rural Mexican American is much more pronounced.

SUMMARY OF AFFECTIVE ORIENTATIONS

It is clear that Mexican American children demonstrate a good deal of affection for the United States. At an early age their affection is often greater than that of Anglo children. Their decrease in affection through the years proceeds at about the same rate as that of their Anglo classmates; at the ninth grade level there is only a

slight difference between the two ethnic groups on most
questions. Much of the decline in affection among Chicanos is due to the steep drop among those residing in a
rural atmosphere and those whose families are closer to
the Mexican culture. The only significant differences between the two ethnic groups appear on questions relating
to Mexico. In these cases, the cultural pride of the
Chicanos becomes evident; even though they are generally
more pro-U.S. than Anglo Americans, they still feel a
special attachment to the country of their ancestral
origin.

On measures of affect for the American polity, Chicanos do not demonstrate the sharp divergence from the dominant culture as they mature that Greenberg found among
black children.[20] The affect of Mexican American children
for the American political community does decrease as
their cognitive ability improves and experiences with the
larger environment increase, but at a rate not dissimilar
to that among children of the core culture.

CONCLUSIONS

Differences in the orientation of Mexican American
and Anglo children with regard to support of the American
political community are not large. While cognition of
verbal symbols of the United States comes later for Mexican
Americans than for Anglos, the Mexican American's affection
initially is generally higher.

Chicano children seem to become aware of the local
polity first and later extend their cognition to the state
and national levels. Even when their ability to verbalize
the names of the governmental levels is not very advanced,
Chicano children do demonstrate a high degree of affect
for the national community. A very high degree of pride
and attachment to the United States characterizes the perceptions of the younger children, to the extent that they
can be considered even more ethnocentric than the Anglos.

Yet disillusionment occurs at a more rapid rate for
Chicanos, particularly for those who are closer to the culture of Mexico. This is likely the result of more severe
rejection by the American society as well as closer cultural ties to Mexico. Rural Chicanos, subject to fewer
contacts with "Anglicizing" agencies than their city brothers, feel less attachment to the United States as they
grow older. Social class does not have a great effect on
the perceptions of these Chicano children but is correlated

with a lower cognition of community symbols. Lower-class
Mexican Americans generally display the greatest affection
when they are young and the least as they near adulthood.

3

ORIENTATION TOWARD
THE REGIME:
GOVERNMENT

INTRODUCTION

In Chapter 2, attention was focused on a comparison
of Mexican American and Anglo children's cognition of and
affection for their political community, the first major
element in David Easton's conceptualization of the political system. A second component of the system is the political regime, which is composed of three basic elements:
(1) values, or the goals and principles guiding the political order; (2) norms, or the accepted operating procedures
for allocating rewards or values--the "rules of the game";
and (3) the structure of authority, or "the formal and informal patterns in which power is distributed and orga-
nized with regard to the authoritative making and implementing of decisions."[1]

The richness of the concept of a political regime
makes it necessary to devote substantial analysis to each
of its components. In this chapter the structure of authority will be examined; the next two chapters will offer
analyses of Mexican American orientations toward the value
and norm components of the regime. David Easton and Jack
Dennis believe that support for the structure of authority
is perhaps the most fundamental requisite of system legitimacy.[2] It is in this subsystem that inputs into the total
system are converted into binding policy outputs or authoritative decisions. In all systems, decision-making roles
are institutionalized, usually in the form of public offices; various officials also may be assigned the tasks
of implementing and obtaining compliance with public decisions. In order for a system to maintain itself, the
decisions of the authority structure must be acceptable to

the members of the polity, i.e., they must be considered legitimate. Easton and Dennis sum up and emphasize this point when they state:

> no system can persist . . . without some struc-
> ture of authority. . . . There must be some min-
> imal input of support for the structure of au-
> thority, and a belief in its legitimacy empiri-
> cally turns out to be the most dependable and
> continuing kind of support. Without this struc-
> ture of authority . . . there could be no polit-
> ical system.[3]

Easton and Dennis have shown that "what is theoreti-cally of highest significance (i.e., authority) empirically plays a crucial part in linking the child to the political system in the United States."[4] Among other things, a child's earliest socialization includes forming images of persons and institutions of authority. As with orienta-tions toward the political community, regime perceptions include cognitive and affective components.

The closest approximation to the theoretical concept of "structure of authority" is the notion of "government." Although a precise definition of the concept is difficult for adults, children have been found able to handle the general idea of government and give it some kind of concrete meaning, however inaccurate, at a very early age. Investi-gators have ascertained that even the second-grade student feels he has some understanding of the concept.[5] His ear-liest cognition involves much personalization—the view of government as composed of a visible person or persons. This early image usually is characterized by highly posi-tive feelings. These favorable orientations toward "per-sonal" government are an important origin of political le-legitimacy as they later spill over to embrace other aspects of the regime.[6]

YOUNG CHICANOS' IMAGE OF
GOVERNMENT

Cognition

What is the specific context of this image of govern-ment among Chicano children, and how does it compare to that among Anglo students? Our sample was offered nine pictorial representations of government--those earlier research determined to be the symbols most frequently selected by children as representing government (see Appendix B). The pattern of response is shown in Table 3.1. The only three symbols selected by more than 10 percent of the total group were the President, Congress, and voting. The order of popularity among the Chicanos was as follows: (1) Congress, (2) the President, and (3) voting. For Anglos, the order was as follows: (1) Congress, (2) voting, and (3) the flag (followed closely by the Statue of Liberty). While Chicanos placed the President among the top three representations of government, the Anglos preferred the U.S. flag. This greater preference for persons among minority group children and for symbolic representations among Anglos concurs with the findings of Greenberg in his study of black children.[7] While the sum perceptions of Chicanos and Anglos do not differ greatly, their developmental patterns through the years do show some variance.

Previous research has posited the theory that the young child first perceives government in the form of a high public authority, especially the President.[8] This is a prime example of the process of "personalization": the child is able to deal with an abstract concept like government by equating it with an easily understood entity --a person. This process is evidenced in our sample, although the Mexican Americans are closer to the ideal type than are the Anglos. Among the youngest Chicanos, the President holds a strong margin as the favorite representative of government over his nearest contender--George Washington. The Anglo third graders' favorite image of government also is the President, but he is picked by a smaller percentage and holds only a slight edge over an institution, the Congress.

The lesser presidential preference of the Anglos may be due to difficulty in separating the office from the man. President Nixon's picture was used, which may have caused a hesitation to select this choice since unsolicited verbal and written comments indicated the incumbent President is quite unpopular with these youngsters. Or a hypothesis tied to socialization theory may be more suitable. Theoretically, a child's political socialization patterns include, with age, a transformation of his early personalization to a growing appreciation of institutions, a process termed "institutionalization." As the child matures, his perceptual ability increases and he sees that government is more than an individual; groups, institutions, and processes become increasingly equated with government. This

TABLE 3.1

Percentage of Mexican American and Anglo Children Selecting Each Picture in Response to the Question, "Which One of These Pictures Shows Best What Our Government Is?"

Grade	Policeman	George Washington	Voting	Supreme Court	Capitol	Congress	Flag	Statue of Liberty	President
				Mexican American Children					
3	0.7	20.0	12.9	4.3	7.9	7.9	4.3	3.6	33.6
5	1.7	4.7	9.9	5.8	14.5	18.6	9.3	7.0	20.9
7	7.3	3.6	9.3	3.1	7.8	26.9	5.7	5.2	12.4
9	6.2	4.0	13.6	2.3	5.6	21.5	10.2	12.4	10.2
Total	4.4	7.3	11.3	3.8	8.9	19.5	7.5	7.2	18.3
				Anglo Children					
3	1.6	10.4	9.6	2.4	11.2	17.6	8.8	9.6	20.0
5	2.4	2.4	4.1	8.1	11.4	34.1	15.4	4.1	13.0
7	5.2	3.0	20.0	6.7	3.0	19.3	13.3	17.0	6.7
9	5.0	1.3	21.3	3.1	4.4	17.5	10.6	11.3	10.0
Total	3.7	4.0	14.3	5.0	7.2	21.7	11.9	10.7	12.3

process is seen in Figures 3.1 and 3.2. Third-grade Chicanos see the government largely in personal terms; a majority select pictures of political authorities, distantly followed by institutions and symbols. Mexican-American third graders select the President and George Washington at almost twice the rate of their Anglo classmates (see Figure 3.3). Thus they come closer to the ideal type postulated by previous studies than do the Anglo children in the present study. Yet at this stage the President clearly is the top choice of both groups. By the fifth grade, authorities, symbols, and institutions are almost equally perceived as government, with institutions selected most often. For Chicanos in the later grades, the institutions of government clearly become the most common cognition. This also is the case for Anglos in our sample.

When one examines the charts of Anglo preferences for the most frequently chosen single representation of government (see Figure 3.4), the process of institutionalization again is illustrated. From an initial low second place, Congress as "government" shoots up to a lofty position by the fifth grade, then diminishes in relative importance and levels off in the seventh and ninth grades. This process also is evident, at a slower rate, in the Mexican-American group. Congress seems to have a very low cognitive profile for younger Chicanos. The peak preference for Congress is not achieved until the seventh grade, after which it proceeds to taper off.

Voting as the essence of government occupies a greatly divergent importance for Chicano and Anglo children. As might be expected, an activity so remote from a young child's experience would not occupy an important position in his cognitive field, as illustrated by the low percentage for both groups in the lower grades. As Anglo children mature and approach the age of franchise, their awareness of its importance to our system's operation increases drastically, until it finally becomes the institution best exemplifying our government. Chicano children do not follow a similar pattern; their ranking of voting as young adults is almost the same as it was in third grade.

Since both ethnic groups were exposed to the same classroom civics instruction, the socializing influences of the extrascholastic community is probably largely responsible for this variance. Voting is not as important to groups more concerned with surviving in an inimical environment as it is to members of the dominant society. Moreover, various sanctions, both legal and extralegal, historically have been used in the United States to discourage

55

FIGURE 3.1

Percent of Mexican American Children Selecting a Political
Authority Figure, A Political Institution or a Political
Symbol in Response to the Question, "Which One of These
Pictures Shows Best What Our Government Is?"

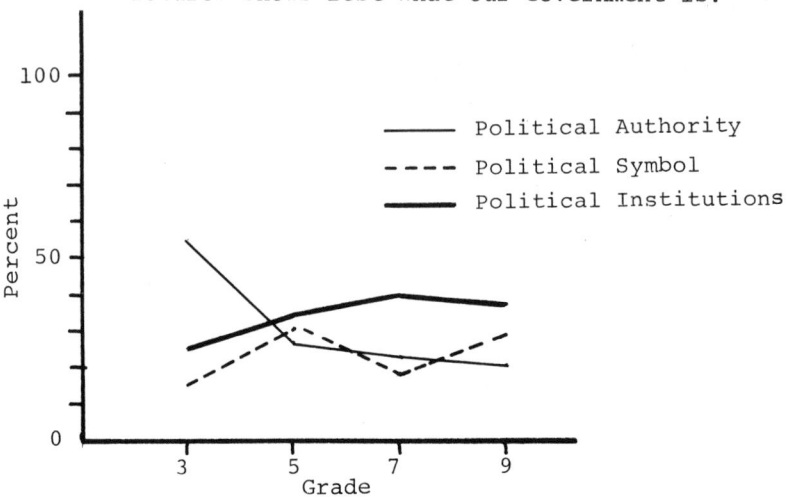

FIGURE 3.2

Percent of Anglos Selecting Either a Political Authority
Figure, A Political Institution or a Political Symbol in
Response to the Question, "Which One of These Pictures
Shows Best What Our Government Is?"

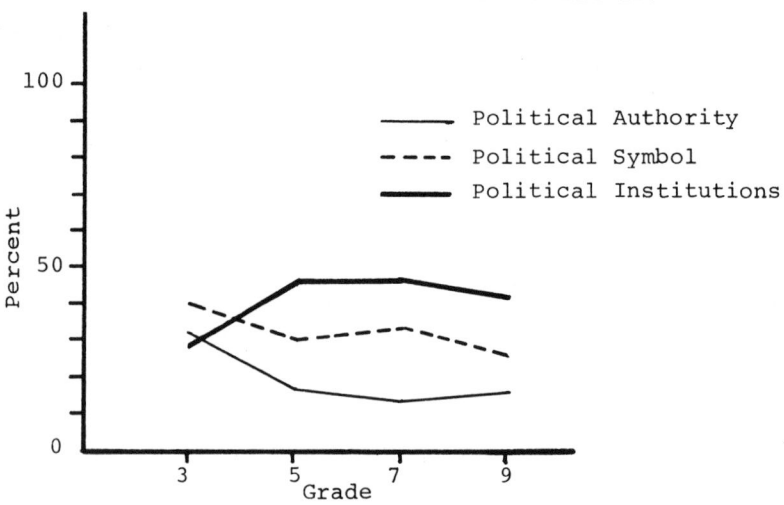

FIGURE 3.3

Choices of Mexican American Children as to
the Best Picture of Government

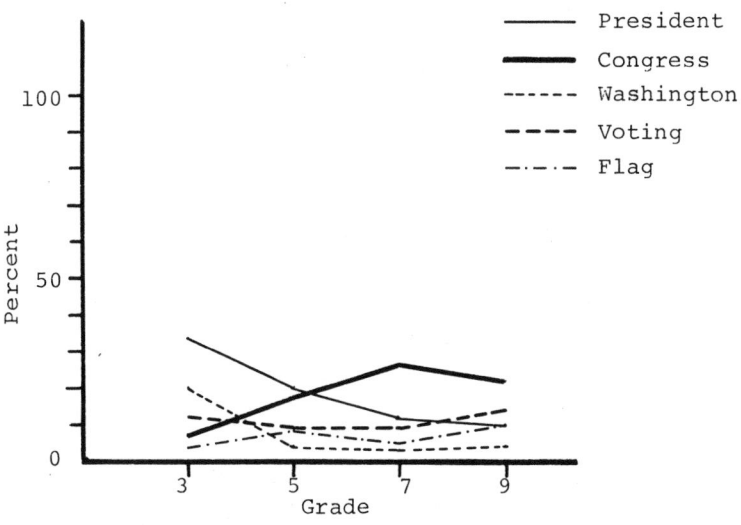

FIGURE 3.4

Choices of Anglo Children as to the Best
Picture of Government

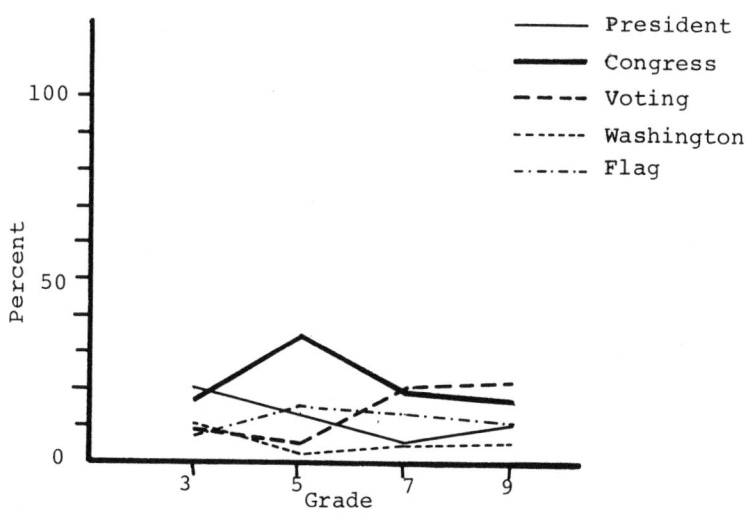

"visible" ethnics from voting. For these reasons and others, voting participation generally is much lower among these groups than among Anglos.[9] Consequently the Chicano child growing up in the California barrio or campo is not going to receive much support from his community institutions or encouragement from his family when it comes to exercising a privilege that is apt to be relatively unimportant to them. The voting process, then, although placed above all but one other representation by ninth-grade Chicanos, is less a picture of government than is the institution of Congress, which usually is stressed in the classroom as an important governmental agent.

When controls for social class are introduced, some interesting comparisons emerge (see Table 3.2). While a large percentage of third graders in both Chicano classes select the President, almost one-third of the middle class select voting as the most popular representation of government, illustrating the quicker cognitive development of the child of higher socioeconomic status. By the ninth grade, Congress is the favorite image for both classes. Middle-class Anglo third graders are most likely to pick Congress as government, while the working class sticks with the President. The ninth-grade working-class Anglos join the ninth-grade Chicanos in seeing Congress as the embodiment of government; however, the Anglo middle class favors voting by ninth grade. Also surprising, in light of past research, is the fact that the Anglo middle-class third graders never selected the President as their favorite.

In sum, the children in this sample seem more advanced in their processes of institutionalization than those of previous studies. The lower level of institutionalization among young Chicano students is closer to the orientation of Anglos in earlier studies than are the cognitions of the Anglos in this study, especially the middle-class Anglo third graders, who already have begun to depersonalize government.

As personalization recedes, Mexican-American children increasingly see Congress as the best representation of government. During these years, the Anglos, who already favored Congress at an earlier age, turn their attention to the voting process. This more abstract concept is less favored by the Chicano ninth graders although it is in second place and gaining popularity. If extended into the future, the Chicano pattern might replicate that of the Anglos. The overall picture might then be considered a lead-lag phenomenon, with the Chicanos developing in the

TABLE 3.2

Percentage, By Class, Selecting Each Picture in Response to the Question, "Which One of These Pictures Shows Best What Our Government Is?"

Grade	Policeman	George Washington	Voting	Supreme Court	Capitol	Congress	Flag	Statue of Liberty	President
Mexican American Lower Class									
3	0.9	20.9	10.4	4.3	70.0	7.8	5.2	3.5	33.9
5	2.4	6.5	5.6	5.6	16.1	15.3	10.5	8.1	21.8
7	5.9	4.4	9.6	2.2	8.1	25.7	6.6	4.4	14.0
9	5.6	4.8	13.6	3.2	5.6	19.2	9.6	12.0	8.0
Mexican American Middle Class									
3	0.0	10.0	30.0	5.0	5.0	5.0	0.0	5.0	40.0
5	0.0	0.0	20.0	7.5	12.5	32.5	5.0	2.5	17.5
7	8.3	2.1	10.4	2.1	8.3	27.1	4.2	8.3	10.4
9	9.8	2.4	14.6	0.0	2.4	22.0	14.6	12.2	17.1
Anglo Lower Class									
3	1.9	13.0	13.0	1.9	13.0	7.4	1.9	14.8	27.8
5	6.5	0.0	4.3	8.7	10.9	19.6	19.6	6.5	19.6
7	5.4	3.6	26.8	7.1	1.8	14.3	14.3	16.1	3.6
9	6.0	1.5	14.9	3.0	4.5	22.4	9.0	13.4	7.5
Anglo Middle Class									
3	1.5	7.3	7.3	2.9	10.3	26.5	14.7	4.4	14.7
5	0.0	4.0	4.0	8.0	12.0	42.7	12.0	2.7	9.3
7	5.4	2.7	14.9	6.7	4.1	22.9	10.8	18.9	6.7
9	4.5	1.1	26.9	3.4	4.5	13.5	12.4	10.1	11.2

same manner as the Anglos but with about a two-year lag. The lesser importance of voting in the Mexican-American community may be the reason the response to voting constitutes the one major difference in the socialization patterns of these two groups of children.

GOVERNMENT AS LAWMAKER

Several studies have shown that when a child assesses government in functional rather than structural terms he will most likely associate government with its lawmaking function.[10] Adults, too, often perceive the government's main activity as the making of laws.[11] When the Mexican-American students were asked, "Who has the most to do with making laws?", their responses formed developmental patterns similar to those for their image of "government." Initially, the President is seen as the chief lawmaker, but he declines rapidly through the years as the groups, Congress, and the Supreme Court become the primary lawmaking agents. By the time political maturation is reached, Congress is far and away the primary legislative institution as the other two agents decline. These opinions, then, substantiate the finding that over the years these Mexican-American youths increasingly tend to see Congress as the center of government. The Anglo pattern is similar.

Another item bears out the increasing importance of Congress in the Chicano children's conception of government. When asked to give an opinion as to "Who does the most to run the country?", they initially favor the chief executive by a tremendous margin. However, by the time they near adulthood, they have completely switched their preferences and give Congress primary responsibility for the country's affairs (see Table 3.3). A growing respect for the role of the U.S. Supreme Court in the affairs of the country also is evident. Once again, the process of institutionalization and the importance of Congress are evident.

Two other items explicitly tapped the students' feelings about "the law": one concerned its mutability, the other its fairness. The youngest Chicanos see the law as very stable, and over one-fourth think that "no laws will change" by the time they are adults. This is probably a result of equating governmental output with the government itself.[12] By the fifth grade, a more perceptive view prevails--responses to the "no change" option drop off greatly,

TABLE 3.3

Mexican American Children's Responses to the Question,
"Who Does the Most to Run the Country?"
(in percentages)

Grade	Congress	President	Supreme Court
3	15.7	75.0	2.1
5	12.8	69.2	3.5
7	29.0	49.2	3.6
9	48.0	30.5	9.0

and the idea that just a few laws will change prevails and
increases with age. A majority of the ninth-grade Mexican
Americans selected this option. Also of note is the fact
that fewer ninth graders than seventh graders feel most
laws will change. Obviously the overall picture is one of
legal stability with only minor changes in the laws over
the years.

The response pattern of their Anglo classmates is
similar except at the initial year of school sampled. The
Anglos see the law (or more likely at this stage, government) as more subject to change--only 13 percent select
the no-change option.

The Chicano youths' concept of legal justice changes
markedly over the developmental years in school. Initially
they overwhelmingly view the law as just, but very soon a
sharp reversal of this feeling begins. As the students
are able to better understand the concept of the law as
separate from government, the belief that "all laws are
fair" shrinks to 17.5 percent by the ninth grade. The fact
that over 70 percent of the oldest Chicanos doubted the
fairness of the laws may be of special significance for
system support. While law is a product of government, a
negative feeling toward its major output also may portend
dissatisfaction with the system itself. Acts of civil
disobedience may be the end result of this situation.

And judging from the results on this item, Chicano
youths would have little difficulty in finding Anglo allies
of similar persuasion. Overall, Anglos are even less inclined to accept the idea that all laws are fair. They
are slightly less supportive in the earliest grade and
very slightly more so in the ninth grade, with a plateau
phenomenon occurring in the middle years (see Figure 3.5).

FIGURE 3.5

Percent, By Grade and Ethnicity, Feeling
that "All Laws Are Fair"

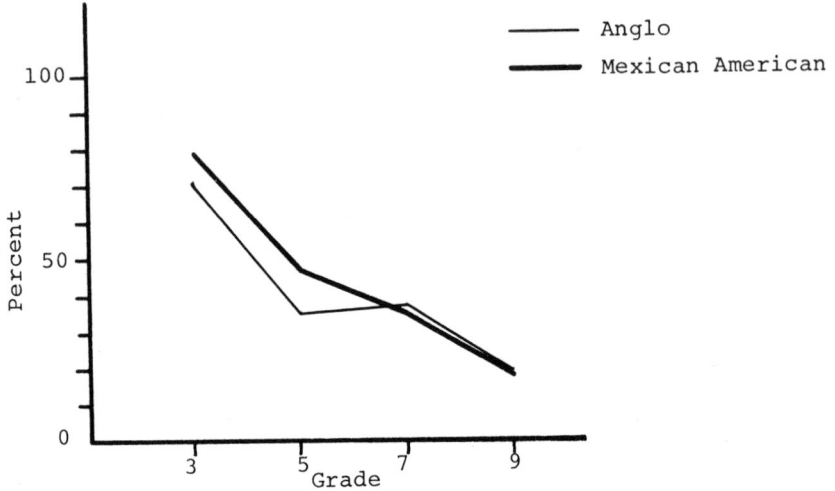

POLITICIZATION

Having provided evidence that Mexican American children have some conception of government while very young,
we may verify this by determining whether these children
really are able to distinguish strictly governmental from
nongovernmental items. If so, the bonds between these
children and authority figures representing government can
more positively be considered the beginning of genuinely
political ties to the system. Since young children are
more aware of individuals than institutions, they were
asked to distinguish between governmental and nongovernmental
occupations. Six choices were presented: two were associated with local governments (policeman and teacher), two
were national government workers (soldier and mailman), one
was not clearly affiliated with any particular level of
government (judge), and one was nongovernmental (milkman).

Table 3.4 illustrates that Mexican American children
can differentiate governmental from nongovernmental figures
from an early age. About 90 percent of the youngest respondents knew that the milkman was not an employee of the
government. Among the public figures, they most easily
recognized the policeman and the judge as working for the

TABLE 3.4

Mexican American and Anglo Children's Responses to the
Question, "Which of These People Work for the Government?"
(in percentages)

Grade	Milk-man	Police-man	Soldier	Judge	Mail-man	Teacher
			Mexican Americans			
3	12.1	75.0	57.9	71.4	25.7	26.4
5	9.3	82.0	58.1	78.5	36.6	34.9
7	10.4	86.5	71.0	82.9	58.5	48.2
9	6.8	70.6	72.9	78.5	68.4	40.7
Total	9.5	78.9	65.4	78.3	48.9	38.5
			Anglos			
3	10.4	69.6	59.2	73.6	25.6	26.4
5	11.4	70.7	71.5	87.8	46.3	31.7
7	7.4	80.0	83.7	71.9	59.3	40.0
9	5.6	63.1	82.5	78.1	60.0	33.8
Total	8.5	70.6	75.0	77.8	48.7	33.3

government. The policeman received the greatest recognition by the Mexican American children; this holds at the
lowest grade level as well as for the entire group. After
the law officer came the judge, followed by the soldier,
the teacher, and the mailman. By the ninth grade, all the
public officials (except the teacher) received roughly the
same recognition, with the judge supplanting the policeman
at the top of the list. The pattern was similar for the
Anglo children, although among them the soldier made the
largest gains through the years until he ranked right below the judge. The teacher's status remained rather ambivalent throughout the years, never considered a governmental employee by as many as 50 percent of any group. It
is probable that the children's perceptions of the teacher
are not unlike those of adults in our society.

One can conclude that Mexican American children are just as able to differentiate the governmental sector from the nongovernmental at an early age as Anglo children. At least they are able to distinguish governmental personnel from those in the private sphere. Young Chicanos are more aware of the police officer's governmental status than are the Anglos, for whom the judge and the soldier stand out.

THE SALIENCE OF GOVERNMENT

To complete our picture of the young Chicanos' perceptions of government, an attempt was made to ascertain whether they felt the government had any impact on the lives of their families and themselves, i.e., whether government is salient for them. Also, there was an investigation of whether the groups differed as to the effect of the various levels of government, or indeed whether they perceived any of the various levels of government at all.[13]

When the pupils were asked whether they thought the U.S. government was very important in what happened to them and to their families, slightly divergent patterns between ethnic groups appear. The most prominent difference is that the Mexican Americans' appreciation of government's impact on their lives falls off quickly and appreciably in comparison with that of the Anglos, although they begin at the same level. The descent continues until the seventh grade and then climbs very slightly (see Figure 3.6).

Controlling for social class reveals some interesting orientation patterns, including converse configurations between classes of Chicanos (see Figure 3.7). Mexican-American children of the middle class see the government as increasingly important in their primary school years; however, its salience decreases sharply during the middle years. The salience of the U.S. government immediately drops for working-class children in primary school, then begins to increase as they continue through school. Anglo middle-class children see the government as much more important than do any of the other groups. Their trend of saliency through the years parallels that of middle-class Mexican Americans. Working-class Anglos evidence a continually decreasing opinion of governmental salience.

One can understand the lower salience of government for the working classes, since all studies show that political interest and participation is positively associated with socioeconomic standing, but why the differential trend

FIGURE 3.6

Percent Positive Responses, By Grade and Ethnicity, to:
"Do You Think the United States Government Is Very
Important in What Happens to You and Your Family?"

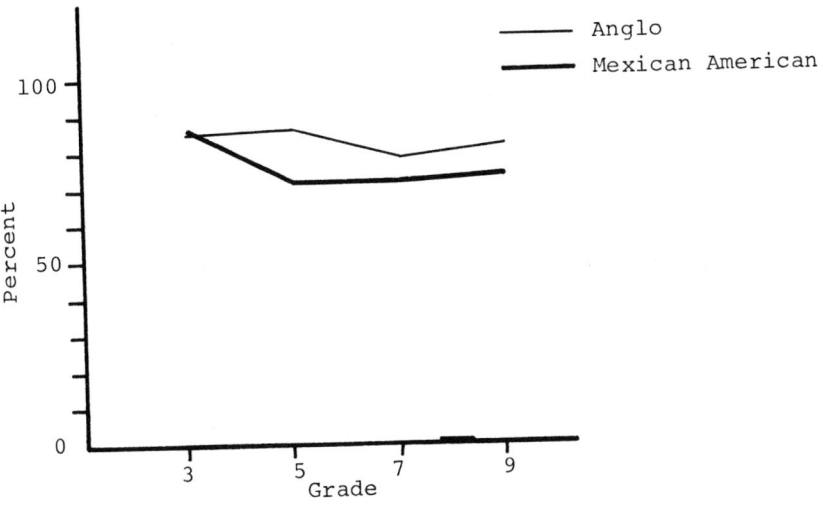

FIGURE 3.7

Percent Positive Responses, By Grade and Ethnicity, to:
"Do You Think the United States Government Is Very
Important in What Happens to You and Your Family?",
Controlling for Social Class

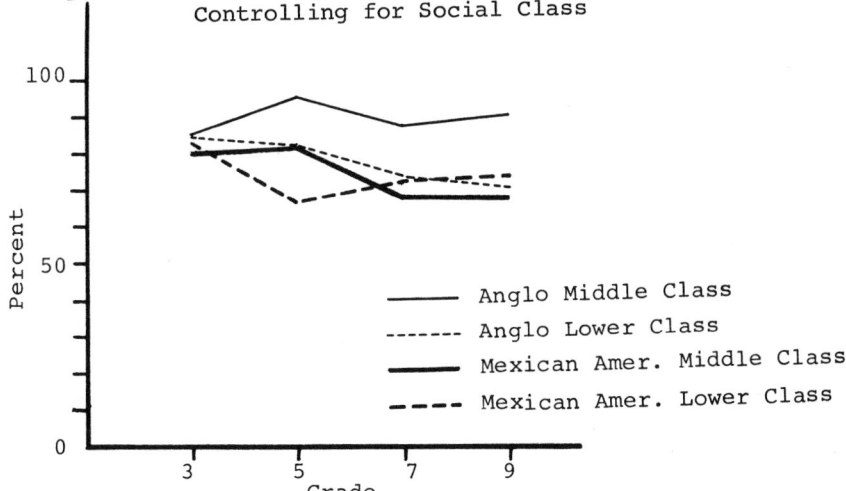

as Chicanos mature? It is likely that middle-class Chicanos are less likely to feel the impact of national governmental policy than are their working-class brothers. As the working-class children mature, they become aware of public policies most likely to affect them and their families, particularly the draft and welfare policies. Thus governmental salience increases for working-class children vis-à-vis their middle-class counterparts.

However, among Chicanos, socioeconomic status is not as good a predictor as Spanish language usage. Those who are closest to the Mexican culture feel the U.S. government is less important to them than those who are more acculturated to U.S. society. Also, this is one of the few items in which the sex of the student has a significant effect on the response. Female Mexican Americans feel less governmental impact than males, who as they grow older no doubt feel the impact of military conscription.

Chicanos feel that the national government has a greater effect on their lives than either the state (California) or city government (see Figures 3.8 and 3.9). Through the early years the same trends are discerned for the latter two levels as for the central government, with the highest salience reported in the third grade but a quick drop in salience to the seventh grade as perhaps a more accurate evaluation is possible. As the "teen" years begin, Mexican Americans begin increasingly to appreciate the impact of the national and local governments on their lives. The importance of state government, however, continues to decline for Chicanos, this being the only deviation from the otherwise parallel orientation of the two groups.

Orientations toward the California government are only slightly affected when controls for class are introduced. Middle-class feelings through the years are relatively stable. The difference mentioned earlier is mainly the result of divergent patterns between the working classes of each group; in fact, the patterns of the Anglo working class and Chicano middle class are most similar. As working-class Mexican Americans near adulthood, they feel the state government is less and less relevant to their circumstances. City government fares only slightly better among lower-class Chicanos, and middle-class Chicanos also feel city government is less important as they mature. Even among the highly aware middle-class Anglos, the salience of city government diminishes sharply as adulthood approaches. Lower-class Anglos give the highest rating to the municipal government.

FIGURE 3.8

Percent, By Grade and Ethnicity, Feeling that the
California State Government Is Important to Them

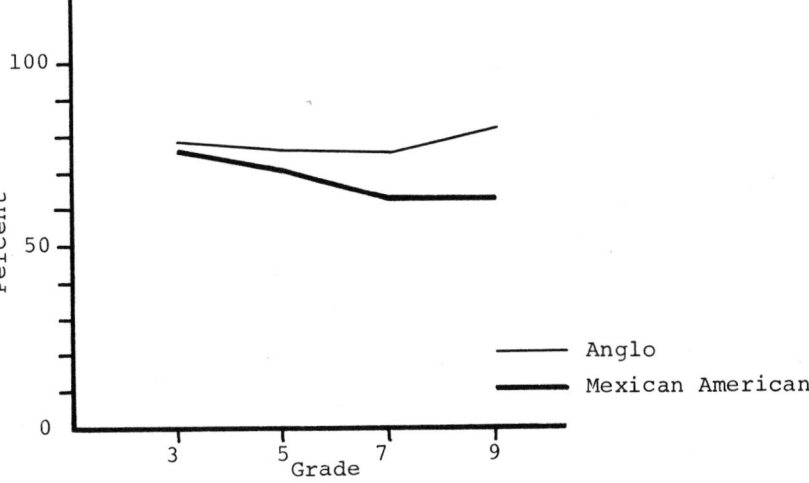

FIGURE 3.9

Percent, By Grade and Ethnicity, Feeling that Their
City Government Is Important to Them

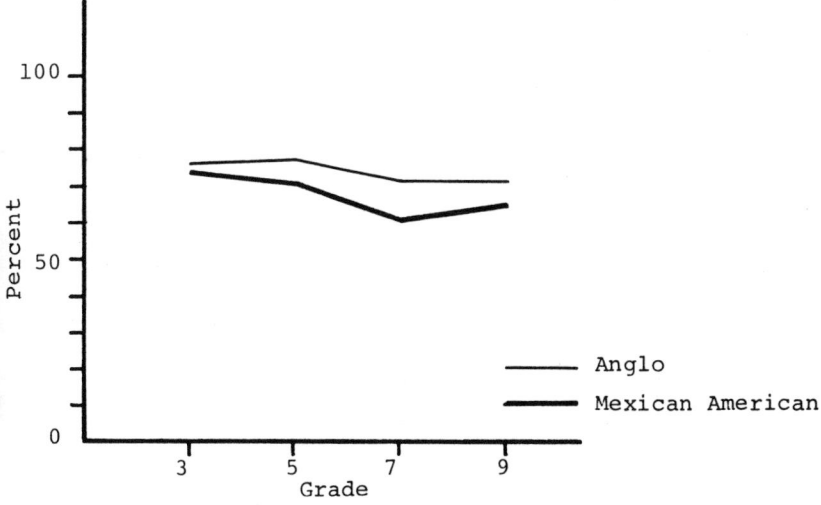

67

Regression analysis shows no difference in the ability of class and ethnicity to cause variance in these attitudes toward the salience of city government. Ethnicity had slightly more effect on orientation toward California government than did socioeconomic status, while attitudes toward the national government were more affected by socioeconomic status than by ethnicity. Ethnicity was most highly associated with attitudes toward state government (gamma = 0.25), then the nation (gamma = 0.21), and least with the city (gamma = 0.19).

Since by far the best predictor of the salience of California government for Chicanos is the use of Spanish, followed by the length of residence in this country, it may be that the families of recently arrived children discussed their move as one to California rather than to Los Estados Unidos, thus increasing the state's salience for their children.

In summary, Mexican American youths first equate government with a person, particularly the President, whom they are aware is a political authority. As they mature, their image of government becomes increasingly institutionalized, with Congress seen as the foremost institution of government. The legislative function of government is emphasized, and its product is viewed as stable and unchanging, if increasingly unjust. The national government is most salient to young Chicanos, followed by those of the state and city in which they reside.

AFFECT TOWARD GOVERNMENT

It is particularly important in a study of support for a political system to assess children's negative or positive judgments of their government. That Mexican American children perceive as visible and salient the existence of an entity entitled "government" has been established. Whether this object is regarded as friendly and competent or hostile and inadequate is of central importance. Of course in reality this affective dimension is not neatly separated from cognition in the child's perception; however, it is analytically useful to separate the two.

As almost all previous research has shown, initial attachment of young children to the regime begins at a very high, positive level. The Mexican American children in the primary school sample are not exceptions, as almost 90 percent see the government in nurturant terms (see

Figure 3.10). Although this feeling declines slightly through the years, the great majority continue to feel protected by the government. Although the diminution of this feeling is greater among the Chicanos during the early years, after the fifth grade their orientation curve runs parallel to, although slightly lower than, that of the Anglos (gamma = 0.29).

Actually, this parallelism is largely attributable to the feelings of the middle classes. Although the initial perceptions of all classes are similar, they vary through the years. Most significant is the continually divergent trend of working-class Chicanos (see Figure 3.11). These children feel less and less sure that government is concerned with their condition until by adolescence their attitudes are significantly different from those of the other groups. No doubt this is an accurate reflection of reality by members of an "invisible minority." This feeling is especially strong among the most "Mexican" of the Chicanos, as measured by Spanish language usage, which is the best predictor of this attitude. Over half (57.7 percent) of Chicanos whose home language is primarily Spanish reject the idea that government cares about them, while only 42.3 percent of the English-speaking Mexican Americans feel that way. The third best predictor, after grade, is area of residence: the northern rural Chicanos feel less certain about the government's concern for them. As they enter adulthood, only a slight majority feel any governmental concern, and this sentiment is falling.

The general idealization of the government and its decline through the years also is shown in Figure 3.12, which indicates the children's evaluation of governmental helpfulness. The youngest children perceive government most helpful, and this feeling declines as the years progress. The Mexican American children are less impressed with the government's role in providing assistance, and this trend continues through the grades; but even at the ninth grade a majority appreciate the government's helpfulness.

However, the Chicano children evaluate governmental helpfulness as lower than governmental concern. If government cares about Mexican Americans, it does not appear to be doing as much in the way of actually providing assistance. As one might expect, socioeconomic level has a significant effect on this attitude (see Figure 3.13). At ages eight and nine, there is very little difference between the categories, although Chicanos of both classes see government as slightly less helpful than do both classes of

69

FIGURE 3.10

Percent, By Grade and Ethnicity, Feeling that "The
Government Cares About Us"

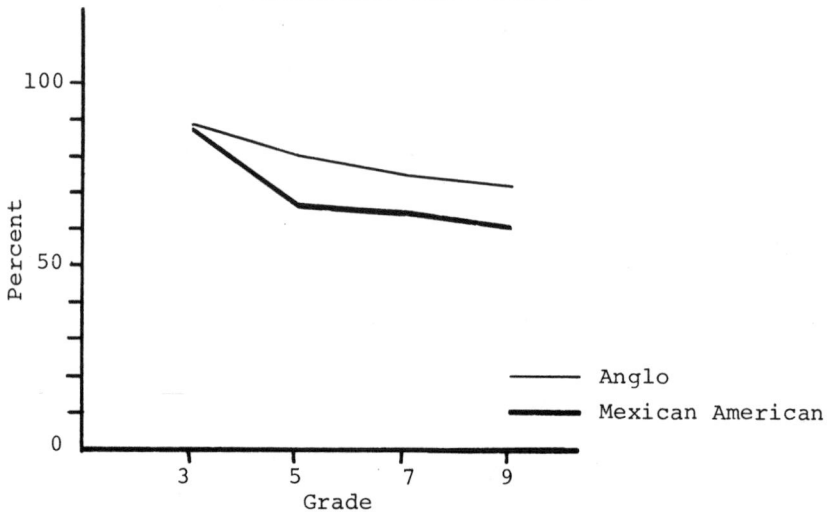

FIGURE 3.11

Percent, By Grade, Ethnicity, and Social Class, Feeling
that "The Government Cares About Us"

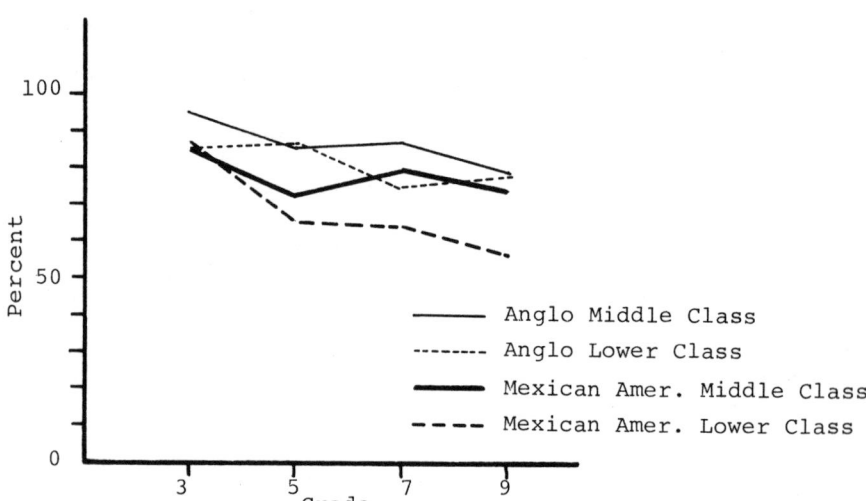

Anglos. But by the ninth grade, working-class children of varying ethnicity feel government is less helpful, and the lower-class Chicanos have the least positive image of government. Fewer lower-class Chicanos feel government is helpful than feel government is concerned.

Do Chicano youths feel the government is a friendly entity? Initially, yes, to a great extent (see Figure 3.14). This very high rating probably can be attributed to the vulnerability theory--that the relatively dependent and vulnerable position of the young child causes him to attribute benevolent characteristics to those in a position to control his fate. If this theory is valid, it would apply only to the younger children in the sample, with a less psychologically compensating perception held by the more mature children, probably from the fifth grade on. This change in perceptual capacity may be reflected in the precipitous drop between the third and fifth grades. At the fifth grade the ethnic groups part company over their evaluation of government friendliness. Although a decline continues for both groups, Mexican Americans more rapidly conclude the government is not friendly. The distance between ethnic groups increases as the youths mature. Grade level is by far the most influential variable on this response for the whole sample (beta = 0.23) and for Chicanos (beta = 0.26).

When the sample is further divided by social class, the differences between the older students of both ethnic groups remain (see Figure 3.15). Regression analysis confirms that ethnicity causes more variation in this attitude (beta = 0.14) than does social class (beta = 0.07). The only difference between classes is a parallel increase in each middle class's view of governmental amity from the fifth to seventh grade.

After grade level (beta = 0.26) and Spanish language usage (beta = 0.13), a heretofore relatively insignificant variable--perception of ethnic discrimination--is the most influential factor on Chicano perceptions of government friendliness (gamma = 0.32). Figure 3.16 shows some significant differences in the results of socialization through the years. Ironically, Chicanos who perceive discrimination are initially the most idealistic about government friendliness. But as they mature, those perceiving discrimination in American society see government as increasingly unfriendly, until by the age of 15 or 16 only 30.7 percent feel government is amicable, while 36.2 percent reject this evaluation. No doubt their experiences with situations of social discrimination produce attitudes that are transferred to the ruling body of the polity.

FIGURE 3.14

Percent, By Grade and Ethnicity, Responding that
"The Government Is Very Friendly"

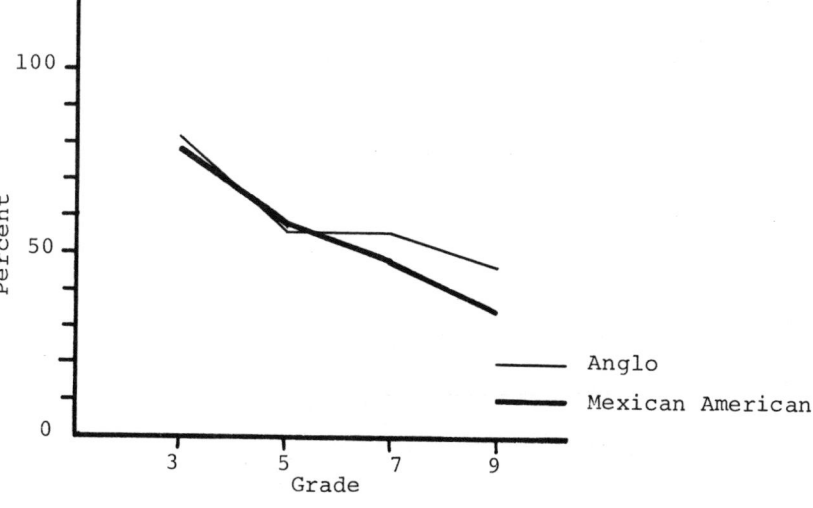

FIGURE 3.15

Percent, By Grade, Ethnicity, and Social Class, Responding
that "The Government Is Very Friendly"

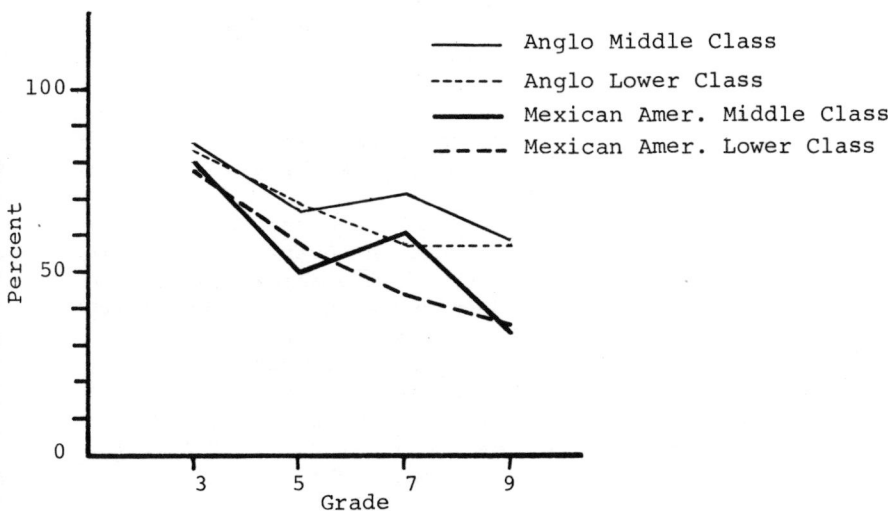

FIGURE 3.16

Percent, By Grade and Perception of Discrimination, of
Mexican American Children Feeling that "The Government
Is Very Friendly"

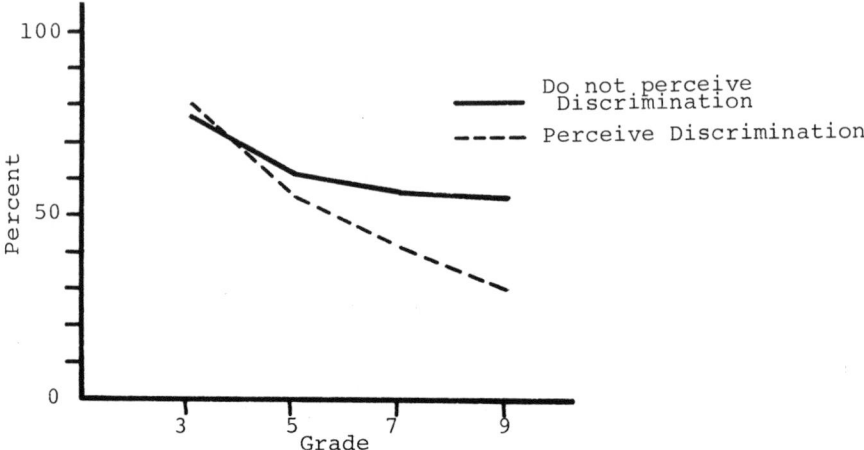

One can speculate that, as children mature, they
realize the government is neither friendly nor unfriendly,
as a person could be, but instead is a complex set of institutions with no single set of attitudes. Yet as they
grow older, Chicano children do not fail to respond to the
item, or answer that they "don't know"; instead, they increasingly respond that "the government is not very
friendly." In the ninth grade as many see the government
as unfriendly as friendly. Among Anglo children, on the
other hand, more than twice as many said government is
friendly as judged it unfriendly; many more took neither
position. One must conclude that whatever characteristics
Chicanos attribute to government, friendliness is not among
them.

These children apparently do not perceive the government as a very threatening force. However, more fear is
evident at the ninth grade than at the third grade. Re-
membering the younger children's view that the government
is very friendly may explain why they fear it less than do
teenagers. Chicanos' fear of the government continues at
about the same level as that of Anglos. Ethnicity seems
to have very little correlation with fear of the government (gamma = 0.02). Socioeconomic status is a better
predictor (beta = 0.06) of responses than is ethnicity

(beta = 0.007). Lower-class Mexican American youths are slightly more afraid of the government throughout their school years, but both Chicano groups generally are below the fear level of Anglos. The most interesting economic group are the working-class Anglos whose attitudes fluctuate the most. At the fifth grade they fear government least, but during adolescence the fear increases until over one-fourth fear the government very much.[14] Among the Chicanos, only Spanish language usage (beta = 0.14) and grade level (beta = 0.10) affect fear of government more than socioeconomic status does.

ROLE PERFORMANCE

How do Chicano children evaluate their government's performance? Three items tap this less emotional affective dimension: students were asked to judge whether government (1) was powerful, (2) knew a lot, and (3) made many mistakes.

Mexican American students of all ages do realize that government is indeed the locus of power in our society and feel only slightly less than Anglos in the sample that this is so (gamma = 0.03, see Figure 3.17). This evaluation is fairly consistent through the years. Controlling for social class brings out significant differences in attitudes; indeed, socioeconomic status is the most powerful predictor of this attitude for the total group and is second only to language for the Chicanos. In the primary grades, the opinions of the lower- and middle-class Chicanos are widely divergent, with the middle class, like the similar Anglo strata, viewing government as more powerful (see Figure 3.18). Government's already relatively low power rating among the working-class Chicanos decreases further during the early years. At the fifth grade, as children's perceptual abilities sharpen and they have increasing experience with socializing agents outside the home, the power evaluation of all but the middle-class Anglos diminishes, particularly that of the middle-class Chicanos who by the seventh grade share the feelings of their working-class co-ethnic. Then, as maturity approaches, all Chicanos raise their estimate of governmental power.

The young Chicanos' view of the government's knowledge-ability is not as high. Initially they perceive the knowledge possessed by the government as greater than·its power. However, unlike their view of power, their assessment of knowledge never recovers from the usual post-

FIGURE 3.17

Percent, By Grade and Ethnicity, Who Feel that
"The Government Is Very Powerful"

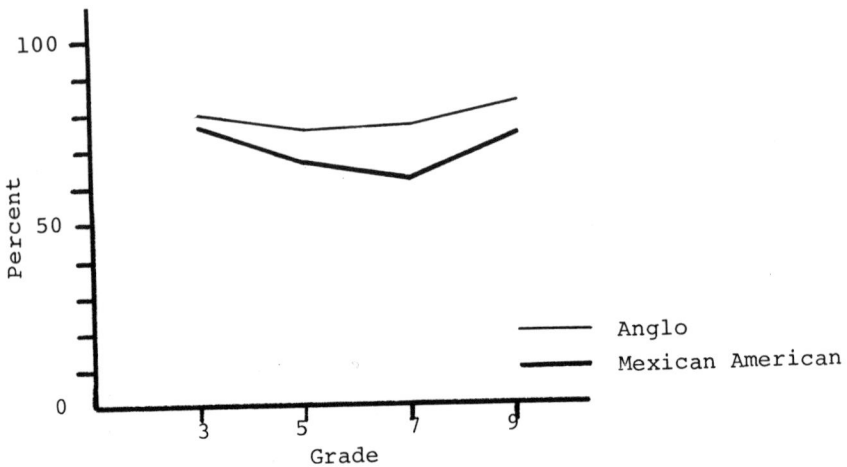

FIGURE 3.18

Percent, By Grade, Ethnicity and Social Class, Responding
that "The Government Is Very Powerful"

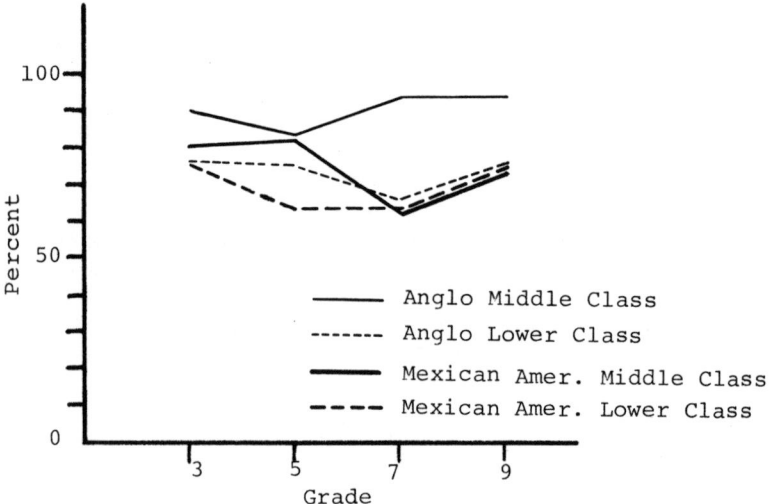

idealization decline (see Figure 3.19). This probably is
an accurate perception, since one's confidence in governmental intelligence sometimes is shaken in adult years by
its seeming ignorance on some issues. Certainly very few
adult Americans would claim omniscience for their government. Yet ethnicity is substantially correlated with this
evaluation (gamma = 0.34) as Chicanos have less faith in
government's knowledge than do Anglos. Since government
seemingly has been unaware of the existence, much less the
problems, of La Raza, this attitude is not surprising.
The disillusionment of Chicanos is much greater through
the years than that of Anglos. Controls for social class
show that this dimension may be substantially affected by
governmental response to the needs and demands of each
group (see Figure 3.20). The less visible Anglo working
class joins the even more transparent Chicano lower class
in an increasingly lower evaluation of governmental knowledge. And among Chicanos socioeconomic status has more
effect on this attitude than any other factor aside from
age and the use of Spanish.

The dimension of government performance involving the
least affect is its infallibility--whether the government
makes many mistakes. A tremendous change occurs in Mexican

FIGURE 3.19

Percent, By Grade and Ethnicity, Agreeing that
"The Government Knows a Lot"

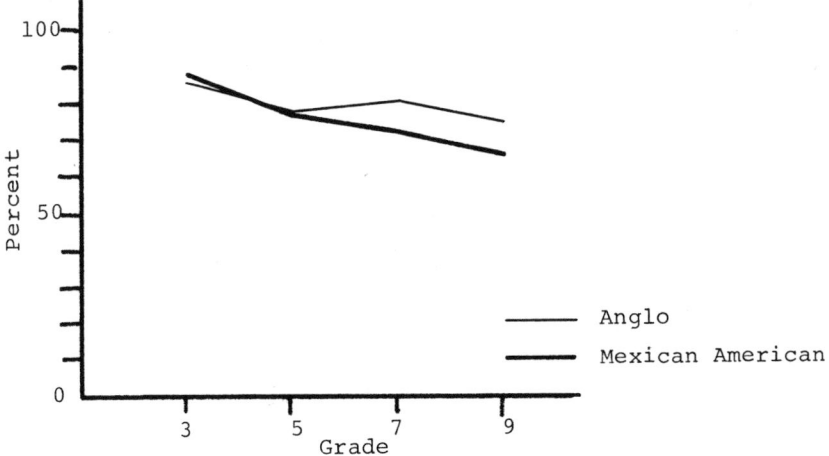

FIGURE 3.20

Percent, By Grade, Ethnicity and Social Class,
Agreeing that "The Government Knows a Lot"

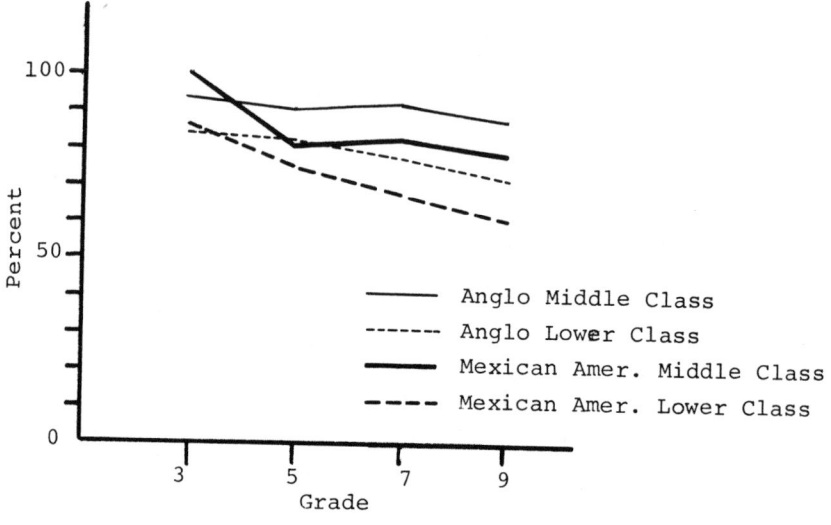

FIGURE 3.21

Percent, By Grade and Ethnicity, Feeling that "The
Government Almost Never Makes Mistakes"

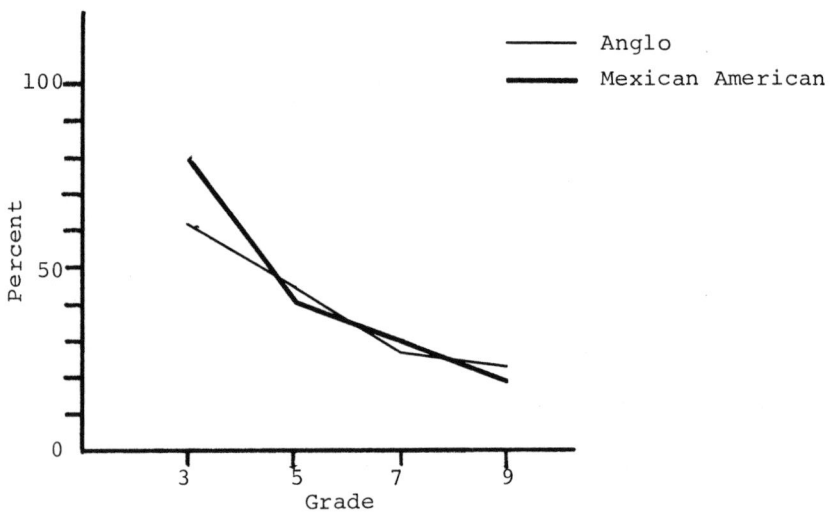

Americans' evaluation of this governmental performance trait during school years (see Figure 3.21). Initially almost 80 percent feel the government is infallible; by the ninth grade fewer than one out of five agree with this evaluation. Greater awareness of the operations of government and increased contact with criticism of governmental activity--particularly through the media, when added to the usual loss through de-idealization--account for this large drop. Grade level is by far the best predictor of this attitude (beta = 0.45), while all others are less than 0.10. Ethnicity is only slightly correlated with this orientation (gamma = 0.05) as Anglos also become disillusioned but to a lesser extent. Controls for socioeconomic status have virtually no effect on the influence of ethnicity.

At this point it may be helpful to review and summarize Mexican American children's affective orientation toward government. The picture is quite complex as the independent variables have differential effects on each dimension. Overall, the picture is one of initially higher affect by the Mexican Americans, a more rapid diminution of this feeling, and a lower evaluation by ninth-grade Chicanos. Generally those Chicanos of the lower class and/or those more oriented to Spanish language exhibit a lower level of affect than their more Anglicized, more affluent co-ethnics.

GOVERNMENT EMPLOYMENT

Another item combining closeness and personal affect toward the government inquired whether or not the students would "like to work for the government someday." At all grade levels, a majority of the Chicanos see themselves as possible public employees. Although idealization declines from a high of 73 percent at grade three, public service still is attractive to over one-half of the Mexican American teenagers. Almost twice as many Chicanos think they might enter governmental positions as rule out that possibility. The Chicanos' responses are in marked contrast to those of the Anglos, more of whom reject future public employment than accept it. Only at the earliest age, with idealization at work, do a slight majority of non-Chicanos hold favorable attitudes.

This finding could be the result of a higher general affection for government among Chicanos. But responses to other items indicate that this generally is the case only

FIGURE 3.22

Percent, By Grade, Ethnicity and Social Class, Responding
that They "Would Like to Work for the Government Someday"

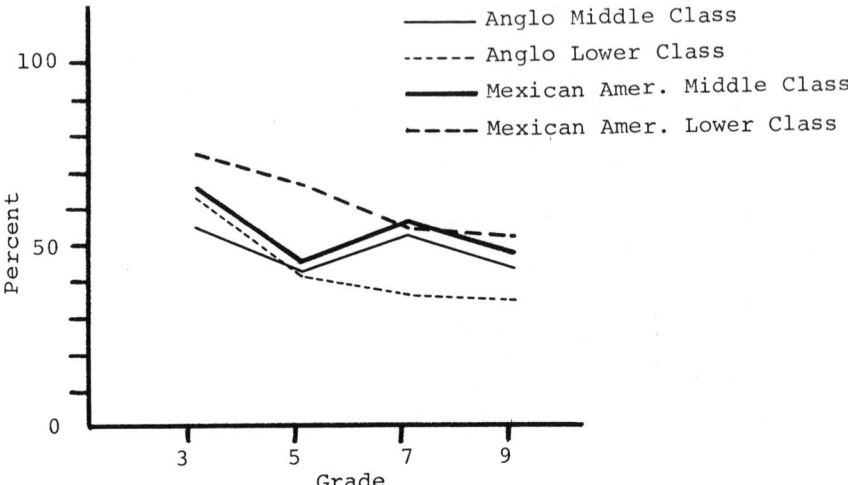

for the youngest Chicanos. Even if this were true, as
idealization gives way to realization, the gap between the
two ethnic groups should narrow; instead, it remains constant through the years. More likely it is a reflection
of the fact that minority groups have been subjected to
less discrimination at the hands of governmental than private employers. Many positions in the lower ranks of the
civil service, e.g., postal service, are held by Mexican
Americans.* It therefore is more likely that Chicano
children come into contact with public employees in a supportive setting, such as among family or friends. Anglo
children, on the other hand, are more likely to have unfavorable opinions related to them by their relatives and
friends concerning the legendary deficiencies of the puc-
lic bureaucracy.

Social class controls demonstrate that, although the
lack of economic opportunity increases the desirability of
public employment for Chicanos, these positions do not ap-
peal to lower-class Anglos (see Figure 3.22). Multiple
classification analysis confirms that ethnicity is a better

*Even so, as of 1972 only 2.9 percent of federal gov-
ernment employees were Spanish-surnamed.

predictor of attitudinal variance on this measure than is
socioeconomic class.

AFFECT FOR VARIOUS LEVELS
OF GOVERNMENT

Might Chicano children have varying degrees of affection for the different levels of American government? It
may be recalled that there were differences in their approval of the national, state, and local political communities. Do these carry over to the structures of authority
in each polity? One "general affect" question was asked
about each of the three levels of American government:
"Does the (United States, California, city) government
make things better, make things worse, or make no difference for most people?"

Overall, the national level of government receives
the highest level of approval among Chicanos. Although
affect does decrease over the years, it probably reflects
a healthy and realistically critical view of the national
government. Support remains above the 50 percent mark.
Even though the evaluational trend is similar for both
ethnic groups (see Figure 3.23), ethnicity is strongly related to this attitude (gamma = 0.31) as the Chicano youths
are less likely to state that the national government
makes things better. Moreover, the divergence in opinions
is greater at each successive stage of development. As
they enter early adulthood, Chicanos are less impressed
with the results of federal activity, and only a slight
majority view it as beneficial.

While controlling for social class does not cancel
the ethnic differences (see Figure 3.24), there are substantial differences between those of varying socioeconomic
standing within each group. Working-class Chicanos initially are as idealistic as those of higher status, but
by the ninth grade fewer than half feel the central government improves the lot of most people; and their support is
on the wane at this point. Although middle-class Chicanos
suffer a more drastic early loss of idealization as reality
testing increases, their approval climbs at a rate similar
to that of Anglo working-class adolescents.

Mexican American young people in California are less
satisfied with their state government, and even this lower
level of support deteriorates over the six-year period surveyed (see Figure 3.25). Ethnicity has a substantial relationship with this attitude (gamma = 0.23), and the Anglo

FIGURE 3.23

Percent, By Grade and Ethnicity, Who Think that "The United States Government Makes Things Better for Most People"

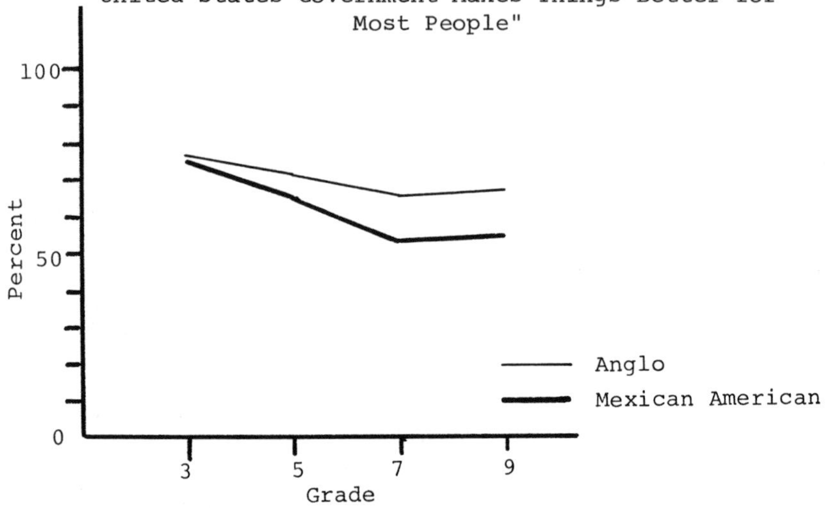

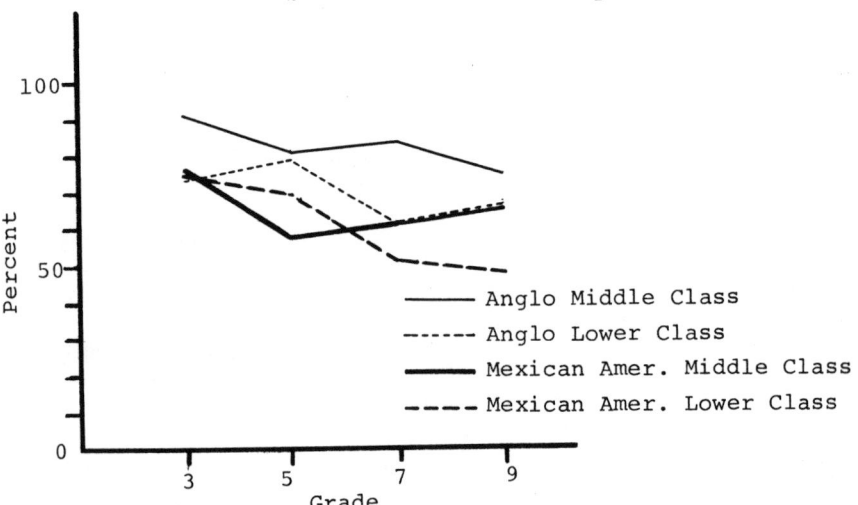

FIGURE 3.24

Percent, By Grade, Ethnicity and Socioeconomic Status, Who Think that "The United States Government Makes Things Better for Most People"

children's attitudes change relatively little over the
years. Significantly, almost one-fourth of the Chicanos
feel that the government of California makes things <u>worse</u>
for most people, while Anglos are more likely to think that
state authorities "make no difference" rather than worsen
conditions. Thus, while Californios are more aware of membership in the state political community and are proud of
it, they see its leadership structure as inimical or irrelevant to their needs.

Controlling for class does not wash out the ethnic
differences (see Figure 3.26). However, a great change in
the opinions of working-class children again is noticed.
Originally, they are second only to middle-class Anglo
youngsters in positive evaluation of the effect of state
government; by the ninth grade they are by far the least
supportive.

Chicanos at all grade levels attribute the lowest
level of governmental worthiness to their city government,
and at all ages think less of its beneficence than do the
Anglos (see Figure 3.27). Almost one-fourth of the Mexican
Americans in third, fifth, and ninth grade consider their
local government irrelevant, i.e., say it "makes no difference." This is a greater proportion than those who consider it a detriment, the reverse of their evaluation of
the state government. Here again, class does not change
the relative position of the ethnic groups, but inclusion
of class does indicate that less than a majority of both
the middle-class and working-class Chicano adolescents feel
the city government improves the people's situation (see
Figure 3.28).

Although it has been found that black affect for government, as measured by these items, undergoes a decline
until recovery takes place in junior high school,[15] this
is not the case for Mexican Americans. Overall, Chicanos
continue to lose confidence in the importance of all levels
of government (see Table 3.5). Only for the national government is there exhibited a very slight rise in approval
between the seventh and ninth grades. Greenberg found
that black ninth graders even evaluated the national government more positively than did third graders.[16] No such
occurrence is found among Chicanos. Governments, especially
the national government, have made some attempts to increase
opportunities for blacks, especially during the civil
rights era of the 1960s. But very little governmental attention has been paid to the plight of Mexican Americans
in the United States. Until quite recently, Mexican Americans deserved the title "forgotten Americans."[17] This lack

FIGURE 3.25

Percent, By Grade and Ethnicity, Who Think that "The
Government of California Makes Things Better
for Most People"

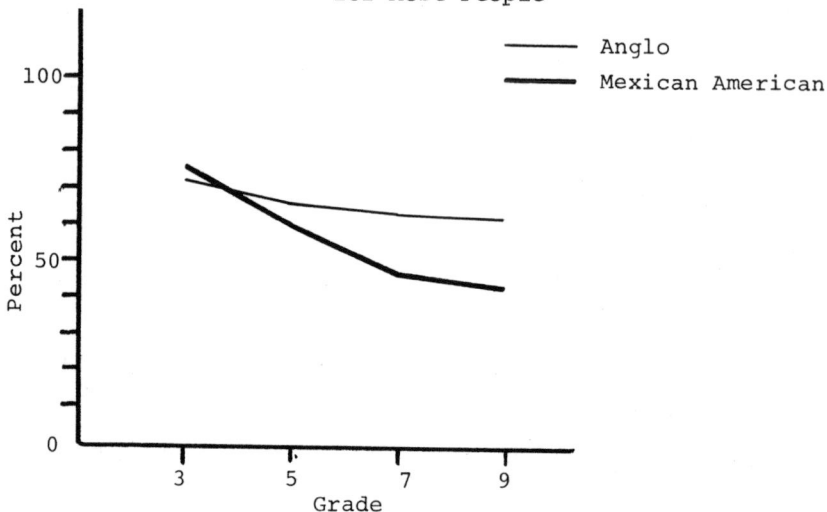

FIGURE 3.26

Percent, By Grade, Ethnicity and Social Class, Who
Think that "The Government of California
Makes Things Better for Most People"

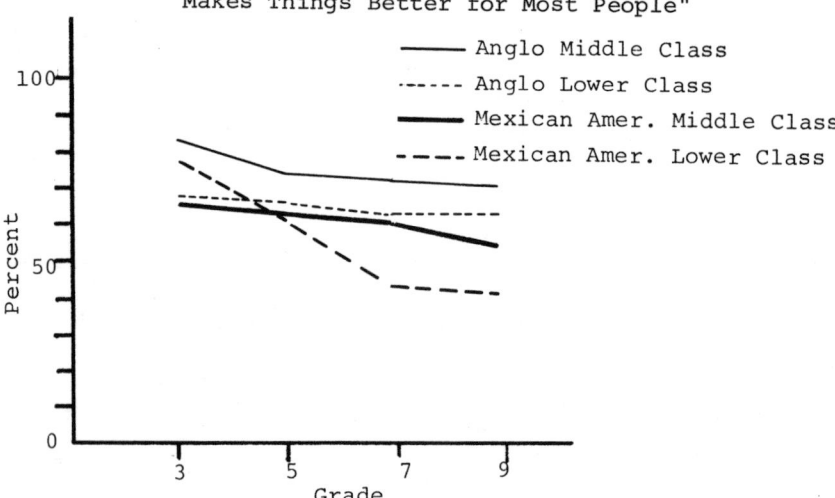

FIGURE 3.27

Percent, By Grade and Ethnicity, Who Think that the
Government of Their City "Makes Things Better for
Most People"

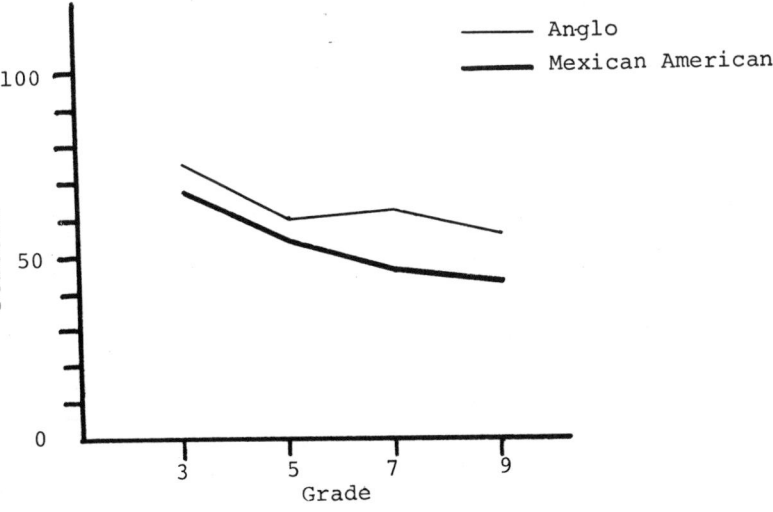

FIGURE 3.28

Percent, By Grade, Ethnicity and Social Class, Who Think
that the Government of Their City "Makes Things Better
for Most People"

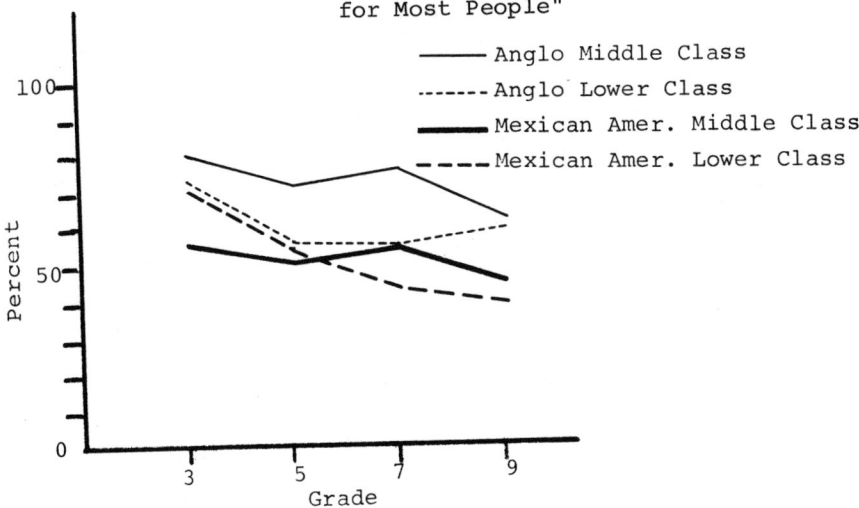

TABLE 3.5

Change Through the Years in Percentage of Chicanos
Responding that Government "Makes Things Better
for Most People"

	Grade 3	Grade 9	Change
National government	75.0	53.1	-21.9
State government	75.7	43.5	-32.2
Local government	68.6	41.2	-27.4

TABLE 3.6

Percentage of Mexican American and Anglo Children
Responding that Government "Makes Things Worse
for Most People"

	Grade 3	Grade 9	Change
Mexican Americans			
National government	5.0	19.8	+14.8
State government	5.7	24.3	+18.6
City government	12.1	18.1	+6.0
Anglos			
National government	6.4	10.0	+3.6
State government	5.6	10.6	+5.0
City government	8.0	10.0	+2.0

of attention by political authorities certainly is reflected in the attitudes of young Chicanos, especially
those of the working class, whose economic deprivation adds
to the problems of ethnic discrimination. There is some
feeling among these students that the national government
is helping matters, while the state government is most often seen as making matters worse (see Table 3.6); and the
city governments are, at best, irrelevant.

SUMMARY

Although there is substantial variation in the attitudes of Chicanos toward the many dimensions of government,
some general patterns can be discerned. Mexican Americans
at an early age perceive government as a person, particularly the President. As they mature, institutionalization
increases and Congress becomes the best representative of
the structure of authority whose stability is rated high
but whose fairness is questioned.

It is the national government that members of La Raza
see as most important and most beneficial to them. The
state government, while having high visibility, is evaluated most negatively. And local governments have low
salience early in life but become more important as Chicanos mature.

In general, very young Mexican Americans have a great
deal of positive affect for the government, usually more
than their Anglo classmates; but by early adulthood the
positions are reversed.

In sum, early attachments to the structure of authority are such that diffuse support for the system is given
a favorable start, even though there is evidence of rapid
erosion, particularly among the rural, more Mexican-
oriented, members of La Raza.

CHAPTER

4

ORIENTATION TOWARD
THE REGIME:
VALUES

INTRODUCTION

We now turn our attention to a second element composing the regime of a political system--its fundamental values or goals.

Underlying most national political systems is a collection of values and principles that express a polity's ideological raison d'etre. Without the direction provided by these normative goals, a political system can be considered primarily a housekeeping entity, performing the necessary system maintenance functions but lacking a philosophical flavor that renders it distinctive from other nations. System values are related in a close, if complicated, manner to the political behavior of the system's members. If the members of any system perceive its characteristic goals as worthy of pursuit or at least do not reject them, the probability they will support that particular system and not another are enhanced considerably. Additionally, consensus on basic political goals produces a "framework of contingent constraints" within which political actions are contained.[1]

In the American political system the chief values of the regime are those associated with the concept of democracy. Such values as individual freedom, fraternity, social and political equality, and the maximization of popular participation in public affairs all have been treated as basic values by democratic theorists. Although the list is not all-inclusive, these values are at least representative of the set of principles that constitutes the ideological foundation of the American democracy.

Since some minimal level of commitment to and support
for democratic values is a condition that contributes
greatly to harmonious political activities within, if not
the maintenance of, the American system, the incorpora-
tion of these systemic values into the belief system of
individual members of the American political system is important. In particular, the "politically relevant" members
of a polity must at least accept, if not further, the
democratic creed.

To accomplish this, political authorities institute
various socializing agencies, especially the schools, for
the purpose of indoctrinating the young with supportive
democratic orientations.[2] School activities are replete
with value-laden patriotic activities, and much of the
curriculum is designed to foster the appropriate civic
values. Although children are not politically relevant,
their early socialization toward democratic regime values
is likely to have a significant impact on their political
attitudes as adult citizens.[3] Several studies have demonstrated that American children are indeed highly supportive
of the values in the democratic creed.[4] However, these
investigations have primarily focused upon children of the
dominant Anglo core culture. Yet the core culture ethos
is being challenged by several subcultural or even counter-
cultural segments, including "hippies" and ethnic minority
groups. Heretofore members of ethnic subcultures largely
have been excluded from the social, economic, and political
activities of the American mainstream. The nonwhite minor-
ities--blacks, native Americans, Orientals, and Chicanos--
have not been politically relevant in the sense that they
have been unable to exert much influence on American
decision-makers. However, one major development in recent
American politics has been a heightened sense of political
awareness and activism among these minorities. Increased
electoral participation, a growing number of ethnic minority public officials, the formation of several ethnic-based
political organizations, and a substantial number of demonstrations and boycotts have provided evidence that members
of ethnic minorities are becoming increasingly relevant to
the politics of the American system.

One may wonder about the political orientation of
these people who for so long have been supportive of this
nation yet for as long have been the objects of political
as well as social and economic racism. Indeed, several
minority group spokesmen have strongly criticized the
values underlying many American institutions, such as the
concepts supportive of a capitalistic economic system.

Does this challenge to many core culture values include disagreement with the basic political values and goals of the American system? Is their orientation toward the philosophic ends of the American polity positive and supportive, or is a divergence from these goals evident? Have the socializing experiences provided by the core culture inculcated democratic values in minority children to the extent that their political behavior will occur within and be bounded by their consensus with the fundamental political values of the dominant culture?

This chapter seeks to provide some tentative answers to these questions through an examination of the political value orientations of Mexican American schoolchildren and a comparison of their views with those of their core culture (Anglo) schoolmates. The results should provide some clues to the future political behavior of Mexican Americans, which will bear directly on the stability of the American political system.

ATTITUDES TOWARD DEMOCRACY

First, an attempt was made to discover whether the children understood what was meant by the term "democracy" --this polity's overarching value. Table 4.1 reveals that the third-grade Chicanos feel they know what democracy is all about. When presented with several alternative definitions only one-fourth did not make a selection (compared to 37.6 percent of the Anglo third-graders). The most popular response is that democracy is "where leaders do what they think is best for the people."

This idea of a "guided democracy" is by far the most popular definition for both ethnic groups in the primary grades and is in keeping with the general attitudes toward authority fostered by the dependent status of young children. However, among Mexican American children the number selecting this response increases over the years, while among Anglos this view declines slightly in the seventh and ninth grades. Since Chicanos' length of residence in the United States and the amount of Spanish spoken in their homes produce the greatest effect on this attitude, the degree of "Mexicanness" could be an important variable here. Some researchers have reported that the majority of Mexicans are oriented to their political system as "subjects--essentially passive and oriented toward the output (policy) rather than the input (participation) side of the system.[5] Alternatively, and more plausibly, it may be that at least the older Mexican American youths are realistically assessing the performance of the American political leaders, who seem to be more self-directed than guided by the wishes of the Mexican American people.

Anglo and Chicano third-graders also differ significantly on their second choice of definitions: the youngest Chicanos are more likely to equate democracy with an affluent society--"where people have lots of things, like cars and television sets." This is not a surprising choice by a group of politically unsophisticated and economically depressed respondents. The effect of economic deprivation is evidenced by the finding that 8.8 percent of the total sample of working-class Mexican Americans support this economic view of democracy, compared to 6.7 percent of the Chicano middle-class pupils. By the fifth grade this conception begins to wither away. At this age, Chicano children become most unsure what democracy means after all, and 40.7 percent do not venture a definition. Thereafter, this doubt persists at a higher level among Chicanos than Anglos throughout the school years. In the ninth grade the largest number of Chicanos still perceive the idea of democracy as benevolent paternalism; the same percentage of Anglos (35.0 percent) now are more sure than their Mexican American classmates that democracy is the reflection of vox populi--"where leaders do what most people want." Again, this may simply reflect the differential level of political influence possessed by each ethnic group.

Do Mexican American youths feel they "live in a democratic country?" They are less likely to think so than their Anglo schoolmates: 45.8 percent of the Chicanos agree, compared to 55.5 percent of the Anglos. Almost half of the members of each ethnic group initially feel they live in a democracy, but by the fifth grade both are much less sure (see Figure 4.1). Subsequently, as their cognitive abilities develop, more children agree with this contention, but the Chicanos continue to be much less sure than the Anglos. By the ninth grade almost 70 percent of the Anglos feel they live in a democracy while only slightly more than half the Chicanos do. Uncertainty also is evidenced by the high rate of "don't know" responses of the total Chicano group (31.2 percent) vis-à-vis those of the Anglos (19.7 percent). Although the number of Anglos who "do not know" decreases rapidly after the fifth grade to 13.8 percent in the ninth, the percentage of Chicano "undecideds" remains high--34.7 percent in the seventh grade and 28.2 percent in the ninth. This uncertainty may be attributed to the fact that, although Chicanos are aware that the

United States calls itself a democracy, they are not as sure as Anglos that this is a proper label. Since they do not receive equal treatment or enjoy equal opportunity, a greater gap appears between the words and the practice. The Chicanos do not reject outright the idea that this is a democracy in any greater proportions than do the Anglos, but neither are they as certain that democracy really holds sway in the United States.

When socioeconomic controls are introduced (see Figure 4.2), the Anglo lower class is seen to have opinions similar to its Chicano counterpart in the primary grades, as about half the members of each feel they live in a democracy. Over three-fourths of the Anglo middle-class third-graders feel this way, but only 35 percent of the Chicano middle class shares this sentiment. At this early age the strongest socializing influence is the family.[6] The low rating by the middle-class Chicanos probably reflects a greater awareness of the sociopolitical status of the Mexican American family in the United States; the Anglo children correspondingly mirror their position. As the more idealistic working-class Chicano youngsters[7] mature and their perception of the environment expands, they come to share the view of the middle-class Mexican Americans. From the age of 11 or 12 on, ethnicity seems to have the greatest effect on this opinion, with both Mexican American classes more doubtful than Anglos about residing in a democracy. Stepwise regression analysis indicates that, after grade (beta = 0.21), Spanish language use (beta = 0.13) and ethnicity (beta = 0.11) are the variables most affecting attitudes on this question.

Chicano students also are more likely than Anglos to agree that "there are other countries in this world that are more democratic than the United States." At every grade level a larger percentage of Mexican Americans than Anglos is in accord with this statement (see Figure 4.3 and Table 4.2). At the ninth grade level slightly more Mexican Americans (29.4 percent) disagree with the statement than agree (28.2 percent); the largest percentage (41.2 percent) expresses doubt. Only at the third grade level are Anglos most inclined to agree that other countries are more democratic. From the fifth grade on Anglo children increasingly see the United States as the most democratic country; by the ninth grade only 18.8 percent feel this is not the case. The number of Chicanos expressing doubt on this item increases noticeably from 23.6 percent in the third grade to 41.2 percent in the ninth grade. It may be significant that the best predictors of this

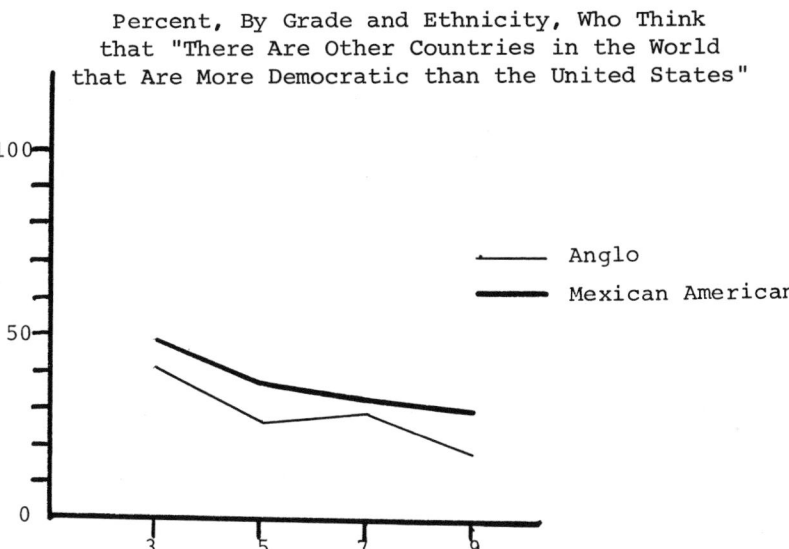

FIGURE 4.3

Percent, By Grade and Ethnicity, Who Think
that "There Are Other Countries in the World
that Are More Democratic than the United States"

opinion for the Chicano children are the degree of Spanish
usage in the home followed by the length of residence in
the United States. The people of Mexico reportedly are
highly imbued with the spirit of democracy,[8] and Americans
of recent Mexican descent may reflect this factor in their
comparison, thus accounting for the relatively high level
of uncertainty.

In sum, it seems that primary school Chicanos are ex-
traordinarily generous in their appraisals of democracy.
They feel that they live in a democracy and that people
in other lands live in countries at least as democratic.
However, as their cognitive abilities develop and their
awareness increases with age, they become increasingly un-
certain about the status of democracy in the United States.
They learn, primarily through vicarious experience in
school, that other countries in the world are less democratic than the United States. Yet their comparison of
everyday experiences with their increasingly sophisticated
concept of democracy probably results in much psychological confusion. A large gap between reality and theory is
noticed. This is manifested in increasingly doubtful responses to items on democracy in the American polity.

TABLE 4.2

Mexican American and Anglo Children's Responses to the
Statement, "There Are Other Countries in the World that
Are More Democratic than the United States of America"
(in percentages; number of responses in parentheses)

Grade	Agree		Disagree		Don't Know/No Answer	
Mexican Americans						
3	48.6	(68)	27.9	(39)	23.6	(33)
5	36.6	(63)	30.2	(52)	33.2	(57)
7	32.1	(62)	29.5	(57)	38.3	(74)
9	28.2	(50)	29.4	(52)	41.2	(73)
Total	35.6	(243)	29.4	(201)	34.7	(237)
Anglos						
3	40.0	(50)	29.6	(37)	30.4	(38)
5	26.8	(33)	31.7	(39)	40.6	(50)
7	28.9	(39)	34.1	(46)	36.1	(50)
9	18.8	(30)	45.0	(72)	35.7	(50)
Total	28.1	(153)	35.7	(194)	35.9	(195)

COMPONENT VALUES OF DEMOCRACY

When democracy is broken up into some of its major
components, civil liberties must loom as an essential feature. And freedom of expression is considered perhaps the
most basic one of these. Young Mexican Americans demonstrate a high level of support for this personal liberty:
two-thirds hold that "anyone should be able to say what he
feels like saying even if it makes other people angry."
In primary school they are not as sure this should be the
case as when they are older, but even so a majority of
third-grade Chicanos would uphold free speech in this case
(see Figure 4.4). The Anglos' attitudes through the years
are almost exactly the same as those of their Mexican-
American classmates in every grade.

The Chicanos' support of individual freedom of speech is less strong than that of the Anglos if that speech is in the form of criticism of the government. They are more prone to agree (39.8 percent versus 35.5 percent) with the proposition that "even if some people do not agree with what the government does, they should go along and should not criticize or complain." Going along with the government is the option of a majority of Mexican Americans in the third and fifth grades, while only the third-grade Anglos would concur. However, the majority opinion switches to the side of the individual by grade seven, and this freedom to criticize governmental policy is upheld by over three-fourths of the Chicano ninth-graders (see Figure 4.5).

Although the effect of socioeconomic status on this opinion is relatively slight and irregular, after grade, area of residence seems to produce the greatest variation in the opinions of Chicanos. Los Angelenos tend to side with the government more than rural Chicanos (gamma = 0.19). Almost 55 percent of the rural Mexican American students disagree with the uncritical acceptance of governmental policy while 47.6 percent of those in urban areas share this sentiment. Figure 4.6 illustrates the dramatic change in attitude through the years toward increased support for disagreement with the government. Both Northern and Southern Californios hesitate to challenge public authority when young, but this reluctance rapidly melts away, particularly among the northern rural group. If this trend continues, adult Mexican Americans would strongly support the individual's right to challenge a governmental policy with which he disagrees.

Another regime value of a democratic system is the ensuring of equal opportunity by the government to all its citizens, often referred to as "civil rights." Less than 10 percent of students in the sample disagreed with the statement that "every person should have the same right as any other person to get ahead." Support for this proposition is uniformly high among both ethnic groups. Initially, at an 80 percent agreement level, concurrence with the statement drops very slightly at the fifth grade level and rises to an apex of 95.5 percent for ninth-grade Chicanos (see Figure 4.7).

A provocative, if slight, divergence in opinions appears between ethnic groups as these school-age children come nearer to adulthood. Although one might expect near universal agreement,[9] 6.3 percent of the ninth-grade Anglos disagree with this general statement of equality of opportunity compared to only 2.3 percent of the Mexican Americans.

FIGURE 4.4

Percent, By Grade and Ethnicity, Agreeing that
"Anyone Should Be Able to Say What He Feels Like
Saying, Even if It Makes Other People Mad"

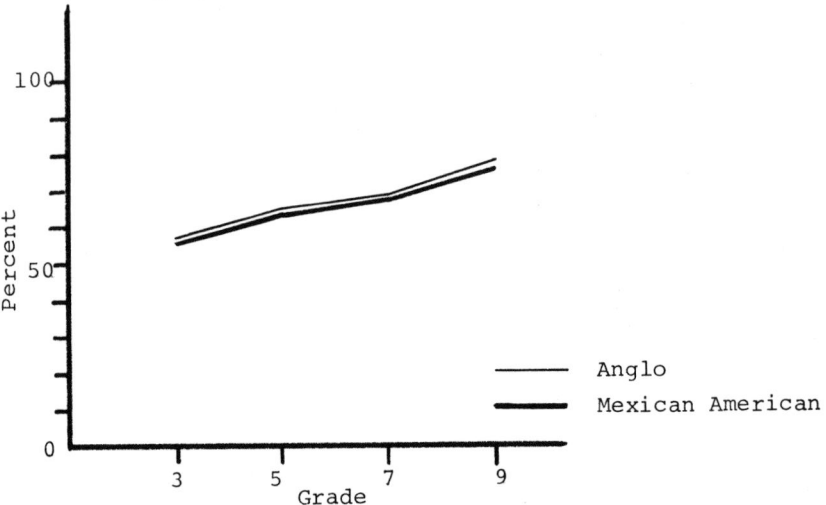

FIGURE 4.5

Percent, By Grade and Ethnicity, Agreeing that
"Even if Some People Do Not Agree with What the
Government Does, They Should Go Along and Not
Criticize or Complain"

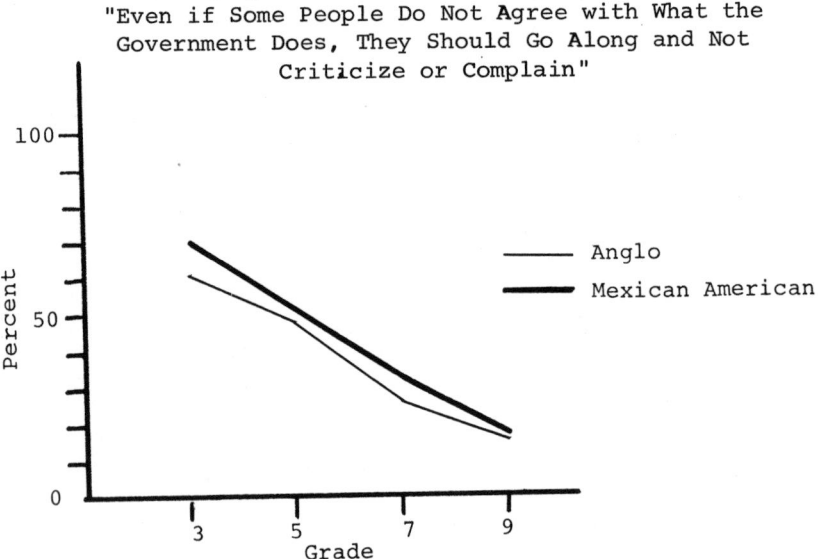

FIGURE 4.6

Percent of Mexican Americans, By Grade and Area of
Residence, Disagreeing that Individuals Should
Go Along Quietly with Government Policy

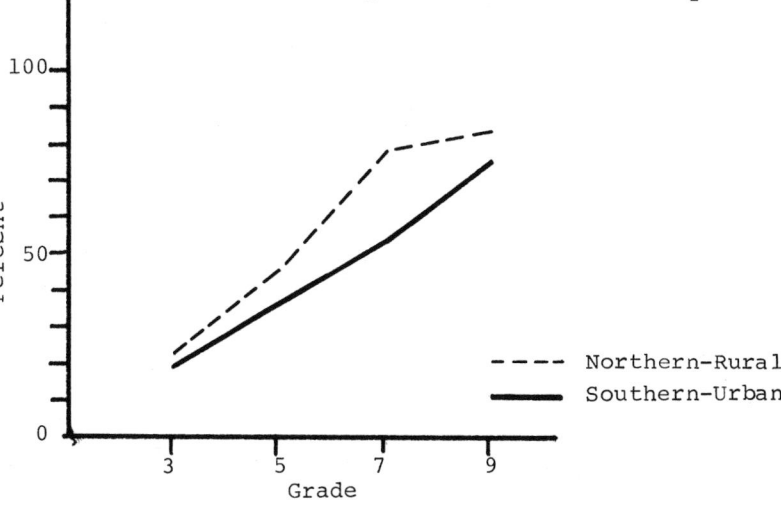

Perhaps this is a manifestation of the "haves" protecting
the status quo while the "less equal" Chicanos are more
concerned with their chances of getting ahead.

The importance of both economic position and ethnicity
is substantiated when controls for economic standing are
introduced (see Figure 4.8). Initially, there is little
variation among socioethnic categories, although the Anglo
middle-class children show the highest level of support,
probably reflecting their familial socialization, since
Americans of higher status are the most fervent carriers of
the democratic creed.[10] As the influence of the family
wanes and extraparental contacts increase, a regrouping
occurs. By the mid-teens, the Anglo middle class and all
the Mexican Americans support this idea at the same level;
the lower-class Anglos lag behind with almost one out of
ten objecting. It is thought by some that the most strenuous objections to the socioeconomic advancement of disadvantaged ethnic groups usually are voiced by those who are
rather insecure in their societal status, namely the members of the white lower class.[11] Although a more detached
and less abstract measurement would be desirable, responses
to this item at least lend weight to this hypothesis.

What are these children's orientations toward nondis-
criminatory treatment of people when group distinctiveness--

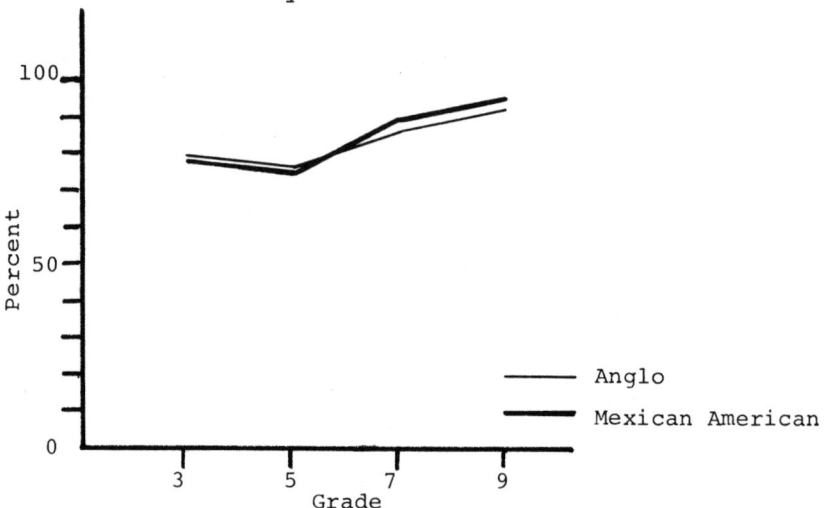

FIGURE 4.7

Percent, By Grade and Ethnicity, Agreeing that
"Every Person Should Have the Same Right
as Any Other Person to Get Ahead"

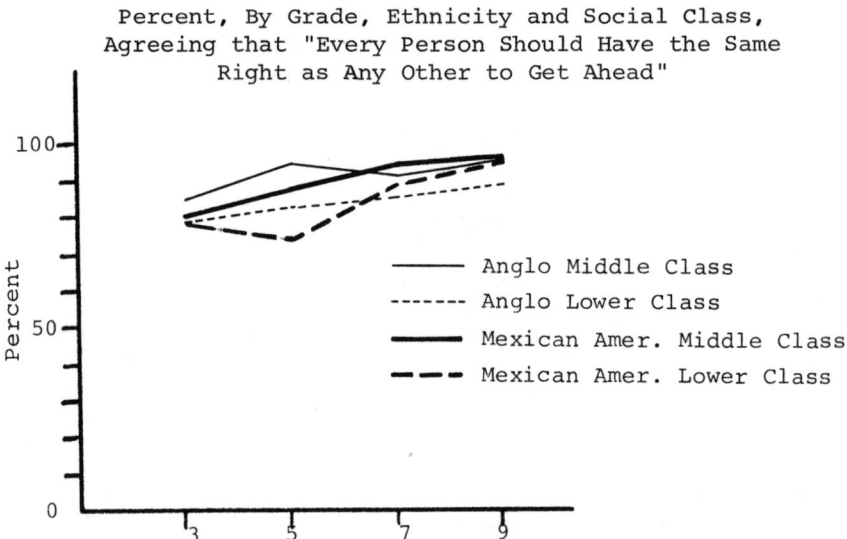

FIGURE 4.8

Percent, By Grade, Ethnicity and Social Class,
Agreeing that "Every Person Should Have the Same
Right as Any Other to Get Ahead"

in this case, ethnicity--is involved? Chicano pupils are
most apt to observe that they are "not treated the same"
as their Anglo counterparts, i.e., they feel racial discrimination is a feature of our democratic polity. This
is consonant with the contention of almost all social observers that discrimination against minority groups is a
very salient feature of American society.[12]

The youngest Chicanos are not as conscious of differential treatment as are their Anglo classmates (see Figure
4.9 and Table 4.3). Minority group parents often are very
protective of their children in the sense that they try to
shield their young from an awareness of their future problems as minority Americans. Since young Chicano children
living in the barrio or rural campo are fairly restricted
in their firsthand contacts with discrimination, this
parental protection may be a very potent socialization factor accounting for lesser awareness of ethnic-based prejudice. However, as Mexican Americans mature and experience
discrimination themselves, those sensing inequality rise
to 71.8 percent of the total ninth-grade sample. This developmental pattern is in marked contrast to that of the
maturing Anglos, whose perception of discriminatory treatment diminishes after the fifth grade, dropping back to

FIGURE 4.9

Percent, By Grade and Ethnicity, Agreeing that
"Anglos and Mexican Americans Are Not Treated the Same"

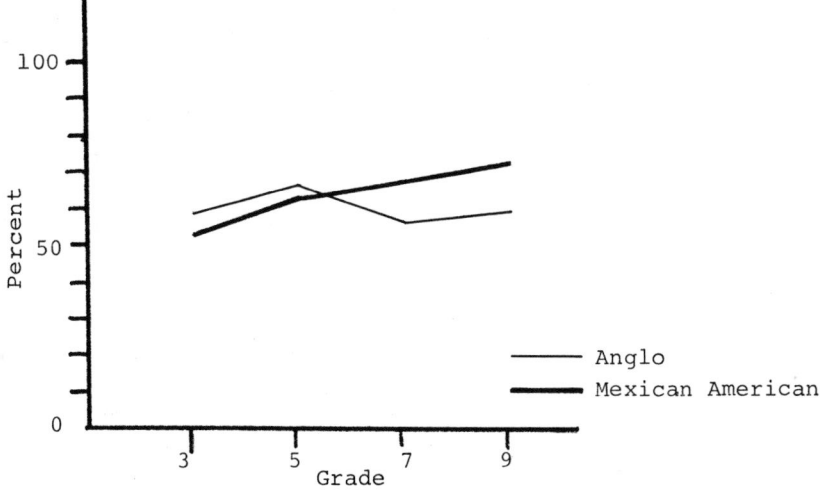

101

TABLE 4.3

Mexican American and Anglo Children's Responses to the
Statement, "Anglos and Mexican Americans Are Not Treated
the Same"
(in percentages; number of responses in parentheses)

Grade	Agree		Disagree		Don't Know/No Answer	
Mexican Americans						
3	52.1	(73)	30.0	(42)	17.8	(25)
5	62.8	(108)	24.4	(42)	12.8	(22)
7	67.9	(108)	19.2	(37)	12.9	(25)
9	71.8	(127)	16.4	(29)	11.8	(21)
Total	64.4	(440)	22.0	(150)	13.7	(93)
Anglos						
3	59.2	(74)	31.2	(39)	9.6	(12)
5	67.5	(83)	24.4	(30)	8.1	(10)
7	56.3	(76)	28.9	(39)	14.8	(20)
9	59.4	(95)	27.5	(44)	13.1	(21)
Total	60.3	(328)	28.1	(153)	11.6	(63)

third grade levels of 59 percent at the ninth grade. Also
worth noting is the fact that uncertainty or ambiguity
about this condition steadily diminishes for the Mexican
Americans ("don't knows" go from 15.7 percent to 9.0 percent): Chicanos know that ethnic discrimination is a characteristic of life in America. Anglo adolescents are
more ambivalent, or perhaps less willing to recognize this
blemish on the face of democracy. This is indicated by
the higher rate of "don't know" responses in the seventh
and ninth grades.

When controls are introduced for social class, ethnicity
remains most important in the third and ninth grades,
while class figures prominently in the developmental pattern of each group (see Figure 4.10). Mexican Americans
of higher economic standing are least likely to charge inequality of treatment while very young. Their increased

FIGURE 4.10

Percent, By Grade, Ethnicity and Social Class,
Agreeing that "Anglos and Mexican Americans
Are Not Treated the Same"

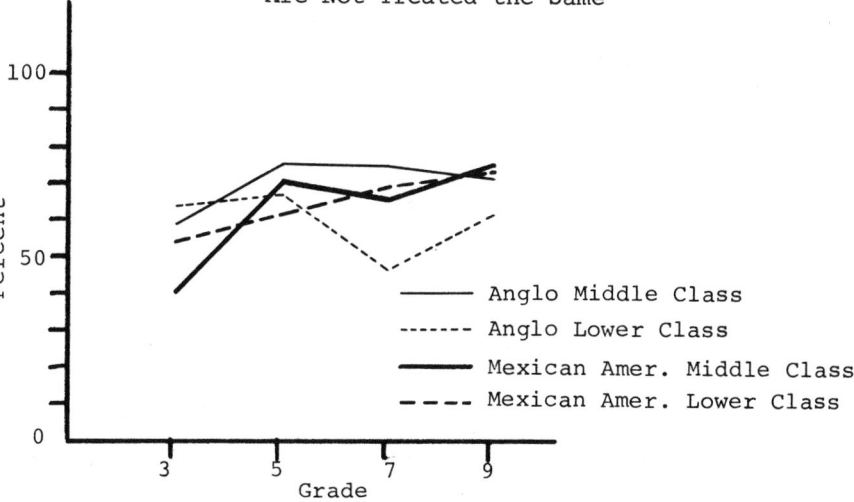

contact with the outside environment, particularly in
school and with peers, forces a dramatic reevaluation of
the situation until, as maturity approaches, they are most
likely to perceive ethnic discrimination. At this stage
their working-class fellow ethnics share the same sentiments, and this attitude still is on the increase for both
classes. Middle-class Anglo admission of discriminatory
treatment is declining at this point, while the working-
class, teenage white is by far the least likely to state
that Mexican Americans and Anglos are not treated the same.
Ethnicity remains the best predictor of this attitude,
when all other control variables are held constant.

INDIVIDUAL PARTICIPATION

One of the arguments posited by philosophers concerned
with the normative bases of democracy is that this ideology
optimizes the individual's opportunity for self-fulfillment.
Democracy is valuable because the individual develops his
psychological and social being as he participates in the
civic activities of the system. Thus a lack of popular
participation is considered undesirable for a democracy,
not because of its systemic effects (which some contend

actually may be beneficial) but because of its violation of the democratic ideal of self-fulfillment.[13]

From this perspective, a maximization of popular participation is a positive benefit in a democracy. Two items in the questionnaire elicited responses dealing with participation of the masses. When asked whether "some kinds of grown-ups should not have a say in what government does," only third-grade Chicanos responded mainly in the affirmative. Mexican American youths in all the other grades, and Anglos of all ages, tend to disagree more than agree with this idea of restriction (see Figure 4.11). From the fifth grade on, the pattern of positive student responses is similar for both groups (gamma = 0.007). However, the pattern of disagreement with the statement, i.e., supporting maximization of popular participation in decision-making, is more revealing (see Figure 4.12). Mexican American antipathy for restricting participation, although initially low, continually increases over the years until it exceeds that of the Anglos. At the third and fifth grade levels the Chicanos' lower response is partially accounted for by their greater number of "don't know" responses (19.3 percent and 15.7 percent, respectively). Anglo disagreement with narrowing participation remains fairly constant throughout these school years.

Dividing the sample by ethnicity and socioeconomic status revealed that those most restrictive in their orientation, i.e., agreeing with the statement, were the middle-class Anglo children (42.1 percent agree), followed by the working-class Anglos (38.1 percent) and working-class Chicanos (36.8 percent); most expansive were the middle-class Mexican Americans (33.1 percent). Middle-class Chicanos duplicate the opinions of the Anglo working class at the ninth grade level. Class is a slightly better predictor than ethnicity on this item.

In responding to an item concerning a restriction on the specific activity of exercising the franchise ("some grown-ups should not be allowed to vote for the leaders of government"), the third-grade Mexican American students again seem most in favor of limiting popular participation. The attitudinal response over the years is almost parallel for both ethnic groups, with an interesting zigzag developmental pattern for each (see Figure 4.13). For some reason, after the rise of an expansive orientation from the third to the fifth grade a more restrictive policy develops in the middle years. After the seventh grade the potential electorate again is expanded--more by the Mexican Americans than by the Anglos. Social class has almost no effect on

FIGURE 4.11

Percent, By Grade and Ethnicity, Agreeing that
"Some Kinds of Grown-Ups Should Not Have a Say
in What Government Does"

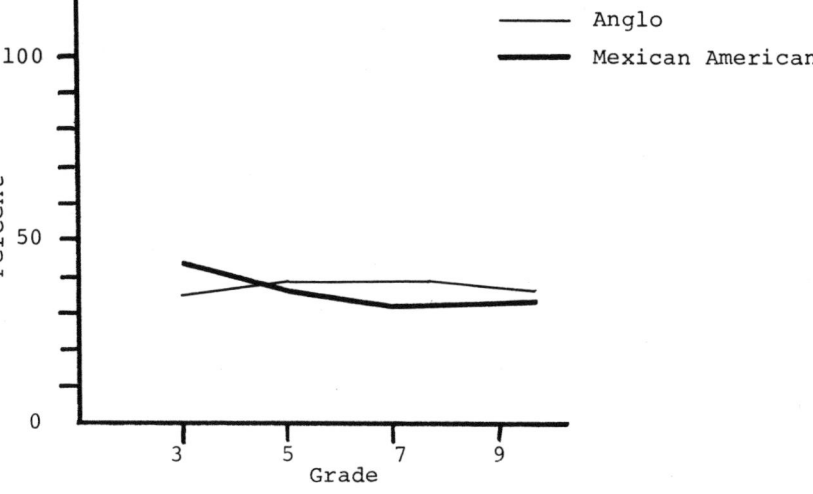

FIGURE 4.12

Percent, By Grade and Ethnicity, Disagreeing
that "Some Kinds of Grown-Ups Should Not Have a Say in
What Government Does"

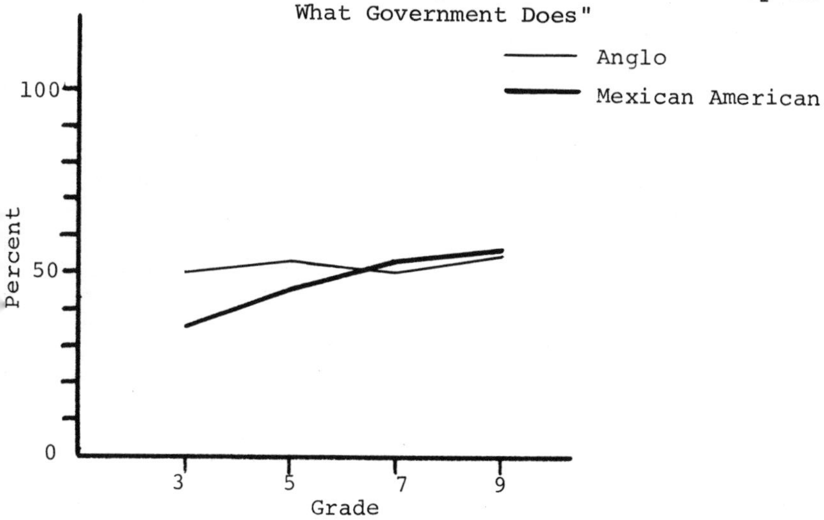

FIGURE 4.13

Percent, By Grade and Ethnicity, Agreeing that
"Some Grown-Ups Should Not Be Allowed to
Vote for the Leaders of Government"

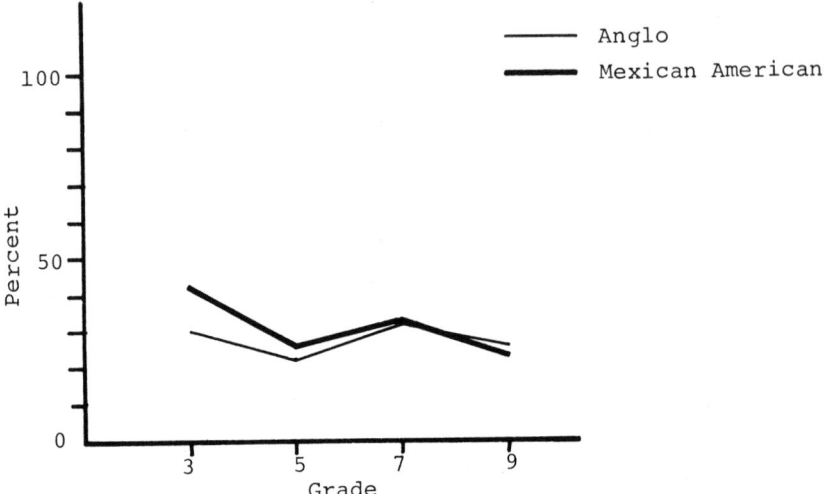

responses to this item, accounting for only 0.1 percent
of the variance.

One major difference in the opinions of each group on
the participation items is that Mexican American third-
graders appear least in favor of expanding the arena of
decision-making. This may reflect the authority patterns
and decision-making processes of their families.[14] This
would be an indirect form of political socialization
through "interpersonal transference," whereby the child
brings his experiences in the family, especially those
with authority figures, to bear on explicitly political
learning.[15] Others also have stressed the importance of
the family in forming psychocultural traits that will affect an individual's later political orientations.[16] Although the literature on the effect of family structure on
the political attitudes of children is abundant, because
of the complexity of variables involved no clearcut asso-
ciations have yet emerged.[17]

Since among Chicanos the best predictor of opinions
on both these items is use of the Spanish language (followed by parents' birthplace and length of residence in
the United States), a less democratic pattern of familial
relationships conceivably may be manifesting itself in the

more exclusionary political attitudes of the youngest Mexican American children.

SUMMARY AND CONCLUSIONS

Young Mexican Americans are quite supportive of the guiding values of the American democracy. In fact, by the ninth grade they are likely to have slightly more supportive attitudes toward democracy than their Anglo peers. Yet as they mature they are not at all certain that the United States is as democratic as it claims to be.

On items involving the relationships between rulers and the ruled, young Chicanos are more likely than Anglos to view democracy in "subject" terms. Although the reasons for this are unclear, this attitude most likely reflects the disproportionately low level of influence of Mexican Americans on governmental decision-makers. However, on questions dealing with mass participation, Mexican American youngsters, on the whole, evidence a higher level of participant orientation than do their Anglo classmates.

Strong support for freedom of speech is evidenced, but it diminishes substantially if this is in the form of criticism of the government. Chicanos' opinions on civil rights are generally more liberal than those of their Anglo classmates, particularly Anglos of the working class.

Values of individual participation are less important to the very young Chicanos, but are increasingly appreciated until they reach at least the level of support by the Anglo ninth-graders. The earlier, more restrictive attitudes are hypothesized to be the result of lesser participation in family decisions.

In sum, Mexican American youths between the third and ninth grades are socialized toward a high level of support of American regime values. There does not appear to be an attitudinal cleavage between Mexican and Anglo Americans with respect to this polity's major goals, i.e., Chicanos desire the same democratic political goals as Anglos.

This finding may provide some insight into the future political behavior of Mexican Americans. The increasing pace of Mexican American political acitivities is likely to follow the ideological course shaped by the children's strong acceptance of democratic values. Demands placed on governmental institutions should not depart from traditional American concerns with freedom, fraternity, and equality. More likely than not, Chicano political pressures will focus on diminishing the great gap, particularly wide for ethnic minorities, between the democratic promise and this system's accomplishments.

5

ORIENTATION TOWARD
THE REGIME:
NORMS

INTRODUCTION

While the goals or values of the American democracy
may be of utmost importance, many would contend that the
system's norms are at least as significant. Easton defines
system norms as the "rules of the game through which they
[the members of the system] conduct their political business."[1] Norms, then, are the all-important means employed
by participants in politics to achieve the ends of the
polity. As rules of the game they have a substantial, if
not determinate, bearing on the objectives sought by members of the political system. Adherence to the norms of a
political system is considered to have an important stabi-
lizing effect upon its functioning. Members of a polity
are expected to conduct themselves in a certain agreed-
upon manner that will promote an orderly method of political activity.

In a democracy these rules of the game include such
norms as an agreement upon decision-making procedures; the
behavior of a "good" citizen--e.g., interest and participation in political affairs; and a viable relationship between those in public office and the electorate. If a
democratic system is to persist, it must inculcate these
standards of behavior in its politically relevant members;
if substantial numbers of these citizens do not learn the
rules of the democratic game, their consequent political
behavior is more likely to be disruptive of the system's
functioning.[2] The orientation of Mexican American children
to several of these regime norms will be examined in this
chapter in order to provide additional evidence concerning
the extent of this subculture's socialization to support
of the system.

However, it also should be noted that, although behavior congruent with a system's norms may be desirable from a systemic perspective because of its contribution to stability and system maintenance, it may be that these same normal activities are dysfunctional for some individual members of the political community. For example, even where Mexican Americans long have participated in the conventional modes of electoral politics, they have yet to achieve a level of success proportionate to their degree of participation.[3] The normal operating procedures of the American system have been biased against this minority to the extent that its members may have built up negative evaluations of the standards, which may diminish or extinguish further normative behavior. As Michael Lipsky puts it, "[Normative] behavior might lead to expressions of apathy and lack of interest in politics or a rejection of conventional political channels as a meaningful area of activity."[4]

Recent activities of Chicanos in this country have renewed interest in the question of whether the participants have been socialized to this system's norms of political behavior. Members of the Chicano community, although considered largely irrelevant to system politics in the past, now are strenuously engaged in political interactions with the decision-makers of the "outside" system. Although the most dramatic examples are protest marches, sit-ins, and other forms of direct confrontation, the more traditional, or electoral, forms of political behavior also seem to be on the increase. Since Chicanos are bound to have a substantial impact on the functioning of the American political system in the near future--that is, their political relevancy is increasing--an examination of their orientations toward the norms designed to regulate their behavior would seem important. Such information should interest minority group members who seek to employ political tactics in line with group dispositions, and therefore be optimally effective. It also should interest system authorities concerned with the stability of the system and the predictability of these groups' political activities.

This chapter examines the development of regime norms among Americans of Mexican ancestry. Although a survey of these attitudes among adult Chicanos would be informative and should be given high priority, an inquiry into the development of political standards among Chicano youths is at least as valuable. Childhood orientations provide clues to the roots of adult attitudes and also may give insight into the political behavior of adult Chicanos. It also is true that much recent political agitation by Americans of

Mexican ancestry, as well as by blacks, and native Americans, is largely a youth movement.[5] Of course, the fact that children's attitudes support a particular mode of political behavior does not guarantee that form of political participation when they become adults. However, it does indicate that children are beginning to develop expectations concerning the relationships between adult citizens and the political world. If children perceive adults as acting in a particular manner, it is more likely that when they become system participants their behavior will be guided accordingly.[6]

PERCEPTIONS OF IDEAL CITIZENSHIP

Focusing first on the children's conception of the ideal "good citizen" in a democracy, we sought to discover what traits this archetypal system member would possess, in the eyes of young Mexican Americans. These children perceive the most salient attribute of a good citizen as obedience to the law, followed by helpfulness and interest in politics and government (see Table 5.1).[7] Obeying the law is uppermost in the minds of the Anglo children as well, although slightly fewer rate it as the most important trait. Legal obedience is selected by over 60 percent of the third-grade and fifth-grade Chicanos; those in the upper two grades select this trait at a rate of 38 percent. The degree of change through the years is less than that among Anglo students, which features an accelerating decline, dropping off to 19 percent at the ninth grade level. The Chicano young see obedience to the law as an extremely important norm of behavior for American citizens. "Someone who helps others" comes in second place among Chicano children but is third in importance to the Anglos. The Chicano students' third choice of traits in a good adult citizen is political interest. Civic interest ranks only fourth out of seven qualities among third-grade Chicanos but is picked with increasing frequency until it is by far the most popular choice of ninth-graders. A similar developmental pattern on this trait also holds for the Anglo students.[8]

One interesting difference exists between the ethnic groups in regard to the qualities of citizenship that are selected less frequently. Among Chicanos, especially the youngest, religiosity is considered a virtue possessed by good citizens, while personal popularity is considered more important by the older Anglos than by Chicanos of the same

TABLE 5.1

Mexican American and Anglo Children's Perceptions of the
Characteristics of an Adult "Good Citizen"
(in percentages; respondents were asked to make
two choices)

Grade	Works Hard	Is Liked	Votes	Obeys Laws	Is Politically Interested	Goes to Church	Helps Others
			Mexican American				
3	37.1	9.3	12.9	62.2	18.6	17.2	35.0
5	29.1	7.0	8.7	62.8	27.9	9.8	47.7
7	21.2	7.3	11.4	38.9	46.6	4.2	39.4
9	11.3	6.8	12.4	37.9	55.4	1.7	39.6
Total	23.8	7.5	11.3	45.4	38.5	7.6	40.6
			Anglo				
3	36.0	8.8	9.6	66.4	26.4	8.8	34.4
5	36.6	8.9	7.3	59.4	30.1	4.9	46.3
7	15.5	11.1	11.1	37.8	49.6	3.0	26.6
9	12.5	10.7	15.7	19.4	60.0	1.9	42.5
Total	24.1	10.0	12.7	44.0	43.0	4.4	37.5

age. These differences probably reflect familial values
in each culture, since religion plays an important role in
the predominantly Catholic Mexican American household.

When asked to rank the citizenship qualities of a
student, Chicano children show much less differentiation
among the various qualities (see Table 5.2). Except for
religious regularity and being liked all qualities draw approximately the same number of responses, particularly at
the lower grades. This adds additional evidence to the in-
ference that youngsters are able to differentiate the essentially nonpolitical role of the nonvoter under 18 years
old from that of the adult participant.[9] Mexican American

students feel it most important that the budding citizen be politically interested, a quality that is most appropriate for a future participant in the political system. This is by far the most frequently selected characteristic among ninth-graders, although the less sophisticated primary-graders think it less important than most other qualities. Diligence and helpfulness again are rated high (as for adult citizens), but obedience is seen as less important for student citizens than for adults. Scholastic achievement (getting good grades) ranks second only to civic interest. Among third-graders, the best student citizen is the most helpful, although most other qualities are almost as desirable. Although it remains important through the years, helpfulness is ranked second to political awareness

TABLE 5.2

Mexican American and Anglo Children's Perceptions of the Characteristics of the Best <u>Student</u> Citizen
(in percentages; respondents were asked to make <u>two</u> choices)

Grade	Helps Others	Obeys	Gets Good Grades	Is Politically Interested	Is Liked	Works Hard	Goes to Church
			Mexican Americans				
3	39.3	37.2	35.0	28.5	6.4	32.1	17.1
5	23.8	39.5	34.8	34.7	9.3	36.0	4.1
7	34.7	23.3	29.5	37.4	8.8	33.2	4.6
9	30.5	13.0	28.8	49.1	10.2	27.7	2.3
Total	31.7	27.5	34.2	38.5	8.5	32.6	6.4
			Anglos				
3	40.8	41.6	20.0	44.0	5.6	34.4	6.4
5	53.6	29.3	22.7	37.4	10.5	35.8	4.9
7	40.7	21.5	14.8	46.6	13.4	29.6	3.0
9	41.9	6.9	23.8	61.9	11.9	25.7	1.9
Total	44.0	23.6	20.4	48.5	10.5	31.1	3.9

by ninth-grade Chicanos. Faithful religious attendance is chosen by many of the youngest Chicanos as desirable for student as well as adult citizens.

The Anglo children rate the qualities of the ideal student citizen in much the same manner, with a few divergences. The largest gap is with regard to scholastic achievement, which is much more important to Chicanos of all ages than to Anglos. On the other hand, the helpful student comes closer to being the ideal citizen for Anglos of all ages. By the time they near voting age Anglos are more prone to think political interest is the most important civic quality a student can have; helpfulness is a popular second choice while obedience rates next to last. Teenage Chicanos spread their choices more, but political interest still is the most desirable trait. Obedience to the laws and academic achievement receive proportionately more support from the oldest Chicanos than from their Anglo classmates.

PREREQUISITES OF POLITICAL PARTICIPATION

Granted that Mexican American youths see political interest as one of the most salient characteristics of a good citizen, does it follow that this ideal democratic man is a model toward which they themselves are developing? The few studies of the political behavior of Mexican American adults generally reveal that they do not participate to the extent that Anglos do.[10] Explanations for their lower level of political participation are many and diverse: discouragement by the discriminatory practices of the larger society, recent migration to the more politically vital cities, generally low socioeconomic status, and such hypothesized cultural traits as "fatalism,"[11] which diminish the importance of political activism. Unfortunately, the extent of Mexican American participation in politics has been the subject of very little investigation, much less the antecedent explanatory factors shaping political behavior. We do know that Mexican American political participation in the larger society is on the increase.

A multitude of studies have demonstrated that certain attitudes are highly correlated with political participation.[12] Among these are political efficacy, or the feeling that one can affect government through his actions; political trust, or the attitude that one's political activities will not be vitiated through the illegal or immoral practices of governmental officials; and a sense of political duty, or the feeling that it is important per se for a citizen to participate in democratic politics. Each of these prerequisites to political action was examined in the sample of young Mexican Americans by the use of three attitude scales.*

As suggested earlier, the presence of these attitudes in children does not guarantee that they will participate in system politics when adults, nor does it assure support for the political regime. It does, however, indicate that the children are beginning to acquire orientations supportive of regime norms.

Political Cynicism

Political cynicism (or the lack of trust) and its converse, trust, have been found to be highly related to political participation.[13] If a person feels distrust of public officials, it is likely to decrease political interest and participation. Adult Mexican Americans in the United States certainly have cause to distrust the American government. The history of contacts between the Mexican American people and the U.S. government is replete with incidents of prejudice and discrimination against the people, some of whose ancestors were brought into the American system through conquest.[14] The stipulations of the treaty settling the war between the United States and Mexico and protecting the personal and property rights of Mexican Americans were largely ignored by the U.S. government. Indigenous political and social organizations were destroyed and new social, economic, and political systems were superimposed on the annexed area. Relationships between governmental authority, particularly law enforcement agents, and Mexican Americans historically have been abrasive. Even today this minority group's relationship to government agencies, particularly those with a great deal of administrative discretion, is characterized by some mutual suspi-

---

*The political efficacy scale (five items) is that adapted by Easton and Dennis from the one used with adult respondents by the University of Michigan Survey Research Center. Measurement of citizen duty is by a three-item scale modified from a Survey Research Center scale of four items. Two items devised for this study form a scale of political trust.

cion and distrust. The small amount of available survey
evidence suggests that adult Mexican Americans possess a
low level of confidence in the political process.[15] Even
though comparable data on the specific dimensions of political cynicism are lacking, it is not unreasonable to speculate that the level of trust in government also might be
low. In turn, this orientation might be passed on to Chicano children.[16]

The political trust scale employed in this study con-
sisted of two items on which the agreement or disagreement
of the student was requested: (1) "I think that whatever
goes on in government is all for the best" and (2) "The
government in Washington can be trusted." Persons disagreeing with both items were judged the most cynical (low trust).

Very young Mexican American children are very trusting of their government and a majority agree with both
items (see Table 5.3). As stated, one might expect negative evaluations of the government's reliability from their
families, but apparently this is not the case, or at least
other positively laden factors override any parental cynicism. This would confirm the suggestion of M. Kent Jennings
and Richard G. Niemi that political cynicism is not an attitude transmitted from parents to their children.[17] Their
comment that "Regardless of parental feelings, children
develop a moderately to higher positive view of the trustworthiness of the national government"[18] would seem to
hold true for Chicanos. Although it has been suggested
that the socializing milieu of the school is an important
contributor to the development and maintenance of political
trust,[19] our data do not support this. During the forma-
tive years of nine through fifteen, when schools should be
perhaps the most influential socializing agent,[20] these
Chicano (and Anglo) youths become increasingly distrustful
of their government. By the ninth grade more Mexican
American youths do not consider the government trustworthy
than extend it their confidence.

The effect of social class on Mexican American's feelings of trust in government was examined not only because
socioeconomic position is a significant factor in the formation of children's political orientation but also because
the current Chicano movimiento is distinguished by its
working-class leadership and support.

When the Mexican American students are analytically
divided into socioeconomic categories, slight variations
in each group's political trust are noted (see Figure 5.1).
At the stage when familial influence is the strongest,
i.e., at the third grade level, middle-class youngsters ex-

TABLE 5.3

Levels of Political Trust Among Mexican American and Anglo
Children
(in percentages; number of responses in parentheses)

Grade	Low Trust		High Trust		Total Number*
Mexican Americans					
3	4.3	(6)	57.1	(80)	140
5	6.4	(11)	45.3	(78)	172
7	15.5	(30)	30.9	(60)	194
9	22.6	(40)	19.2	(34)	177
Total	12.7	(87)	36.9	(252)	683
Anglos					
3	6.4	(8)	54.4	(68)	125
5	8.1	(10)	39.0	(48)	123
7	15.4	(21)	30.9	(42)	136
9	21.9	(35)	16.9	(27)	160
Total	13.6	(74)	34.0	(185)	544

*Includes medium levels of trust.

press the greatest trust in government. This may reflect
a less negative political evaluation by the more affluent
families. During the years when the children's perceptual
abilities develop rapidly and when the most influential
socializing agents are the school and peers, the cynicism
of both groups increases at a comparable rate. As the
age of political maturity approaches, the declining trust
of middle-class children levels off; however, among working-
class children, trust declines even more sharply. Since
at this stage experiences with the outside world are the
most influential socializing factors, it is not improbable
that adverse experiences as a member of an impoverished
ethnic minority are being reflected.

The only similar study of political cynicism among
Chicano students also revealed that ninth-grade Mexican-

FIGURE 5.1

Feelings of High Political Trust Among Mexican
American Children, By Class

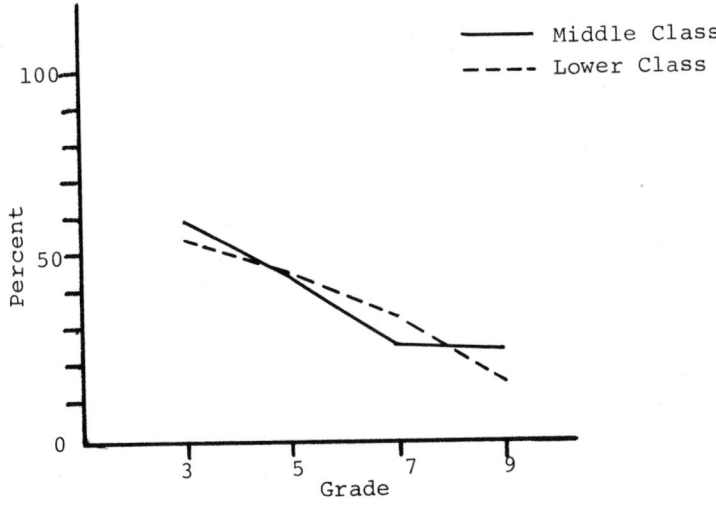

FIGURE 5.2

Percent Chicanos, By Grade and Spanish Language Use,
Exhibiting High Political Trust

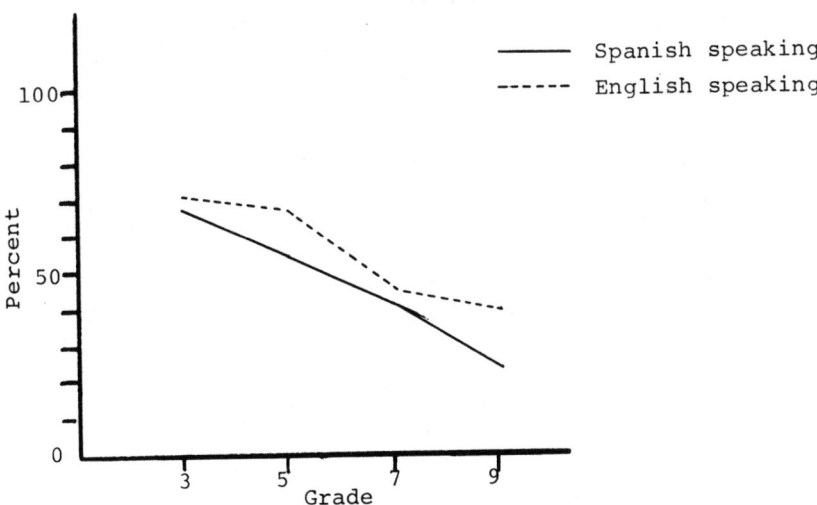

American students differed from their Anglo and black classmates in that they were more cynical.[21] Although the study's small sample precluded effective controls for socioeconomic class, the investigator hypothesized that "low socioeconomic status . . . may have more strongly influenced these Mexican Americans' political beliefs than did presumed cultural traits."[22] This substantially correlates with the findings of this study, which demonstrates that differential levels of trust among Mexican American adolescents are partially a product of class standing. However, regression analysis demonstrates that, for the total sample, ethnicity is a better predictor of political trust than socioeconomic class, when all other variables are held constant.

For Chicanos, the most powerful predictor of political cynicism is the degree of Spanish language usage. This variable is based on the relative use of Spanish and English by the child and his mother in the home. The level of Spanish usage may be the most accurate reflection of the extent of a group's cultural assimilation. Therefore, Chicanos who are least assimilated into the core American culture in terms of economic status and language are most distrustful of the system that has not yet incorporated them. Of the Spanish-speaking Mexican Americans, 31 percent are highly trustful of the government, with a decline in support from 51 to 12 percent from the third to ninth grade, while 43 percent of the English-speaking Mexican Americans (and 25 percent of these ninth-graders) exhibit high trust in government (see Figure 5.2). The second most influential factor is the area of residence. The trustworthiness of government is more suspect to the northern rural group than to the Chicanos of Southern California.

In sum, Mexican American children generally trust the American government about as much as do their Anglo schoolmates, but the cynicism level in both groups is high. The rural, lower-class, mainly Spanish-speaking Chicanos are most distrustful. These children of Mexican descent apparently do not have a low level of trust when they first contact the political system.[23] Growing up in their particular circumstances, however, exerts a tremendous negative influence on their level of confidence.[24]

Sense of Political Duty

Another attitude that can be an important requisite for citizen participation is the sense of political duty.

A citizen in a democratic society is expected minimally to take part in political activities by casting a ballot.[25] Although various motivations lie behind electoral participation, the internalized obligation of the voter certainly is a significant orientation.[26] Three items designed to measure the degree of socialization to the norm of political duty through electoral participation were included in the questionnaire.*

Mexican Americans in the United States, as a consequence of separation from the larger society, have largely retreated from "outside" politics. To the extent that they do participate politically, it is primarily within the parameters of the barrio society.[27] Consequently Mexican American parents might be expected to pass feelings of political distance on to their children. In addition, the rural background of Mexican Americans and their low economic position both imply sociological variables correlated with a low sense of electoral participation, making it less likely that Mexican American youths would have a strong sense of political obligation to the American government.

Research on the sense of civic obligation of black children has concluded that members of this distinctive disadvantaged ethnic minority have not been socialized to feel a sense of political duty to the same extent as their white counterparts.[28] In fact, of the measures of attitudes conducive to political participation used in this research, political duty has been found to be the one most highly correlated with race.[29]

For all these reasons, one might hypothesize that Chicano children would be less socialized to support the regime norm of citizen (electoral) duty than would their Anglo classmates. As expected, at all grade levels, Mexican-American youths manifest lower levels of political obligation than do Anglos (see Table 5.4). At both the third grade and ninth grade levels, almost twice as many Chicanos exhibit a low sense of electoral obligation as do their non-Mexican American cohorts. When high and medium levels of citizen duty are combined, 87.7 percent of the

---

*The children were asked to agree or disagree that (1) "So many other people vote in the national elections that it doesn't matter much whether or not any one person votes"; (2) "A lot of elections are not important enough for a person to bother with"; (3) "It isn't so important to vote when you know the people you vote for don't have a chance to win."

119

TABLE 5.4

Sense of Citizen Duty Among Mexican American and Anglo
Children
(in percentages)

Grade	Low	Medium	High	Total Number of Responses
Mexican Americans				
3	27.9	60.7	11.5	140
5	11.9	57.0	31.4	172
7	6.7	48.5	44.8	194
9	6.2	37.3	56.5	177
Total	12.1	50.2	37.6	683
Anglos				
3	15.2	58.4	26.4	125
5	2.4	50.4	47.1	123
7	2.2	39.7	58.1	136
9	3.2	28.8	68.2	160
Total	5.5	43.2	51.3	544

Chicano students feel it is important, per se, to vote,
while 94.7 percent of the Anglos feel the same way. Perhaps because of the emphasis that civics teachers place on
voting,[30] belief in the significance of voting increases
tremendously through the school years. By the time these
students are three years from voting age, 56.5 percent of
the Chicanos and over two-thirds of the Anglos exhibit a
strong disposition toward exercising the suffrage.

Stepwise regression analysis reveals that socioeconomic
class produces slightly more variation in the citizen duty
scale than does ethnicity. The lowest socialization of
this norm occurs among the lower-class third-graders within
each ethnic group, with a much larger gap between the Anglo
third-graders of each level than between the two Mexican
American classes (see Table 5.5). Among those ranking low
on this attitudinal scale, variations in social status make

TABLE 5.5

Sense of Citizen Duty Among Mexican American and Anglo
Children, Controlling for Social Class
(in percentages; number of responses in parentheses)

Grade	Low		Medium		High	
Mexican American Middle Class						
3	25.0	(5)	60.0	(12)	15.0	(3)
5	10.0	(4)	50.0	(20)	40.0	(16)
7	6.1	(3)	30.7	(15)	63.2	(31)
9	7.3	(3)	31.7	(13)	61.0	(25)
Total	10.0	(15)	40.0	(60)	50.0	(75)
Mexican American Lower Class						
3	28.7	(33)	60.8	(70)	10.5	(12)
5	11.3	(14)	58.9	(73)	29.9	(37)
7	7.3	(10)	52.9	(72)	39.7	(54)
9	5.6	(7)	33.2	(49)	55.2	(69)
Total	12.8	(64)	52.8	(264)	34.4	(172)
Anglo Middle Class						
3	8.9	(6)	61.8	(42)	29.5	(20)
5	2.6	(2)	50.7	(38)	46.7	(35)
7	1.4	(1)	29.8	(22)	68.9	(51)
9	2.2	(2)	28.1	(25)	69.7	(62)
Total	3.6	(11)	41.5	(127)	54.9	(168)
Anglo Lower Class						
3	23.6	(13)	42.7	(29)	23.7	(13)
5	2.1	(1)	49.0	. (23)	49.0	(23)
7	1.8	(1)	50.0	(28)	48.2	(27)
9	4.5	(3)	29.9	(20)	65.7	(44)
Total	8.0	(18)	44.4	(100)	47.5	(107)

less difference for Chicanos than for Anglos. The middle
classes of both groups display similar patterns with an increasing sense of civic obligation. Although middle-class
third-grade Chicanos initially rank lower than their Anglo
peers, they display a similar developmental pattern of
very rapid socialization to this norm, with a leveling off
at the seventh grade level. The lower classes are slower
to develop a high sense of electoral obligation and may
still be developing it in the ninth grade. Lowest in sense
of civic obligation at all stages is the Mexican-American
working class (34.4 percent high obligation). The combined
effects of ethnic discrimination plus low socioeconomic
status apparently are too great to be overcome by curricular
attempts at instilling this sense of civic duty.

Partial correlation analysis also points out that the
best predictor of orientations toward citizen duty is the
degree of Spanish language usage of the respondent (beta =
0.17). Thus the most "Mexican" American children display
the lowest sense of civic electoral obligation. Slightly
over 30 percent of the more Spanish-speaking feel highly
obligated to vote, while 43.5 percent of those who use
more English are so inclined.

Because of the highly supportive results of their responses to other items in this study, these particular
opinions of the Spanish-speakers do not appear to reflect
greater loyalty to another political system such as Mexico.
Instead, the specific nature of the attitude being measured
--the importance of participation in elections--must be
taken into account. Until a recent court decision over-
ruled it,[31] California's election code disenfranchised all
but those literate in English. Citizens whose main language
was Spanish and who were not literate in English hardly
could be expected to feel a sense of obligation toward a
duty they had never had the privilege of exercising. It
is estimated that California has about 250,000 permanent
residents who own property, pay taxes, and are subject to
laws but, because they do not know English, are prohibited
from becoming citizens of the United States and California
and therefore cannot qualify to vote. Although there is
no specific data on this point, it is very likely that some
Chicano children in the sample have parents who are not
U.S. citizens and thus are ineligible to vote. This es-
trangement from the suffrage undoubtedly affects the attitudes of Mexican American parents, who in turn transmit
them to their children. In view of this absence of attitudinal and behavioral cues supporting electoral participation, the existence of a high-level sense of civic duty

in even a relatively small percentage of Spanish-speaking
children is surprising.

Political Efficacy

The feeling that one's political activities have some
effect on the political system is among the most widely
investigated regime norms.[32] Most of this research can be
traced back to the early works of the voting behavior researchers at the Survey Research Center, University of
Michigan, who defined political efficacy as "the feeling
that individual political action does have, or can have,
an impact upon the political process . . . that political
and social change is possible, and that the individual
citizen can play a part in bringing about this change."[33]
A sense of political efficacy has been shown to be associated with political interest, increased political participation, and positive attitudes toward the political
system (or legitimacy), personal trust, education, and
income.

The most complete analysis and discussion of children's
responses to this regime norm is contained in an article
by Easton and Dennis.[34] They found that five items used
in previous research have the greatest significance for
childhood socialization studies, and these were incorporated in the present study to form a scale of political efficacy. Their "most important conclusion" was that children have begun to develop a sense of political efficacy
by the third grade.[35] At this early age, the child's image
of government is quite diffuse and his responses on these
items are interpreted as projective attitudes about the
proper behavior of adults; he is learning to think about
adults and politics in a manner that will influence the
way he thinks about himself as he matures politically.
Easton and Dennis state:

> We can . . . interpret the attitudinal component
> [political efficacy] . . . as a first but critical
> step in the child's acquisition of an orientation
> to political efficacy as it related to himself.
> He is building up an emotional frame of reference
> or loose attitudinal structure through which he
> has come to think about and view expected rela-
> tionships between adult members of the system
> and the authorities.[36]

Easton and Dennis, reporting on the attitudes of a national sample of 12,000 white, middle-class students, reveal that by early adolescence most pupils develop strong feelings of political efficacy, supportive of the regime.[37] However, differences have been found among subgroups in the American population. Children from families of lower socioeconomic standing have been found to lag behind those of higher status in developing this norm.[38] Several studies have found that black children feel less efficacious than their white classmates, from an early age.[39] However, an investigation that compared levels of political efficacy of a small sample of blacks, Anglos, and Mexican Americans in a common setting discussed no significant differences among the groups.[40] However, in the ninth grade all three groups felt less efficacious than the white eighth-grade students in the studies reported earlier.

For several reasons, it was hypothesized that Mexican American children would manifest lower levels of political efficacy than their Anglo classmates. As mentioned earlier, Mexican Americans have been politically as well as socially and economically suppressed, with the result that their level of politicization toward system politics is low.[41] When they have participated in system politics, their efforts have been rather ineffective, as measured by favorable governmental response to their needs. Two values ascribed to the traditional Mexican American family also may depress feelings of efficacy in Chicano children. If Mexican Americans really do perceive themselves as subjects rather than masters of their destiny,[42] the youngsters would be likely to feel less confident or able to manage political forces. Moreover, children traditionally are relegated to a very subordinate status in the family,[43] a position that could be projected into later political roles. In any case the family generally is thought to be the agent of socialization with the greatest impact on the early development of political efficacy.[44]

Our hypothesis is supported by the responses of the sample, as indicated in Table 5.6. Mexican American children initially manifest lower levels of political efficacy, and, although there is a slight increase through the school years, the increase is less than half that among Anglos. In fact, the percentage of Chicanos who feel low political efficacy is greater in the ninth grade than in the third.[45] Over half the oldest Anglos feel strongly that citizens can affect their government (high efficacy), while only a little over one-quarter of the Mexican American ninth-

TABLE 5.6

Sense of Political Efficacy Among Mexican American and
Anglo Children
(in percentages)

Grade	Low	Medium	High	Total Number of Responses
		Mexican Americans		
3	17.1	65.6	17.1	140
5	16.9	65.6	17.5	172
7	17.6	57.1	25.3	194
9	18.1	54.1	27.7	177
Total	17.4	60.3	22.2	683
		Anglos		
3	12.8	61.6	25.6	125
5	13.8	43.6	32.5	123
7	12.5	44.9	42.7	136
9	9.4	38.2	52.5	160
Total	12.0	48.8	39.3	544

graders concur. During adolescence some movement from medium to high levels of efficacy is evident among the Mexican Americans. However, through the school years a hard
core of feelings of low efficacy persists.

Evidence concerning the effect of social class on attitudes of political efficacy in children is mixed.[46] For
our sample, when all other independent variables are held
constant, social class has less effect on this attitude
than ethnicity, which is the strongest predictor of all
the variables. The effect that socioeconomic status does
have on the orientations of Mexican Americans on this
variable is shown in Table 5.7.

Third-grade lower-class Chicanos show a higher level
of political efficacy than their middle-class schoolmates.
This may be one example of the higher rate of positive,
idealistic responses given by the youngest, lower-class

Chicanos to most items in this study. Over the next four
years, the number of middle-class Chicanos who feel high
efficacy doubles and then almost doubles again in the following two years. After an early dip, the lower-class
Chicanos demonstrate attitudes of higher efficacy at a
slow, steady rate, but at the ninth grade they still lag
considerably behind middle-class seventh-graders. The
rise in feelings of efficacy among Chicano working-class
children, after an early decline, probably reflects the
influence of the school and its attempts to inculcate democratic norms. Working-class children apparently are more
susceptible to such school socialization than those of
higher economic status.[47] The trend toward an increased
sense of political efficacy is reversed among the most
mature middle-class Chicanos. It may be that, as they
approach adult status, they become more aware of the actual
efficacy of their people, and their attitudes begin to reflect actual political potency gleaned from experience with
government and its agencies rather than abstract acceptance
of a regime norm.[48]
   The importance of culture as a determinant of feelings
of political efficacy may be demonstrated by the finding
that, among Mexican Americans, the variable most affecting

TABLE 5.7

Sense of Political Efficacy Among Mexican American
Children, By Socioeconomic Class
(in percentages; N = 683)

Grade	Low	High	Change
	Middle Class		
3	10.0	10.0	0.0
5	15.0	20.0	+5.0
7	16.3	38.8	+22.5
9	17.0	24.3	+7.0
	Lower Class		
3	18.2	18.2	0.0
5	16.9	14.5	-2.4
7	16.9	21.3	+2.4
9	17.6	28.0	+10.4

this attitude is the amount of Spanish language usage (or
degree of acculturation), while among Anglos grade level
is the best predictor. Whether this strong effect of membership in a distinctive culture results from value differences, family relationships, or, more directly, the greater
alienation of those least accepted into the American "core
culture" can only be answered by further investigation.

In sum, Mexican American youths feel substantially
less confident than Anglos that their activities as citizens affect governmental decisions. Unlike their Anglo
peers, a majority of Chicano adolescents feel only moderately, rather than highly, efficacious by the time they
are a few years from voting age. Attitudes of nonefficacy
prevail through the years for a significant number of Chicanos.

Summary

Ethnicity has been seen to be a very important variable with respect to the development of support for the pre-
participative regime norms of political trust, duty, and
efficacy. In general, Mexican American children trust
their government less, feel more futile about exerting influence on it, and are less motivated to participate in
elections than their Anglo peers. In its earliest stages,
differences in orientation between the two ethnic groups
generally are narrow, as the third-grade Chicanos are
slightly more trusting but feel less efficacious or elec-
torally duty conscious. However, later socialization produces a divergent and less positive orientation for Chicano
youths, particularly those who reside in rural areas, are
of the lower class, and are least acculturated. The gulf
that develops between Mexican- and Anglo-American children
as they mature may indicate that ethnic differences in political orientation may be more the product of a minority's
negative experiences with secondary socializing agents
than a reflection of familial inculcation of distinctive
cultural values.

MAJORITY RULE

One major feature of democratic decision-making theory
is majority rule. Although much debate has taken place
over the various consequences of this procedure, the conditions under which it should be used, and the dilemmas in-

herent in its application, most democratic theorists see
it as the optimal rule for decision-making in a system
where each person's political power theoretically is equal
to every other's.[49] Thus a decision made by simply tally-
ing the ayes and nays on any one issue becomes the official
decision and is to be accepted by the losing minority--if
not as the permanent outcome at least as a decision rightly
arrived at.

How do the Chicano pupils feel about majority rule as
the decision-making norm in our political system? Only at
the third grade level does a majority agree that "If most
people agree to do something, everyone should go along with
it" (see Figure 5.3). Support for this principle declines
steeply over the next six years until 72.9 percent oppose
it in the ninth grade. However, among Anglo children the
proposition does not gather majority support at any level,
although agreement falls off less sharply. Apparently,
these young people are demonstrating their nonconformity
in reacting to this question. The item is not couched in
a political context per se and this might make a difference
in the response.

ELECTION AND CONTROL OF OFFICIALS

In a democracy, all citizens are urged to participate
in government even to the extent of running for office.
Usually implied is the norm that people seek public positions to serve the polity. Mexican American youths see
candidates for high public office as motivated primarily
by a desire to "change things that are not good in government" (see Figure 5.4). While this reason is least often
given by the youngest Chicanos, it rises in popularity until over half (53.7 percent) select it. This trend shows
the mirror image of respondent feelings that candidates
run for office to preserve the status quo. Over half the
third-grade Chicanos think candidates "want to keep things
as good as they are in our country," but less than 10 percent of the oldest Chicanos agree. More than one-quarter
of these ninth-graders think selfish motives--such as
prestige or money--underlie races for office. This represents only a slight increase over the 20 percent of third-
graders who select this motive.

The Anglo children in the sample hold parallel but
stronger views on the reform-based motivations of public
candidates. The developmental pattern is similar for the
"conservative" motive, although it is less strongly held·

FIGURE 5.3

Percent, By Grade and Ethnicity, Agreeing that
"If Most People Agree to Do Something,
Everyone Should Go Along with It"

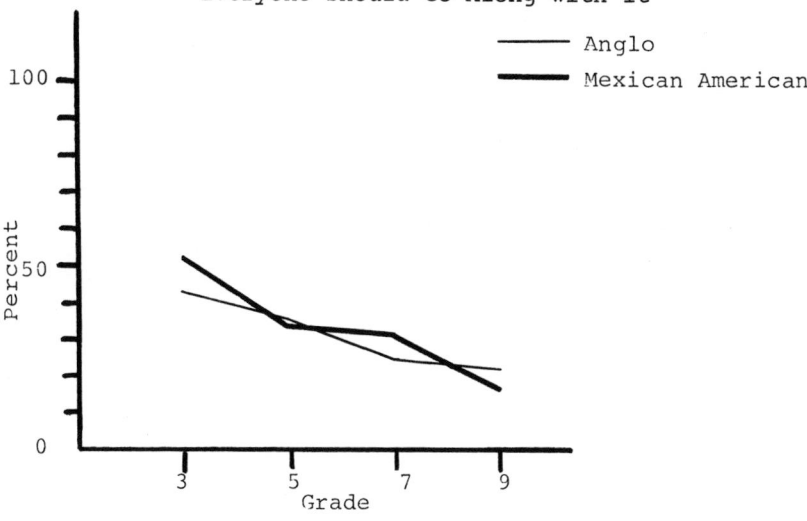

FIGURE 5.4

Motivations of Candidates for Public Office

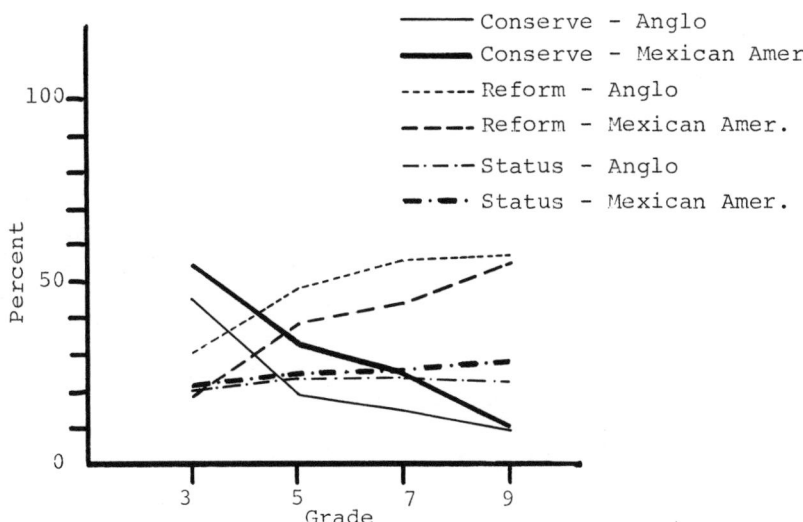

by Anglos than by Chicanos. Anglos ascribe selfish motivations in almost exactly the same proportion as Mexican Americans at each year until a slight difference appears at the ninth grade.

Overall, then, the only difference between the two ethnic groups is that the Mexican Americans tend to believe candidates are attempting to preserve the status quo more often than Anglos do, although this is the most popular choice only among the Chicano third-graders. After the fifth grade, reform is seen as the primary objective. Selfish motivations finally are accorded a middle position, with teenage Chicanos seeing this as the reason for candidacy more often than do Anglos.

The most "democratic" method of selecting officials is, of course, by popular election, with the winning candidate minimally receiving a plurality of the votes cast. Correspondingly, a majority of Mexican American children feel the most important characteristic of a public leader is approval from most of the people (see Table 5.8). Only the youngest Chicanos think intelligence is a more desirable qualification for a leader. Respect for intelligence and education traditionally has been high among Mexican Americans, as well as in Mexican culture. This apparently is communicated to the youngest children by the most influential socializing agent at an early age--the family. Anglo third-graders do not place as high a premium on intelligence, preferring a majority-supported official at all grades. Yet the highest frequency of responses favoring majority representation is among Chicano ninth-graders.

It may be of interest that 51 of the Chicano respondents viewed old age as the most important criterion for a leader while only three of the Anglos did. Over 90 percent of these Chicano respondents were in the elementary grades, while the Anglos were in the highest two grade levels. Respect for age is found more often in both traditional and European societies than in the modern American community. Mexican American culture, with a mixture of traditional-rural and European elements, probably features more respect for the elderly than does the American core culture with its emphasis on youth.

Overall, Chicanos demonstrate expected support for election of candidates by majority vote. The lack of early support for this norm probably results from their greater tendency to personalize government and its components. After this initial discrepancy, support for this regime norm increases to an extent even greater than that demonstrated by the comparable Anglo group.

TABLE 5.8

Qualifications of Governmental Leaders Preferred by
Mexican American and Anglo Children
(in percentages)

Grade	Strength	Intelligence	Majority Support	Age
		Mexican Americans		
3	12.9	42.1	27.9	6.4
5	4.7	32.6	54.1	2.3
7	2.1	27.5	61.7	0.0
9	1.1	22.6	63.8	0.6
Total	4.7	30.5	53.4	2.0
		Anglos		
3	8.0	32.8	53.6	0.0
5	2.4	34.1	54.5	0.0
7	3.0	25.9	59.3	1.5
9	3.8	21.3	60.0	0.6
Total	4.2	27.9	57.2	0.6

Once an official is elected, he is expected to remain
responsible to his constituency. Although the importance
he attaches to communications from his constituents may
vary, few would contend that they do not give such communications at least minimal consideration.[50] The sample
members were asked their opinions on the President's reaction to a letter received from a member of the public.
The youngest Chicanos think the President "cares a lot"
when they write to him (see Table 5.9). However, their
evaluation of presidential responsiveness drops quite rapidly through the years as their attitudes become more
realistic. Ninth-grade Chicanos primarily feel the President will "care a little" about their communications; the
next highest response is that he "does not care" at all.
This is not a surprising pattern of reaction, on the whole;[51]
most adults probably feel their missives to the executive

TABLE 5.9

Mexican American and Anglo Children's Perceptions of
Presidential Response to Communications
(in percentages)

Grade	Cares a Lot	Cares Somewhat	Cares a Little	Does Not Care
	Mexican Americans			
3	76.4	8.6	8.6	5.0
5	47.1	26.2	12.8	13.4
7	27.5	27.5	25.4	15.0
9	13.6	26.0	31.1	28.8
Total	38.9	22.8	20.2	16.1
	Anglos			
3	63.2	15.2	8.0	18.7
5	37.4	27.6	18.7	16.3
7	33.3	25.2	20.0	17.0
9	12.5	20.6	40.0	21.9
Total	35.1	22.1	22.8	16.9

have little impact but are not ignored entirely. The Anglo response is quite similar, the major difference being that Anglos are not as optimistic in the early grades nor as pessimistic as Chicano teenagers.*

*A stepwise linear regression analysis reveals that area of student residence is the independent variable with the greatest effect on this opinion (beta = 0.28). However, the statistical interpretation ignores a unique but important set of circumstances surrounding the responses to this item. The day the survey was conducted, a child from one of the schools in the northern sample received a response to a letter to the President that said, in effect, "Thank you for your suggestion, but you take care of your business and the President will take care of his." Repre-

SUMMARY AND CONCLUSIONS

Mexican American children's socialization toward regime norms is quite similar to that of Anglo children in its earliest stages, although some slight variations, perhaps attributable to the cultural values of the traditional Mexican family, are apparent. However, on attitudes considered prerequisites of political participation--such as a sense of political trust, citizen duty, or political efficacy--later socialization produces a divergent and less positive orientation for Chicano youths, particularly those who reside in rural areas, are of the lower class, and are least acculturated. Smaller differences are noted with respect to norms, such as majority rule, that do not imply interactions between the political decision-makers and those seeking to influence them.

Since Mexican-American adolescents have perceived that norms regulating certain types of citizen political activity are irrelevant or inapplicable with regard to their own experience, it is not surprising that much recent Chicano political activity has taken the form of strikes, boycotts, walkouts, demonstrations, and other behavior that places stress on the system. Ironically, these "abnormal" behaviors, if effective, may be experiences that eventually could increase the level of support for traditional democratic norms.

---

sentatives from the major news services and television networks descended (literally, in helicopters) upon the school, and the story received coverage in the national media.

Appropriately enough, our results show that the Northern California children were much less inclined to believe in the efficacy of their communications than their fellow students in Southern California.

6

THE POLITICAL AUTHORITIES: NECESSARY BUT NOT SUFFICIENT?

INTRODUCTION

In Chapter 3 we saw that Mexican American children, like their Anglo counterparts, develop a notion of government fairly early in childhood. This image initially is personalized, focusing on such governmental figures as the President, and becoming more institutionalized as the child matures.

The importance of individual public figures to political socialization has been stressed in much of the literature. David Easton and Jack Dennis view the child's earliest and highly favorable contact with public figures as the key to the legitimacy of the political system.[1] These researchers contend that the President and the policeman are the most visible and salient authorities for the young child, and they also emphasize the impact of favorable perception of these authorities as initiating points of positive system support. From the system viewpoint, it is very important that children see these authorities in a highly idealized manner--benevolent, caring, and helpful-- since these orientations form a bridge to a more diffuse support for the total system.

Fred Greenstein also found that children see public figures in a highly personal and positive manner and contended that this early feeling forms a foundation for system stability.[2] Some consider these positive valuations of a very personalized yet diffused image of government to be the result of the child's psychological need to attribute benevolent characteristics to authority figures because of his position of vulnerability and helplessness.[3] However, later studies have criticized this vulnerability-anxiety hypothesis by demonstrating that children vary a great deal in their levels of anxiety as well as their degree of affect for the President, and that the generalized relationship does not hold for all cases.[4] In a more recent article, Dean Jaros and his associates demonstrated that children of an American subculture, the Appalachian poor, do not share these highly positive evaluations of governmental authorities.[5]

In this chapter we shall examine how Mexican American children feel toward various governmental authority figures and postulate some implications for their future orientation toward the political system.

THE PRESIDENT

Cognition of the President

In comparing responses on the items "Who does the most to run the country?" and "Which one of these pictures shows best what our government is?", Chicanos, like Anglos, pick the President as the most salient figure (see Chapter 3). This accords with most previous research, which strongly emphasizes the importance of this early recognition of the President.

What constitutes a Chicano child's view of the President? Are their perceptions fairly accurate vis-à-vis Anglo children? Are Chicano children's orientations transferred during the process of institutionalization toward support for the system? If so, what implications does this suggest for adult system support?

As was pointed out, the President is the most significant public authority for young Chicano children. Obviously he is recognized as a very important representative of the government, i.e., his visibility is very high. But is the chief executive also very salient? Does the child feel this authority figure has any impact on his own life? When children were asked to relate various authority figures to their families ("Who helps your family the most?"), the responses indicated a feeling that the President is indeed "close" to the child's personal environment. The youngest Chicanos rate the President far more "helpful" than any other public authority, second only to their fathers (see Table 6.1). Although this ranking is similar to that of the Anglo group, young Chicanos feel a bit closer to the President. This early high level of saliencey, in terms of helpfulness, falls off quickly for both groups.

TABLE 6.1

Mexican American and Anglo Children's Responses to the Question, "Who Helps Your Family the Most?"

(in percentages; number of responses in parentheses)

Grade	Policeman		Soldier		Father		Teacher		President		Governor		Don't Know/No Answer	
Mexican Americans														
3	11.4	(16)	2.9	(4)	41.4	(58)	3.6	(5)	26.4	(37)	13.6	(19)	0.7	(1)
5	7.6	(13)	0.6	(1)	65.1	(112)	0.0	(0)	8.7	(15)	17.4	(30)	0.6	(1)
7	3.1	(6)	4.1	(8)	75.1	(145)	0.0	(0)	4.1	(8)	9.3	(18)	4.1	(8)
9	3.4	(6)	1.7	(3)	76.8	(136)	0.0	(0)	2.8	(5)	7.3	(13)	7.9	(14)
Total	6.0	(41)	2.3	(16)	66.2	(452)	0.7	(5)	9.5	(65)	11.7	(80)	3.5	(24)
Anglos														
3	8.8	(11)	3.2	(4)	52.8	(66)	1.6	(2)	21.6	(27)	8.0	(10)	4.0	(5)
5	4.1	(5)	0.8	(1)	77.2	(95)	0.8	(1)	7.3	(9)	7.3	(9)	2.4	(3)
7	6.7	(9)	3.7	(5)	74.8	(101)	0.7	(1)	5.9	(8)	4.4	(6)	3.7	(5)
9	6.3	(10)	3.8	(6)	72.5	(116)	1.3	(2)	2.5	(4)	6.9	(11)	6.9	(11)
Total	6.4	(35)	3.1	(17)	69.5	(378)	1.1	(6)	8.8	(48)	6.6	(34)	4.4	(24)

Controlling for social class reveals that the difference in salience between the ethnic groups reflects mainly the feelings of middle-class, third-grade Chicanos, who feel the President helps their families as much as their fathers do (see Table 6.2).

Apparently the President also is very close in the sense of being incorporated into the child's moral standards. A majority of Chicano third-graders think it is more wrong to disobey the President than their parents, teacher, or a policeman (see Table 6.3). This attitude continues into junior high school until the President is edged out by the policeman in the ninth grade. The Anglo pattern is similar.

TABLE 6.2

Mexican American and Anglo Children's Responses to the Question, "Who Helps Your Family the Most?", Controlling for Social Class
(in percentages)

Grade	Police-man	Soldier	Father	Teacher	Presi-dent	Gover-nor
Mexican American Working Class						
3	12.2	2.6	41.7	2.6	24.3	15.7
5	6.5	0.8	63.7	0.0	10.5	17.7
7	2.9	3.7	77.9	0.0	4.4	8.1
9	4.0	1.6	76.0	0.0	3.2	8.8
Mexican American Middle Class						
3	5.0	0.0	40.0	10.0	40.0	5.0
5	2.5	0.0	80.0	0.0	2.5	15.0
7	4.2	6.3	68.8	0.0	4.2	12.5
9	2.4	2.4	82.9	0.0	2.4	2.4
Anglo Working Class						
3	11.1	3.7	44.4	1.9	24.1	9.3
5	2.2	2.2	73.9	2.2	8.7	8.7
7	10.7	3.6	64.3	1.8	7.1	7.1
9	9.0	7.5	64.2	0.0	4.5	7.5
Anglo Middle Class						
3	7.5	3.0	61.2	1.5	19.4	7.5
5	5.4	0.0	81.1	0.0	6.8	6.8
7	2.7	5.5	83.6	0.0	5.5	2.7
9	4.8	1.2	83.3	2.4	1.2	7.1

TABLE 6.3

Chicano Children's Selections of Whom It Is Most Wrong to Disobey
(in percentages; number of responses in parentheses)

Grade	Mother	Teacher	Policeman	President	Father	Don't Know/No Answer
3	9.3 (13)	5.7 (8)	10.7 (15)	51.4 (72)	5.0 (7)	17.1 (24)
5	14.0 (24)	4.7 (8)	15.1 (26)	30.8 (53)	12.8 (22)	22.7 (39)
7	14.0 (27)	3.1 (6)	13.0 (25)	26.9 (52)	10.4 (20)	31.1 (60)
9	10.2 (18)	1.7 (3)	17.5 (31)	15.8 (28)	15.3 (27)	36.2 (64)
Total	12.0 (82)	3.7 (25)	14.2 (97)	30.2 (206)	11.1 (76)	27.4 (187)

138

Another measure of closeness may be the communication distance between the President and the child. If a child writes a letter, will it have any impact on the President? As discussed in Chapter 5, young Mexican-American children are more likely than Anglo children to think it will make an impression. However, as Chicanos develop mentally and physically they begin to feel more distant from the President and at high school age are more likely than Anglos to say the President will not care about their communications.

Affect for the President

The President is visible and salient, but how is he perceived in terms of affect? Is he benevolent or malevolent, kind or uncaring? Chicano children initially are extremely affectionate toward the President, but this liking drops off precipitously (see Figure 6.1). Affection is divided evenly in the fifth grade and swings heavily against the President in the seventh. In the ninth grade a majority of Chicanos (53.1 percent) state that they "don't like him very much." While a general decline of affection also is displayed by the Anglo sample, the change in attitude is less dramatic. The Anglos do not care for the President as much initially, but at the seventh grade admirers still hold a slight margin over those disliking him.

Since higher idealization seems evident among the young Chicanos, it may be that Chicano children feel more vulnerable than do Anglos. Young Mexican Americans certainly do exist in a more hostile social environment than children of the majority culture, and perhaps they are more "anxious" than their Anglo primary school classmates. Both groups drop below majority "liking" for the President by the fifth grade. The children are becoming less idealistic and more realistic in their perceptions of the President by this time.

Since the President is viewed in such highly favorable terms by the youngest children, a spillover to other parts of the regime could occur and this might provide a singularly important foundation for system stability. As Easton and Dennis have stated, "early idealization of the office [of the President] may leave enough respect as a latent force to sustain a belief in its legitimacy. If so we have come upon a major taproot of diffuse support in a system."[6] The responses of the older children, in addition to being less idealistic, more probably indicate their evaluation of the current presidential incumbent than of the presidential office.

FIGURE 6.1

Percent, By Grade and Ethnicity, Responding
"I Like the President Very Much"

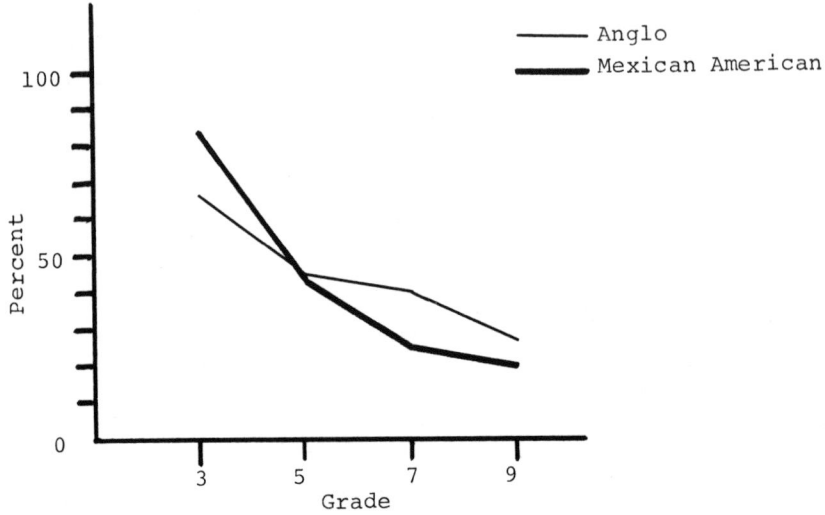

FIGURE 6.2

Percent, By Grade, Ethnicity and Social Class,
Stating "I Like the President Very Much"

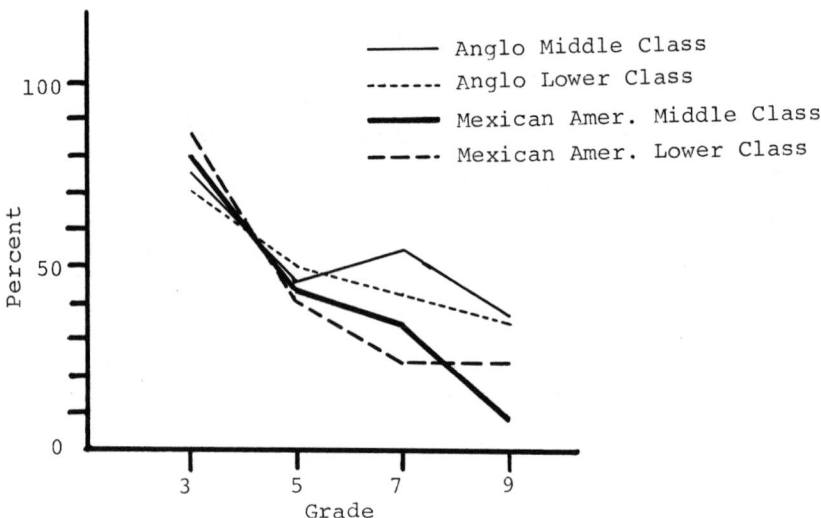

Controlling for social class graphically illustrates the change in both the perceptual abilities of the maturing children and the effect of their experience with different socializing agents as they pass through childhood into adolescence (see Figure 6.2). Although the effect of ethnicity continues, both lower-class Anglos and Chicanos continue to like the President less and less through the fifth and seventh grades. The disaffection of middle-class Chicanos proceeds more slowly, and the Anglo middle class rallies behind the President. However, as the decline in lower-class affect levels off in the next two years, the middle classes grow disenchanted. Only 9.8 percent of the middle-class Chicanos like the President very much; 58.5 percent "don't like him very much."

According to the developmental profile of Richard Dawson and Kenneth Prewitt, the most influential socializing experiences of the middle years are those of the school environment, proceeding through direct political learning, while in later years direct contact with political reality, both personally and through the media, is the main characteristic of the socialization process.[7] This may help to explain why the generally more "aware" middle-class Chicanos, exposed to more criticism of the President in their adolescent years, show a sharp drop in affection. Yet social class is one of the least significant variables affecting this attitude. Age (grade level) is, of course, the most powerful, explaining 13 percent of the variation of responses on this item (beta = 0.35). Ranking second in explanatory power both for the total group (beta = 0.16) and the Chicanos (beta = 0.17) is geographical area of residence. It is among the Mexican-American third-graders of Southern California that the highest degree of idealization is present. A tremendous reversal in feelings toward the President occurs in the next few years until over half these children "don't like (the President) very much" by the ninth grade. The rural Chicanos of Northern California initially like the President less, and their feeling of relatively less affection continues through the years until leveling off at a level similar to that of their southern co-ethnics. Spanish language usage among Chicanos is the next most significant predictor (beta = 0.12) as the more Spanish-oriented children tend to like the President less.

Is this most salient and very close public authority a person to be feared? Twice as many Mexican-American children (14.3 percent) as Anglos (7.2. percent) initially fear the President, adding weight to the vulnerability hypothesis. The Mexican Americans' apprehension declines to almost zero by high school, while fear among Anglos remains virtually constant.

Ethnicity is as good a predictor as grade on this variable. Socioeconomic class is less a factor than either of these control variables. The effect of socioeconomic status on Chicano attitudes is minute. The most influential variable is the amount of Spanish used by the young child and his parents (beta = 0.19). Fear of the President is expressed more frequently by less assimilated Mexican Americans. Since at least one author contends that the folk value system of rural Mexico includes a view of the world outside the family as hostile and threatening,[8] this might explain the greater fear among the less assimilated Mexican American youngsters.

Chicanos initially feel the President also is a very friendly figure, much more than do the younger Anglos. However, this feeling among Chicanos shows a rapid decline until it falls below the Anglo "presidential friendliness" curve in the middle school years (see Figure 6.3). This curve is almost an exact replica of the "likeableness curve." Controls for social class make little difference in Chicano perceptions of friendliness at any grade level.

In sum, these measures of presidential affection demonstrate that the President suffers a tremendous loss in popularity among Chicano children over the years, although initially he ranks extremely high on their affection list.

Evaluation of the President's
Role Performance

How do Chicano children evaluate the role performance qualities of the President? Although it is particularly difficult to distinguish the affective from the cognitive components of these evaluations, we attempted to do so by asking the children to give their views on presidential helpfulness, power, knowledge, and diligence. Based on the research by Easton and Dennis, the order of these traits, as listed, is toward increasing cognitive and decreasing affective content.[9]

Although all young children see the President as very helpful, Chicanos see him as especially benevolent (see Figure 6.4). While all young people's ratings of presidential helpfulness decline over the years, the drop among Mexican Americans is comparatively steep. When socioeco-

FIGURE 6.3

Percent, By Grade and Ethnicity, Agreeing that
"The President Is Friendlier than Most People"

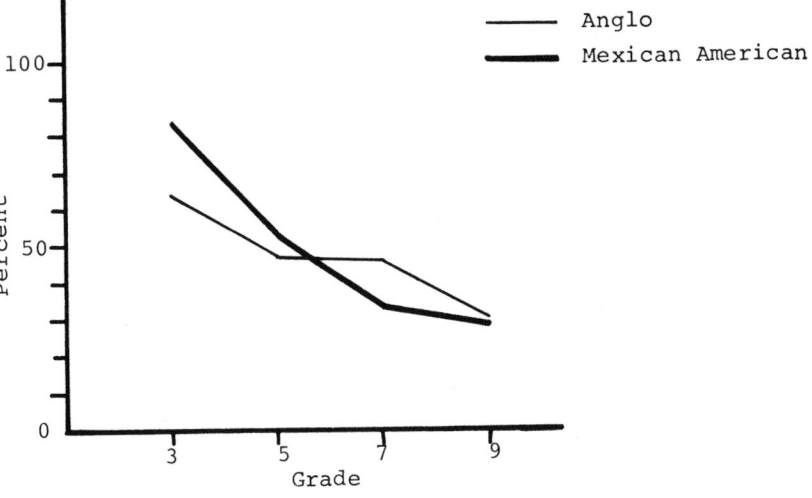

FIGURE 6.4

Percent, By Grade and Ethnicity, Agreeing that
"The President Is More Helpful than Most People"

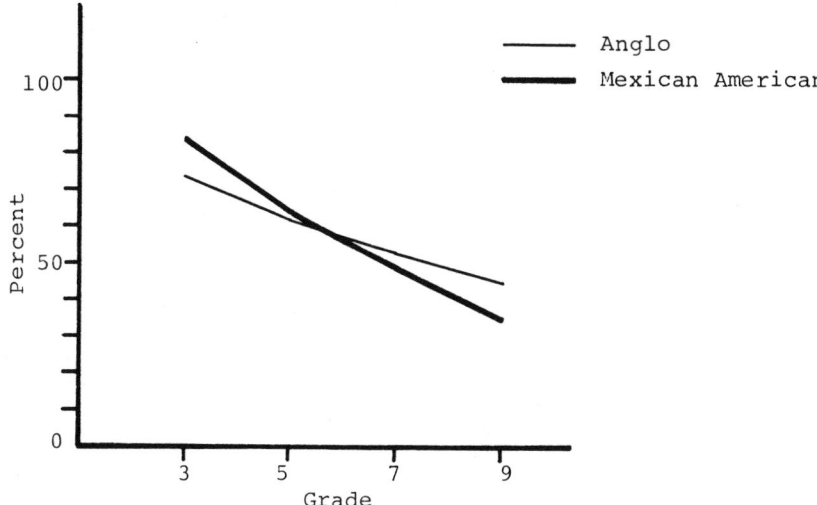

nomic standing is introduced, the lower-class Mexican-American pupils again are the most idealistic in the earliest grades and exhibit a great disillusionment through the years. Although middle-class Chicanos in the ninth grade do not consider the President any more helpful than do their co-ethnics of lower status, initially they had lower estimations of presidential benevolence. A majority of both classes of teenage Anglos view the President as helpful, and this rating changes very little over the later years. But the Chicanos' view of presidential helpfulness at this age continues to grow more negative, reflecting what they have learned from increasing contacts with the real political world.

When Chicanos evaluate presidential power, only the youngest believe that "the President can make everybody do what he wants them to do" (see Figure 6.5). Of the Anglo third-graders, 58 percent reject this statement. However, by the fifth grade the divergence between the two ethnic groups narrows considerably, and by the age of 15 or so their attitudes are similar on this point.

Socioeconomic class is more highly correlated (gamma = 0.35) with attitudes toward presidential traits than is ethnicity (gamma = 0.22). Working-class children are more impressed by the coercive power of the President than are those of higher economic standing, regardless of ethnicity.

An independent variable that had relatively little effect on the attitudes examined up to this point is the sex of the respondent.[10] However, on the measure of presidential power, Chicano attitudes are affected more by sex than by any variable other than age or Spanish language use. Young Mexican American girls are more impressed with the President's ability to force compliance than are their male classmates. This also was true of Anglo females, but to a lesser degree. Perhaps the greater dependency and subordinate status of little girls in the traditional Mexican American family accounts for some of the difference in response.[11]

The next two dimensions examined include the least affective content: presidential knowledgeability and diligence. The usual very high rating in estimates of presidential knowledge is given by the youngest Chicanos. Again the perceptions of the two ethnic groups cross in the middle grades, a phenomenon largely attributable to the sharp plunge in the Mexican American evaluation (see Figure 6.6). While 47 percentage points separate the rankings of third-grade Chicanos from the ninth-graders, the Anglos' opinion descends by only 20 points. As Mexican American youths

FIGURE 6.5

Percent, By Grade and Ethnicity, Agreeing that
"The President Can Make Everyone Do What
He Wants Them to Do"

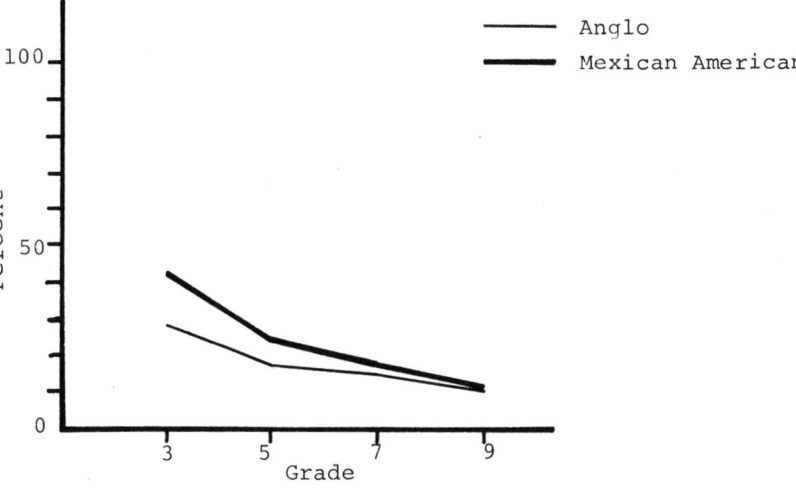

FIGURE 6.6

Percent, By Grade and Ethnicity, Agreeing that
"The President Knows More than Most People"

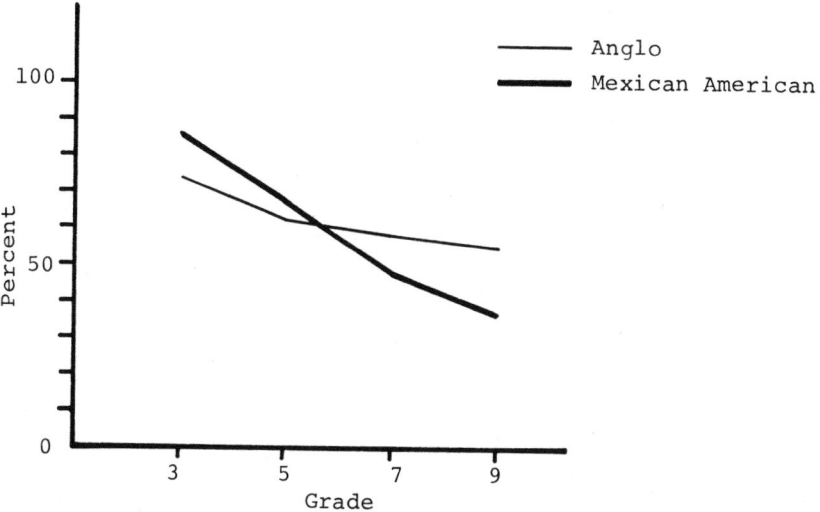

mature, they become more and more critical of presidential knowledge while Anglos' estimates remain above the majority mark.

The socioeconomic standing of Chicano children has very little effect (beta = 0.008) on their evaluations of presidential knowledge. It does separate the higher evaluations of the Anglo middle class from the less favorable opinions of the working class. However, economic status does not change the discrepancy in responses to this item given by the two ethnic groups.

The older Chicanos do not assume the President works very hard; in fact, in the ninth grade more (42.9 percent) think he "does not work as hard as most people" than the reverse (41.9 percent). This can be contrasted with ninth-grade Anglos, a majority of whom (53.8 percent) feel the President works harder than most. This dimension of presidential role performance shows the most rapid drop in Chicano ratings: between the third and fifth grade the drop is from 82.1 to 47.7 percent. During this period young Chicano children probably become aware of their socioeconomic situation. They know that their fathers work extremely hard, in the fields or factory. The comparison between the President's work and that of the immediate family is inevitable, with the resultant drop in presidential rating. This observation is supported by the fact that the early sharp drop is explained largely by the reactions of the youngest, very idealistic nucleus of the Chicano working class (see Figure 6.7). Except for these feelings of the younger children, who probably reflect the economic status of most Chicano families, Mexican American children rate presidential diligence only slightly lower than do Anglos. Again, as the children's cognitive ability develops and their extrafamily experiences increase, ethnicity (especially if measured solely by language, beta = 0.19) divides the perceptions of the children.

A comparison of Chicano perceptions of all presidential traits (see Figure 6.8) demonstrates that the President initially is seen in a very positive, idealized light along all dimensions. Those dimensions embodying the least affective content (diligence and knowledge) decline less precipitously and level off sooner. Where the traits involve greater affect, the ratings decline more sharply. ("Power" seems to be a unique dimension; perhaps the lower rating is due to the actual "distance" of the President, and the students find it difficult to believe the President can exercise direct control over them.)

What do the children see as the President's primary responsibilities? School-age Chicanos overwhelmingly see

FIGURE 6.7

Percent, By Grade, Ethnicity and Social Class,
Agreeing that "The President Works Harder than
Most People"

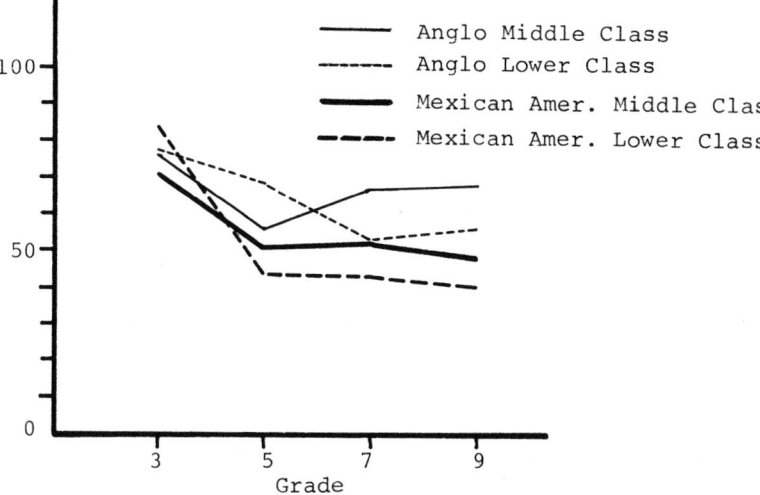

FIGURE 6.8

Mexican American Children's Perception of Presidential
Traits, By Grade

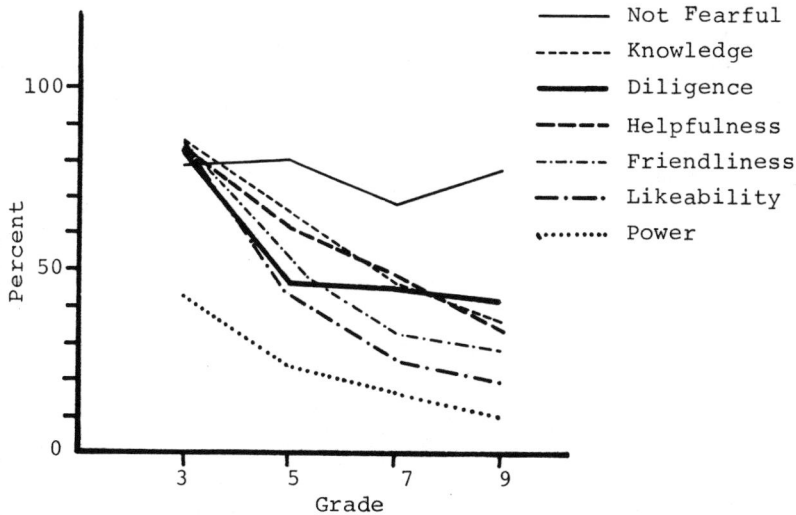

the President as responsible for running the country well (see Table 6.4). His role as top administrator is favored over any other by a two to one margin. Their perception of the President's job does not change much over the years. In the early years this view most likely mirrors the child's dependence on and vulnerability to the most salient authority figure in government. A similar proportion of Anglo children also see the President primarily as the top manager for the nation.

Chicanos think that the two next most important duties of the President are to "stand for our country" and "help people in our country." The symbolic role of the chief of state is particularly salient in our presidential system of government: the President, as the only elected representative of a national constituency, must assume ceremonial as well as governmental duties. The importance of this strategic position for presidential power has been noted by many students of the Presidency, and Chicano children seem to pick this up at all ages. The President's responsibility for the welfare of the citizens is the third most attractive choice for young Mexican Americans. No clear developmental change is evident for Chicanos as contrasted with Anglo children, who demonstrate a rising preference for this presidential role until it is the second choice in the ninth grade. Children in both ethnic groups also see the President as an important law enforcement authority initially, but this role dwindles to minor importance over the years.

Overall, the President's domestic chores, both symbolic and governmental, are seen as his role much more frequently than his participation in international affairs. A substantial number of third-grade Mexican Americans stress the President's role in making friends with other countries, as do over one-third of the working-class Chicanos. The third-grade Anglos emphasize keeping the country out of war, but his peacemaking duties then quickly shrink in importance.

The overall pattern shows little differentiation of roles at the third-grade level, probably due to low cognitive ability. Presidential responsibilities become more clearly distinguished through the years as the children begin not only to differentiate each duty but also to stress the President's domestic role. It is true, however, that his "administrative role" continues to remain important. Perhaps this is because the general nature of the question indicates overall responsibility for the nation's course--a position not unexpected in a presidential system of government.

TABLE 6.4

Mexican American and Anglo Children's Perceptions of the President's Job
(in percentages; respondents were asked to make two choices)

Grade	Keep Us out of War	Make Friends with Other Countries	Help People	Stand for Country	Enforce the Laws	Run Country Well
			Mexican Americans			
3	24.3	30.7	25.7	24.9	25.7	61.4
5	26.2	19.7	32.5	34.3	15.7	66.3
7	21.2	19.7	31.6	35.8	7.3	53.3
9	24.3	14.7	30.5	29.1	6.8	63.9
Total	23.8	20.7	30.4	31.5	13.0	61.1
			Anglos			
3	32.0	18.4	23.2	22.4	21.6	60.0
5	17.1	21.2	37.4	23.5	13.8	65.1
7	20.0	17.1	43.5	20.7	5.2	64.4
9	17.6	14.4	45.0	29.4	1.9	62.3
Total	21.4	17.5	38.1	24.3	9.9	63.1

Summary

The President does seem to provide a very favorable point of induction into the political system for young Mexican Americans, and if, as generally hypothesized, this feeling spreads to other elements of the regime, it may be an important source of system stability. However, as Chicanos mature they appear to become much more critical of the President than do Anglos, even though the Anglos in this study generally are less satisfied with the President than those in surveys conducted under previous administrations (with the possible exception of the middle class).

While earlier studies appear to stress the presidency as the most important and valuable basis of system support, later research modified that conclusion by pointing out that responses seem to be substantially affected by the incumbent of the Presidency.[12] The early studies, done while the office was occupied by popular Presidents--Eisenhower and Kennedy--reflected this fact, especially as the effect of idealization faded through the years. Studies conducted during the Johnson and Nixon administrations show a marked decline in presidential affect, adding evidence to the contention that the Presidency is very difficult to separate from the President.

Do these Mexican American children actually realize who the incumbent President of this country is? Table 6.5 assures us that even the third-graders are overwhelmingly able to select the current President. The youngest Chicanos are very slightly less sure than the Anglos. Although George Washington (15.0 percent) is the greatest distractor for both groups at this early level, John F. Kennedy (9.3 percent) and Lyndon B. Johnson (5.7 percent) are substantial selections of Chicanos but not of Anglos. Correct recognition increases through the next several grades, but teenage Chicanos in the ninth grade show a reluctance to pick Richard M. Nixon as the "top leader" in the country today. The Chicanos' lower rate of recognition vis-à-vis that of their Anglo classmates is paralleled by the increased selection of John F. Kennedy and of "no choices." Obviously affect plays a large role in response to these questions in the higher grades. Former President Diaz of Mexico is selected by a few Mexican American children at every grade level (a total of 1.6 percent), while only 2 out of 544 Anglos pick him. In the earlier grades, this probably reflects the mention of the name of the long-time President of Mexico by members of the family or broadcasters on Mexican media programs. At the higher grade levels, it is possible that cultural nationalism plays the key role.

TABLE 6.5

Mexican American and Anglo Children's Choices of the "Top
Leaders in This Country Today," Controlling for
Social Class
(in percentages)

Grade	Washington	Nixon	Kennedy	Diaz	Johnson
Mexican American Working Class					
3	12.2	68.7	11.3	0.9	4.3
5	5.6	71.8	14.5	1.6	0.8
7	2.9	80.9	5.1	2.2	1.5
9	0.8	76.8	10.4	1.6	0.0
Mexican American Middle Class					
3	15.0	65.0	0.0	0.0	15.0
5	5.0	82.5	7.5	0.0	0.0
7	0.0	79.2	14.6	2.1	0.0
9	2.4	80.5	7.3	0.0	0.0
Anglo Working Class					
3	7.4	75.9	7.4	0.0	1.9
5	13.0	84.8	2.2	0.0	0.0
7	0.0	78.6	7.1	1.8	0.0
9	3.0	86.6	6.0	0.0	0.0
Anglo Middle Class					
3	11.8	86.8	1.5	0.0	0.0
5	5.6	90.1	4.2	0.0	0.0
7	8.7	82.6	8.7	0.0	0.0
9	3.5	87.1	8.2	1.2	0.0

THE POLICEMAN

The local law enforcement officer always has occupied
a prominent position in the political socialization literature dealing with public authorities. In an early study,
Mary Ellen Goodman suggested that the policeman plays an
important role in the inculcation of political values in
children as young as age four.[13] Easton and Dennis' study
of the contribution of public authorities to the origins of
political legitimacy emphasizes the policeman's role.[14]

They speak of the young child's "head-and-tails" initial
contact with government, the head being the President, the
tail the policeman. A respect for general political authority is the most significant spinoff from early obedience
to the police officer. Among young black children, in
fact, the policeman is a more powerful authority figure
than the President, and intially his role attributes also
are given a more positive rating.[15] That young Chicano
children recognize the policeman as a public authority
was confirmed in Chapter 3, as he received greater recognition in this respect than any other figure (see Table
3.4). Granted this early recognition, how do Chicano children feel about the law enforcement officer?

In order to directly measure affect toward the police,
the Mexican American and Anglo youngsters were asked whether
they liked the policeman or not (see Figure 6.9). Even
though primary school Chicanos like the police almost as
much as they do the President, their affection also declines almost as fast. By early high school, almost half
Chicanos say they do not like the police very much. Young
Anglo children in our sample generally felt the same, but
with a higher degree of ambivalence ("Don't Know/No Answer" = 31.3 percent) than enmity (26.9 percent). The affection curve of the Chicanos descends at a fairly uniform
rate while that of the Anglos plateaus in the middle years
before plunging again as adolescence begins.

Ethnicity correlates substantially with this general
measure of affection for the policeman (gamma = 0.34).
Social class controls have generally the same effect on
this item as on previous ones regarding the President.
Chicanos remain united in their attitude (gamma = 0.26),
while the Anglo classes diverge at various stages of development.

Among Mexican Americans, general affect for the policeman is most highly correlated with area of residence
(gamma = 0.37). The rural Northern California children
are much more likely to say they "do not like him very
much," especially when quite young, than are those in
Southern California (see Figure 6.10). However, by the
ninth grade over half of both regional groups feel enmity
toward the police. After age (beta = 0.31) and area of
residence (beta = 0.22), Spanish language use has the
greatest influence on this attribute.

Is the early affection for the policeman the result
of his friendly personal qualities? Young Chicanos do
not think he is as friendly as the President (see Figure
6.11). By the seventh grade more think he is _not_ friendly

152

FIGURE 6.9

Percent, By Grade and Ethnicity, Who Like the
Policeman Very Much

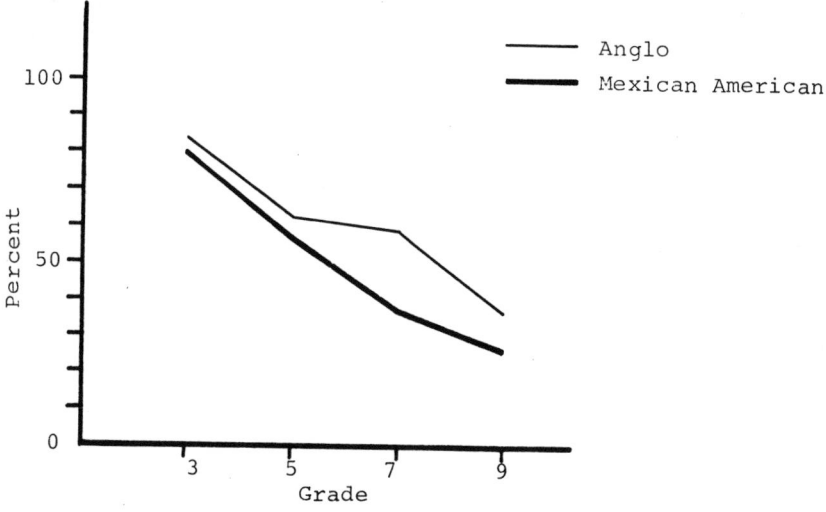

FIGURE 6.10

Percent of Mexican Americans, By Grade and Area of
Residence, Who Do <u>Not</u> Like the Policeman Very Much

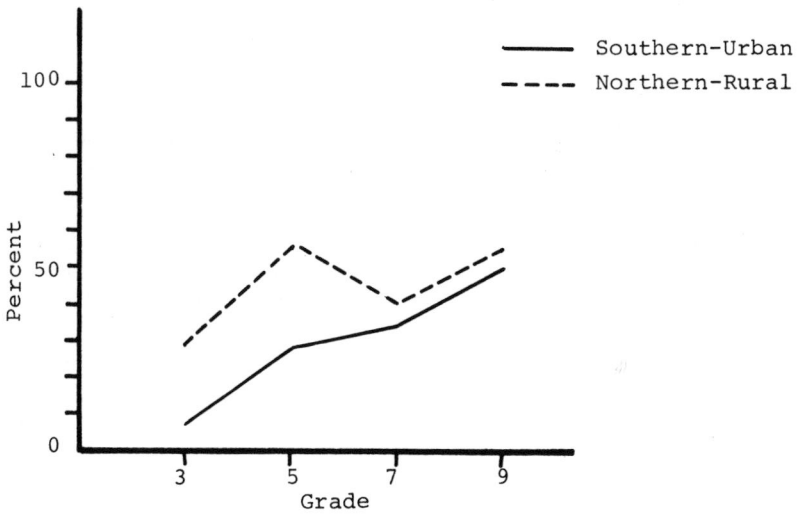

FIGURE 6.11

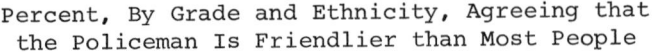

Percent, By Grade and Ethnicity, Agreeing that
the Policeman Is Friendlier than Most People

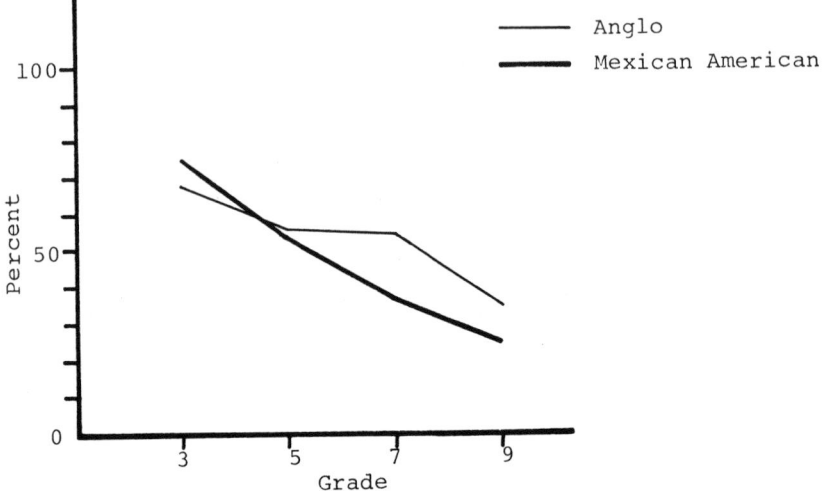

than see him as amicable, and by the ninth grade a majority
say the police officer is not very friendly at all. Their
Anglo classmates originally appreciate police friendliness
less but eventually rate the policeman higher on this dimension. As in the evaluation of general affection, the change
of opinion among the Anglo fifth- and seventh-graders levels
off, while that of the Chicanos continues to descend. A
much greater degree of uncertainty is displayed by the Anglo teenagers, while the Chicanos are less ambivalent.

Social class produces little variation among the Chicano students; the working-class youngsters are more prone
to idealize the policeman in the third grade, but by the
time they are teenagers they think less highly of him than
do middle-class Chicanos. This class gap in affection is
more pronounced among the Anglos. However, the importance
of ethnicity holds up even in the higher grades as intra-
ethnic group class differences are much smaller than those
between Chicanos and Anglos. Although grade is the independent variable that best predicts this response (beta =
0.29), ethnicity explains more of the variation than does
class. For the Chicano group, the use of Spanish is by
far the best predictor of this attitude (beta = 0.19),
after grade (beta = 0.34).

The policeman is not a fearful figure for the youngest Chicanos, and only 8.6 percent are afraid of him as
compared to almost twice as many Anglos. Significantly,
however, during the next two years fear of the policeman
increases among young Mexican Americans while it declines
among the non-Hispanos. These first two years are probably
more valid measures of the dimension than is the response
at the higher grades because small children are not yet
socialized to the value of not showing or admitting fear.
The reactions of the seventh- and ninth-graders, not controlling for bravado, are almost exactly the same for
both ethnic categories (gamma = 0.04). Young Chicanos fear
the President, distant as he really is from the immediate
scene, more than the policeman. As the reality of the
situation emerges over the years, fear of the President
falls below that of the police. Socioeconomic class is
not very strongly associated with this attitude.

The dimension of police helpfulness taps a mixture of
affective and cognitive orientations. It is most likely
that children in the earlier grades react largely along
affective lines, not having had much actual experience
with police officers. As the children begin to see the
policeman in a more realistic light, a more balanced orientation probably results. As adolescence begins, the maturing young person is more likely to have firsthand contacts with law enforcement officers. In their early years
both Chicanos and Anglos view the policeman as a helpful
authority; this feeling declines as idealization subsides.
During the middle years--as the children begin to form
their opinions on a more solid cognitive foundation--a
spectacular divergence of orientation occurs between ethnic
groups (see Figure 6.12). The policeman's stock among the
Anglo children rises toward its initial ideal level; among
Chicanos the rate of decline quickens. With the onset of
adolescence the opinions of both groups become less favorable. By early adulthood the gap between the groups is
quite large. Over one-fourth of the Chicanos say the police are not as helpful as most people, while a slight majority (57.6 percent) think they are more helpful than
most. Almost three-fourths of the Anglos see the police
as very helpful and only 13.8 percent think the contrary.
As many Anglos either "don't know" or do not respond as
take the position that they are not very helpful. Figure
6.13 illustrates that these different orientations are not
the result of class differences.

While ethnicity correlates highly with perceptions
of police benevolence (gamma = 0.26), multivariate analysis

FIGURE 6.12

Percent, By Grade and Ethnicity, Agreeing that
the Policeman Is More Helpful than Most People

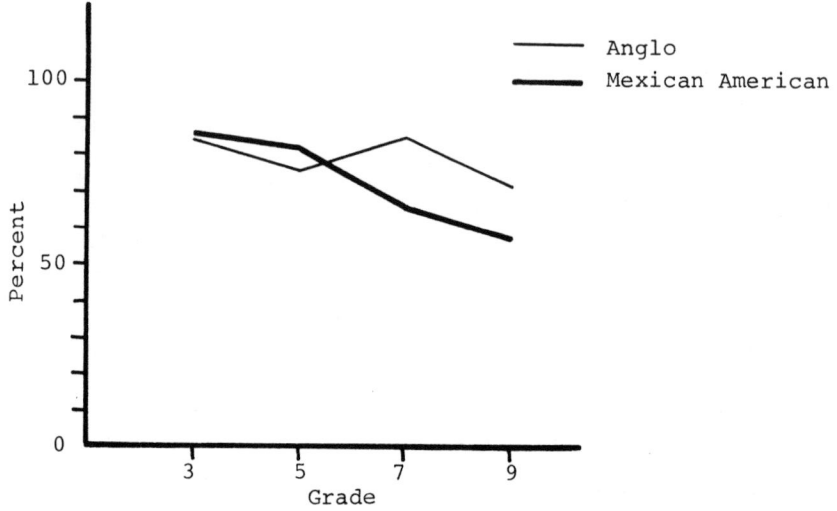

FIGURE 6.13

Percent, By Grade, Ethnicity and Social Class,
Agreeing that the Policeman Is More Helpful
than Most People

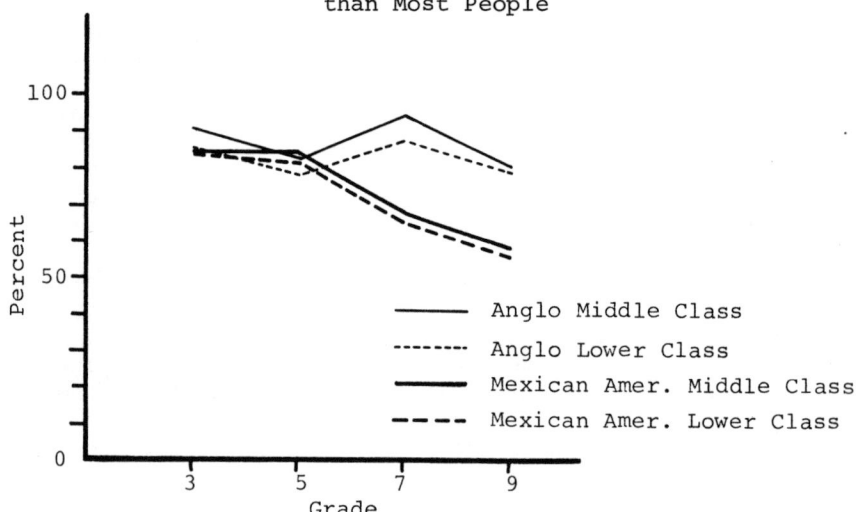

reveals that it is again the Spanish language usage of the respondent that is most influential (beta = 0.17). The more Spanish is used, the lower the estimation of police helpfulness.

As an elaboration of their perception of police benevolence and helpfulness, the students were asked to rate the relative importance of various police functions. Overall, Chicanos feel that it is most important that the police "help people who are in trouble" (see Figure 6.14). While this dimension is rated second by third-graders, it rises in the middle years, eventually to rank at the top of the list. So while the importance of police assistance to the public rises as Chicano children mature, their rating of actual police performance of this task diminishes. This gap between expectation and evaluation probably reflects disenchantment with actual police performance in providing assistance to persons of Mexican ancestry.

The youngest Chicanos rank the policeman's duties in the same order as do the Anglos: (1) apprehension of law-breakers, (2) assistance to those in need of help, and (3) enforcement of the law. As noted, by early adulthood Chicanos rate public assistance most important, followed at a distance by arrest and enforcement functions. In contrast young adult Anglos rate all the police duties at almost

FIGURE 6.14

Ratings of Policemen's Duties by Grade and Ethnicity

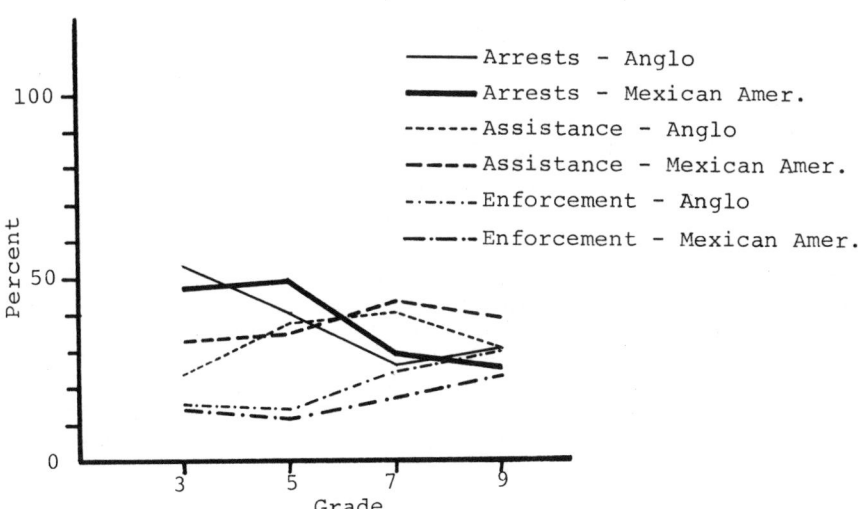

157

equal importance--within one percentage point of each other
--with the arresting functions leading the group. While
it is not surprising that all young children see the primary function of policemen as "catching crooks," it is interesting to note the developmental pattern of each group's
opinion of the arrest function. For Chicanos this duty
continues to diminish in importance through adolescence;
however, for members of the dominant culture this function
becomes increasingly important as adulthood approaches.
The contrast in developmental patterns suggests that the
Anglo concern for "law and order" (minority group critics
equate this with repression of ethnic minorities) is not
judged as important by minority group members, who are more
likely to be on the receiving end of this particular activity.

As we move into the images of the police that involve
less emotion, the children were asked to rate the level of
knowledge of the policeman. Here again, the Chicano youths
initially rate the policeman higher than do the Anglos, although he is rated lower than the President. This high
opinion declines over the years for both groups, but at a
faster rate for the Chicanos; the curves cross in the middle grades until at the highest grade the police are considered more knowledgeable by Anglos than by Chicanos, although the difference is not great. Ethnic differences remain when social class controls are introduced (see Figure
6.15). However, the opinions of the Anglo working class
are closer to those of the Chicanos than to their fellow
ethnics of higher socioeconomic standing.

There is an interestingly different pattern of developmental socialization with regard to police "power" between Chicanos and Anglo youngsters (see Figure 6.16). Only
the youngest Mexican Americans hold that the policeman has
the power to "make people do what he wants." A dramatic
change of opinion occurs in the next two years, and by
grade five a majority state that he does not have this kind
of authority. In contrast the number of Anglo students who
see the police as powerful increases during the same period.
Both groups then show a decline until the seventh grade
when they turn upward but remain below the earliest level.

Controlling for social class illustrates that the early
divergent trend between the two ethnic groups is primarily
the result of early and drastic changes in orientations by
the Chicano working class (see Figure 6.17). An idealized
view of police power by the Chicano lower class plunges
over the next two years to the lowest level of all categories, where it remains while other adolescents see the

FIGURE 6.15

Percent, By Grade, Ethnicity and Social Class,
Agreeing that the Policeman "Knows More than
Most People"

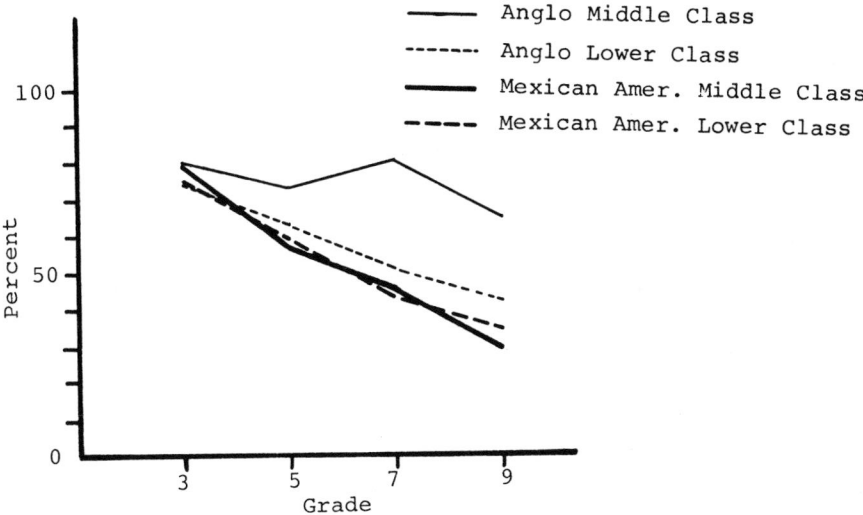

FIGURE 6.16

Percent, By Grade and Ethnicity, Agreeing that
the Policeman "Can Make People Do What He Wants"

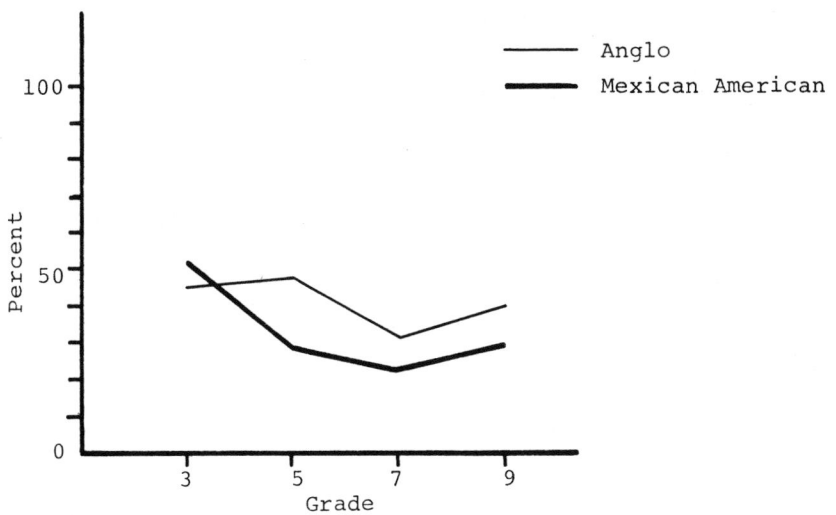

FIGURE 6.17

Percent, By Grade and Ethnicity, Agreeing that
the Policeman "Can Make People Do What He
Wants," Controlling for Social Class

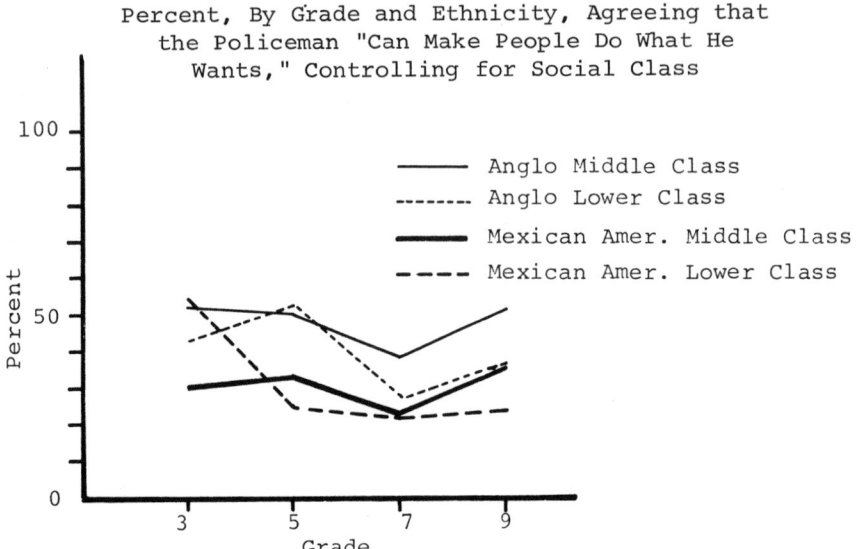

policeman's authority as increasingly important. Still,
ethnicity remains a stronger predictor of views on police
power than does socioeconomic class.

After age the best predictor of this opinion is the
sex of the child, both for the total sample (beta = 0.13)
and for the Chicano group (beta = 0.12). While 61 percent
of the male Mexican Americans hold that the policeman "cannot make people do what he wants" only 42 percent of the
girls believe this. No doubt this is a result of the difference in authority positions of men and women in the
American (Anglo and Mexican) culture, with the resultant
greater submissiveness-dependence of females.

Why does the relatively higher idealization of the
policeman diminish so rapidly for young Chicanos? Since
school experiences are objectively the same for both groups,
other agents of an extrascholastic nature must dictate the
difference. Some light is cast on this dimension by examining the pupils' proposed reactions to a hypothetical situation in which they are confronted with police power, i.e.,
given an order by a policeman. In this case, however,
the order is "wrong." The child is asked how he would
react to this situation. Very few young members of either
group would disobey police authority. As Chicanos mature,
however, their resistance to "invalid" police authority

stiffens (while that of Anglos declines after the fifth grade) until three times as many Chicanos would not follow an incorrect order as would Anglo young adults.

The switch in opinions of Anglos and Chicanos between the third and the fifth grade with respect to the power possessed by police is the reverse of the responses of primary schoolchildren who would carry out a police order unquestioningly, i.e., the unchallenged compliance of Chicano children increases as their evaluation of police power decreases. The Anglos' unquestioning obedience decreases as their perception of coercive power increases. Apparently, while the youngest Chicanos do not think the policeman can force people to comply with his directions, they still would view the order as legitimate and comply voluntarily.

Some of the variance in compliance with police authority may be explained by the differential treatment of Mexican Americans and Anglos. Discriminatorily harsh treatment of visible ethnic minorities by police officials has been well documented, and Mexican Americans have received more than their share of "police brutality."[16] The unfavorable experiences of family members with law enforcement agents and their own firsthand experiences as they grow older should be reflected in the attitudes of young Chicanos.[17]

A measure of comparative treatment by the police produces major differences along ethnic lines (gamma = 0.40). Almost a third of the Chicano third-grade children feel the police discriminate against them and their people (see Figure 6.18). At this stage their opinions are largely a reflection of familial attitudes. As Mexican American youths progress through school this feeling diminishes, although remaining above that of the Anglos. From a low point at the fifth grade, these feelings of relative persecution climb until in the highest grade studied they are almost at the earliest high level. The opinions of the teenage Chicanos, especially when compared with the ever-declining and -diverging Anglo feelings of discrimination, probably result from their personal, firsthand experiences with the police in their community.

With the exception of very young middle-class Chicanos, social class is not as significant a factor affecting this attitude as ethnicity (beta = 0.15 for ethnicity, 0.05 for socioeconomic class). As one might expect, by far the most powerful predictor of this opinion among Chicanos is the relative perception of ethnic discrimination in general (beta = 0.19, gamma = 0.39). Although initially both those

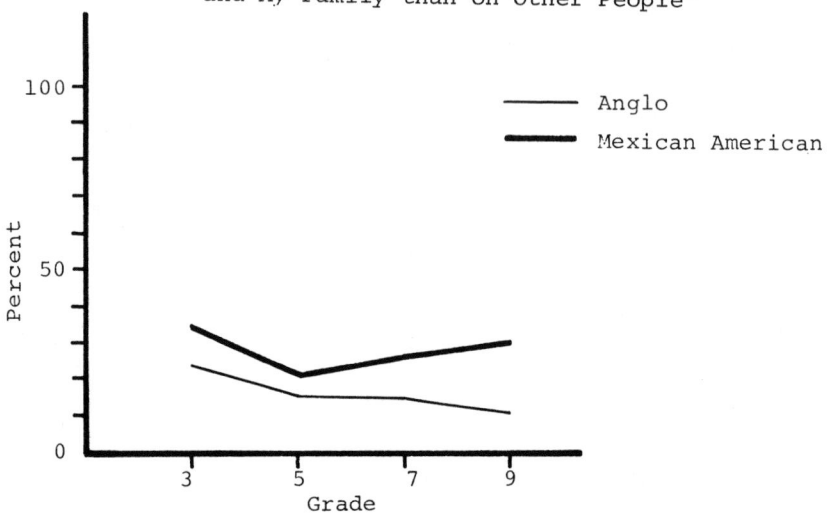

FIGURE 6.18

Percent, By Grade and Ethnicity, Agreeing that
"the Police Are Harder on People Like Me
and My Family than on Other People"

—— Anglo
━━━ Mexican American

Percent

100

50

0

3   5   7   9

Grade

FIGURE 6.19

Percent of Chicanos, By Grade and Perception
of Discrimination, Agreeing that "the Police Are Harder on
[Them and Their Families] than on Other People"

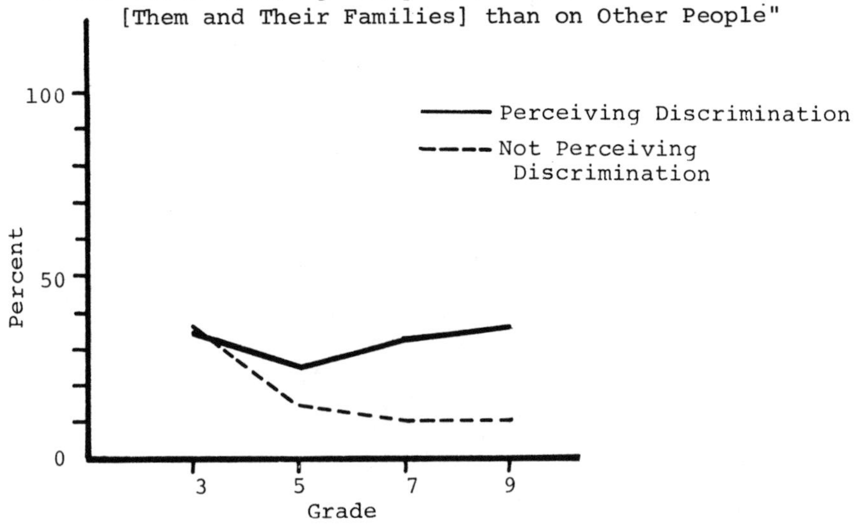

—— Perceiving Discrimination
---- Not Perceiving
     Discrimination

Percent

100

50

0

3   5   7   9

Grade

who do and those who do not perceive discrimination feel similarly (a little over one-third feel police persecution), a growing divergence occurs with maturity (see Figure 6.19). Over the first two years in school, as the curriculum is filled with stories involving positive qualities of policemen, the perception of discrimination by police declines among both groups. At the fifth grade, however, although this feeling continues to diminish slightly among those children who do not feel discrimination, it climbs steadily upward for the others, reaching a level of 35.4 percent.

Moreover, the Mexican Americans who have been in this country for the shortest period of time and who tend to use more Spanish also are most likely to perceive harsh treatment by police.

Perhaps the evaluation of the policeman least emotionally tinged involves his diligence, since this should have the least direct impact on a youth's daily experience. The correlation of ethnicity with police diligence is indeed one of the lowest (gamma = 0.13). As they mature Mexican Americans, as well as Anglos, feel less and less that police work relatively hard (see Figure 6.20). Among third-graders Chicanos are more likely than Anglos to think the "policeman works harder than most people," but by the

FIGURE 6.20

Percent, By Grade and Ethnicity, Agreeing that
"the Policeman Works Harder than Most People"

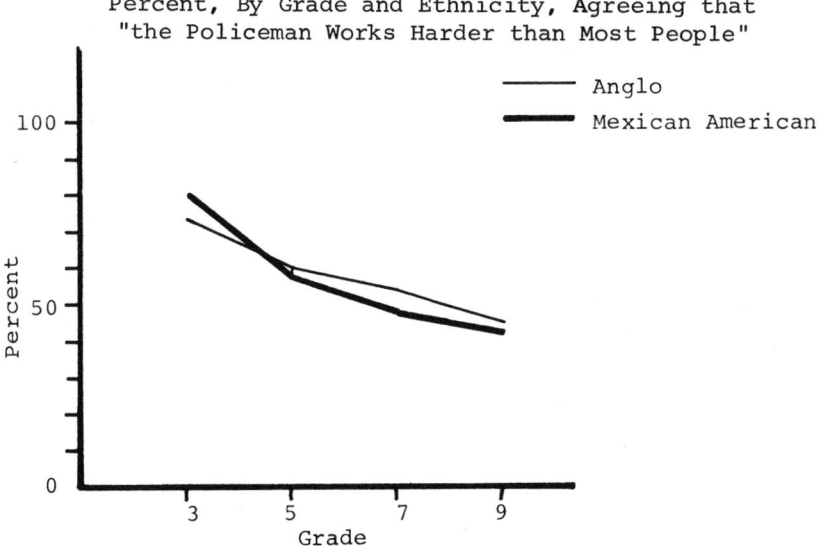

163

fifth grade their opinions have changed relative to those of their non-Chicano classmates. This feeling continues to develop among Mexican American youths until, at the ninth grade level, more think the policeman's work is lighter than that of most people than feel his duties are relatively hard.

Introduction of class variables produces a familiar pattern. Working-class Chicanos in the third grade rate the policeman's diligence highest; their middle-class compatriots rate it lowest. Socioeconomic standing does have some effect, particularly in the middle grades, as working-class Anglos share the feeling of Chicanos. However, as the children grow older, they diverge along ethnic lines (ethnicity beta = 0.15).

On the industriousness dimension, the most important independent variable, including age, is area of residence for Chicanos (beta = 0.30), which is highly correlated (gamma = 0.46) with attitudes. While 60.5 percent of the urban Mexican Americans think the police work relatively hard, only 39.1 percent of those living in a rural area share this view. Farm labor, especially the type done by the Chicano field hand, is very strenuous. In comparison to the work of their family members, police duties must seem soft. The gap of almost 30 percentage points between the attitudes of urban and rural Chicanos remains constant throughout the school years. Whether under the influence of family in the early years, peers, or direct experiences, rural Chicanos are aware of the difference in physical labor between the police and his primary reference groups.

In general Mexican Americans are socialized toward a less favorable attitude toward the police than are Anglos. On measures of affect, the pattern is one of slightly lower affection in the early grades, with an increased downward divergence as Chicanos grow up. Their evaluation of job performance generally is higher than that of Anglos, primarily because of the very positive views of the working-class third-graders. The only exception to this trend is the Chicano children's perceptions of police diligence. As with the more affective dimensions, the Chicanos' perceptions of police performance of their duties decline more steeply over the years than those of the Anglos.

Secondary socialization experiences outside the family are likely to contribute greatly to the serious erosion of support for the police as the Chicanos mature. Their contacts with the police are likely to occur in an unfavorable context, and they hear reports, from friends and through the media, of unfavorable incidents involving police and Mexican Americans. They come to feel that, while the police should be assisting persons in need, instead they are disproportionately harassing Chicanos. These views are particularly strong among the less assimilated and discrimination-perceiving Chicanos.

The police do not seem as important public figures in legitimizing system authority for Mexican Americans as for Anglos. While the policeman is seen as having more coercive power than the more distant and abstract President, the lower level of affect, the resistance to unjust use of police authority, and the tremendous deterioration of the policeman's position over time indicate that the policeman has a smaller role in Mexican American children's socialization toward system support through the acceptance of public authority than for Anglo children.[18]

OTHER PUBLIC AUTHORITIES

While the President and the policeman are the most salient public authorities for the Anglo children in our sample, Chicanos feel one other governmental figure is more important to their own welfare than the policeman, and that is the state governor (see Table 6.1).[19] The incumbent governor of California at the time of this study, Ronald Reagan, is hardly a typical governor with regard to level of publicity. As a former movie actor, presidential candidate, and governor of the most populous state, he receives an inordinate amount of public attention. In addition, his positions on public policies within the state are quite controversial. It is not surprising, then, that third-grade youngsters find Reagan highly visible. Why he is also considered quite salient is another matter. Although no systematic evidence is available, the comments of many Chicano influentials to the author indicate that Mexican Americans in California have not been very satisfied with Governor Reagan's conduct of state government, and he has been sharply criticized for his policy of, at best, "benign neglect" toward the Chicano community. It is therefore quite unlikely that the young children would pick up favorable comments from the neighborhood or family setting. More than likely, their greater affect is only another indication that the youngest Chicanos usually rate public authorities higher than do Anglos of similar age. Indeed, by the time they are teenagers, the Chicanos' opinion on this matter is very similar to their non-Hispanic classmates.

It may be of interest to educators to note that, although Mexican Americans in the earliest grade consider their teacher relevant to the family's welfare at a frequency twice that among Anglos, not one Chicano has this opinion after the fourth grade. Several Anglo children continue to consider the teacher helpful. This may indicate something about the relationships of Chicano students to (almost exclusively) Anglo teachers or to an academic curriculum dominated by Anglo culture.

THE FATHER

It is no surprise that the father turns out to be the most important authority figure in the opinion of most of the sample (see Table 6.1). In the first two grades the Chicano child's father shares the credit for helping his family with public officials more than the Anglo father does. However the "subjective helpfulness" of Mexican American fathers continues to increase as the children approach maturity. In comparison after the seventh grade the Anglo fathers begin to diminish in importance.

This is not simply a reflection of the children's affection for their father, since both groups appear similar in this respect. Chicanos like their fathers almost as much in the ninth grade as they do in the third. Anglos' affection for their fathers, as measured by their agreement with the statement "I like him very much" is similarly high, although it varies more through the years (see Figures 6.21 and 6.22).

On the most purely affective dimensions of helpfulness and friendliness, fathers are rated similarly high by both ethnic groups with only a slight loss over the years, although Chicanos slightly emphasize the friendship dimension. However, with regard to fear of the father, some differences appear. Chicano youngsters in the third grade show little paternal fear yet this increases rapidly in the next few years until almost one-third admit to fear of their fathers. Anglo paternal fear, while initially higher, is rather constant (and comparatively lower) through these school years. Social class differences change the ethnic differential very slightly.

On the less affect-laden evaluation of their fathers' diligence, knowledge, and power, the general pattern among Chicano youths shows declining estimates, highest on the diligence scale and lowest on that of knowledgeability. The sharp decrease in estimates of paternal knowledge

FIGURE 6.21

Father Traits as Perceived by Mexican American Children

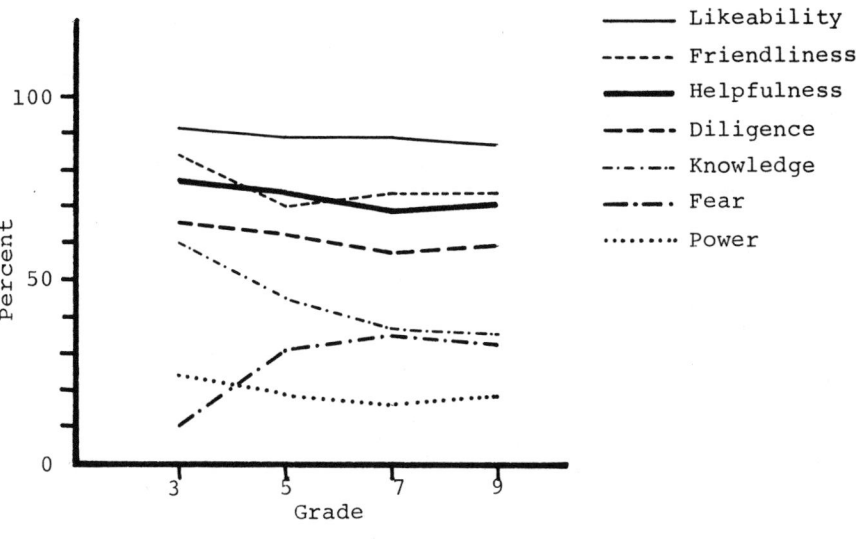

FIGURE 6.22

Father Traits as Perceived by Anglo Children

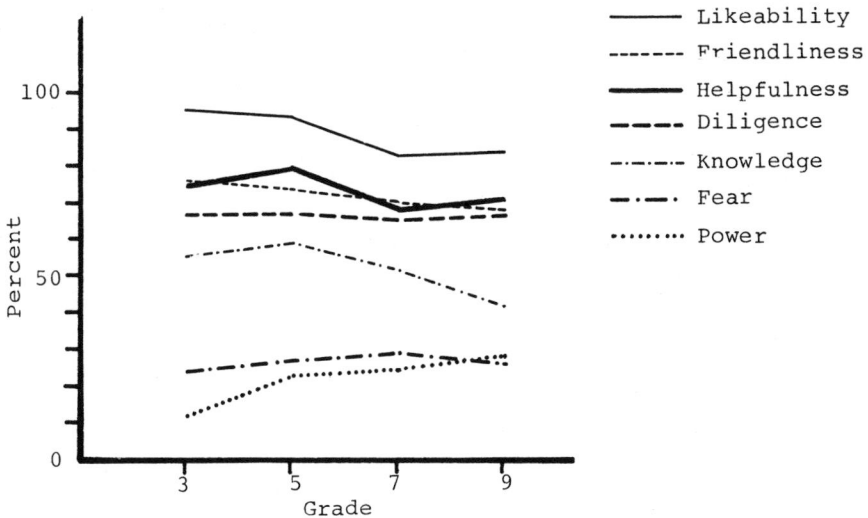

through the years probably marks the youths' growing realization that their parents have not had the opportunities
for formal education that Anglos enjoy. The median number
of school years completed by Mexican Americans 25 years
of age and over in California is 10.6; for Anglos it is
12.4.[20] That the children may realize their fathers' actual level of educational achievement is suggested when
controls for class, which is highly correlated with education, are introduced (see Figure 6.23). Middle-class Anglos (which in this sample include several families of professionals) rate their fathers' knowledge much higher than
does any other group. The rating of ninth-grade middle-
class Chicanos is midway between that of their Anglo counterparts and the two lower-class groupings, with working-
class Mexican Americans at the very bottom of the scale.

Ratings of their fathers' diligence show little variation through the years for both ethnic groups. The fact
that the Chicano fathers' ratings are slightly lower than
those of the Anglos may be due to the fact that the unemployed (mostly Mexican Americans) brings the values down
considerably. This is supported by the opinions of the
oldest and thus most cognitively aware Chicanos. Of the
middle-class Chicanos, 71 percent say their fathers work

FIGURE 6.23

Percent, By Grade and Ethnicity, Agreeing that
Their "Father Knows More than Most People,"
Controlling for Social Class

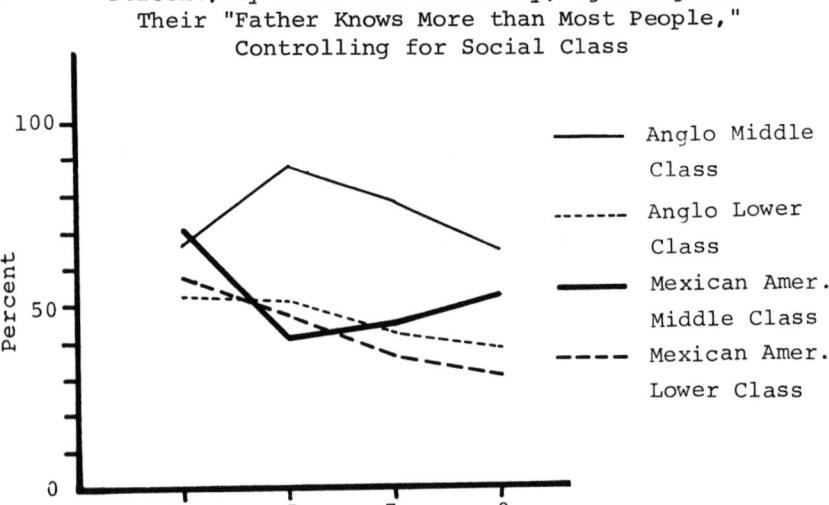

harder than most people; only 58.4 percent of the lower class respond similarly.

Although all students realize that very few private individuals in our society can "make most other people do what [they want]," Chicanos come to feel their fathers are relatively less powerful than Anglos. Their ratings of father power are lower at all grade levels except at the most idealistic age of nine, and they generally decline through the years. In contrast the Anglos initially are less idealistic, but as their cognitive abilities increase so do their ratings of their fathers' power.

Of course the important question for the purposes of this study is the following: What political implications do these orientations toward fathers have?

Some of the earlier empirical studies, finding a close correlation between the young child's attitudes toward his father and public authority, hypothesized this to be a result of "transference." Through this psychological process the youngster, having close emotional ties to his father, transfers his feelings to the more distant public authority figures.[21] This theory was based primarily on inductive speculation concerning the reason for these high positive ratings for authority figures in government, and was partially the result of insufficient data. Later more detailed studies, however, indicate that children "do not confuse familial authority, as manifested by father, with the political authorities in the outside world."[22] Not only are children able to differentiate private from public images but they also show an increasing differentiation among various public authorities depending on each one's specific role attributes.[23]

Rather than transferring feelings from the father to public figures, the child apparently attributes to public authorities the characteristics of a culturally "ideal adult." Using a sophisticated computer analysis of the effects of predictor variables on dependent variables, Easton and Dennis remark: "We would have expected affect for President to be associated with affect for father, but this association does not occur. Indeed none of the father evaluations is related to the child's image of the President--to any significant degree."[24]

A further analysis, this time involving simple correlation between the children's ratings of their fathers with the ratings of the President led Easton and Dennis to conclude:

> Freudian intimations notwithstanding, once again
> we do not observe a close association between the

> child's liking for his father and his liking
> for the President. On this general evaluative
> dimension [affect], there appears to be little
> significant generalization of sentiments
> [transference] for the parent to the President.[25]

However, they did find that on the "power" dimension some
correlations exist between the children's ratings of their
fathers and the President and policeman,[26] thus applying
the transference theory on a much narrower basis of perceived _performance_ characteristics rather than affect.

However, Easton and Dennis do suggest that the broader
area of family relationships, including internal communication patterns and relationships between child and parents,
may have a substantial effect on sentiments toward public
authorities.[27] This thesis also is common in other socialization literature. Robert Hess has mentioned that his
cross-national research suggests that family authority
patterns may be a crucial factor in the idealization of
public authorities.[28] In his studies of foreign societies,
Robert Levine also hypothesized that the authority structure of the extended family is an important socialization
variable.[29] And Kenneth Langton has done some intricate
work on the comparative influence of each parent and varying family structures on the political attitudes of children, although primarily with regard to allocative (electoral) rather than system politics.[30] These kinds of relationships are very difficult to evaluate because of the
detailed knowledge of intra-familial relationship patterns
that would be necessary in order adequately to explain
political socialization.

Within the limits of our data, does having a Mexican
or Chicano father seem to be a significant variable affecting attitudes toward public authorities? On the item of
highest general affect--likeableness--the father initially
ranks higher than the two most important public authorities
(see Figure 6.24). But, more importantly, this feeling
for the father continues at a constant level across the
grades while it plummets for the President and the policeman, with the latter having a slight edge after the initial
evaluation. A very similar distinction is made by Chicano
children on the friendliness dimension (see Figure 6.25),
although the President initially ranks as high as the father. As we move into the more cognitive roles, the gap
between the father and the public figures begins to close.
In fact, on the helpfulness dimension (see Figure 6.26)
the youngest Mexican Americans see both the policeman and

FIGURE 6.24

Relative Likeability of Authority Figures as
Perceived by Mexican American Children

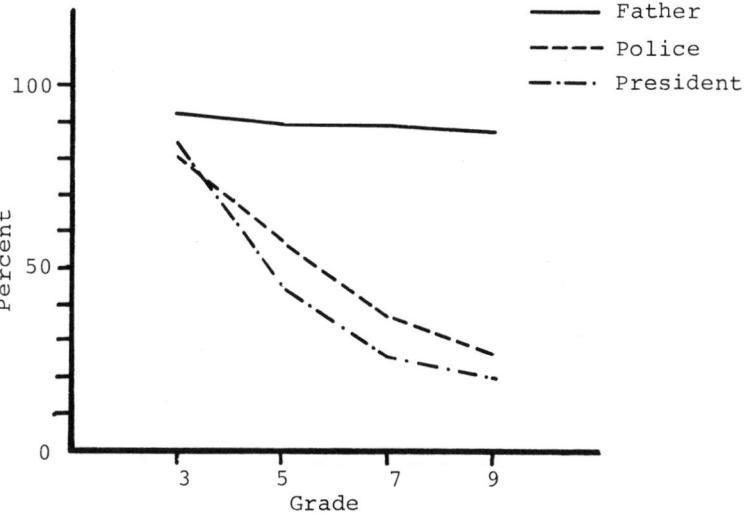

FIGURE 6.25

Relative Friendliness of Authority Figures
as Perceived by Mexican American Children

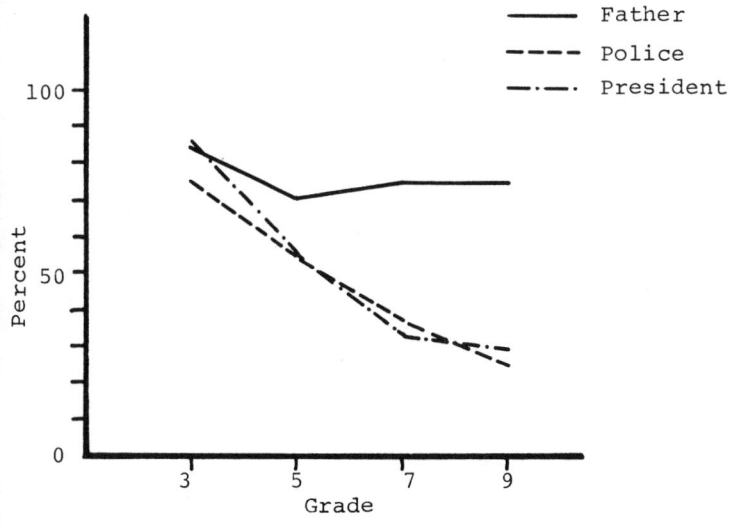

FIGURE 6.26

Relative Helpfulness of Authority Figures as
Perceived by Mexican American Children

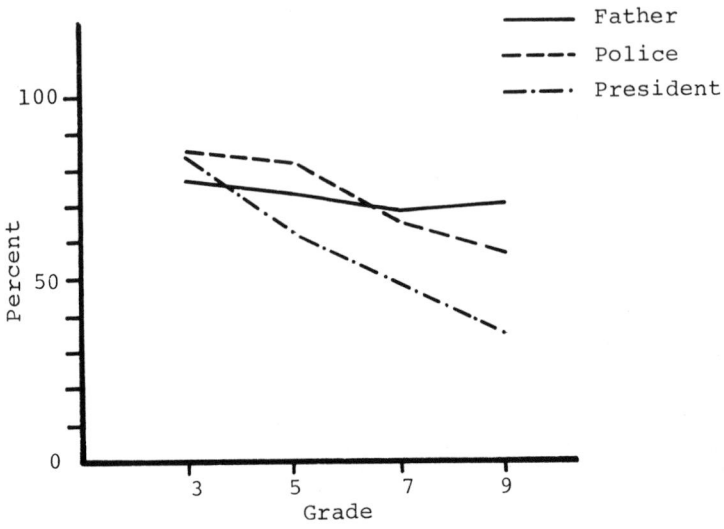

FIGURE 6.27

Relative Diligence of Authority Figures as
Perceived by Mexican American Children

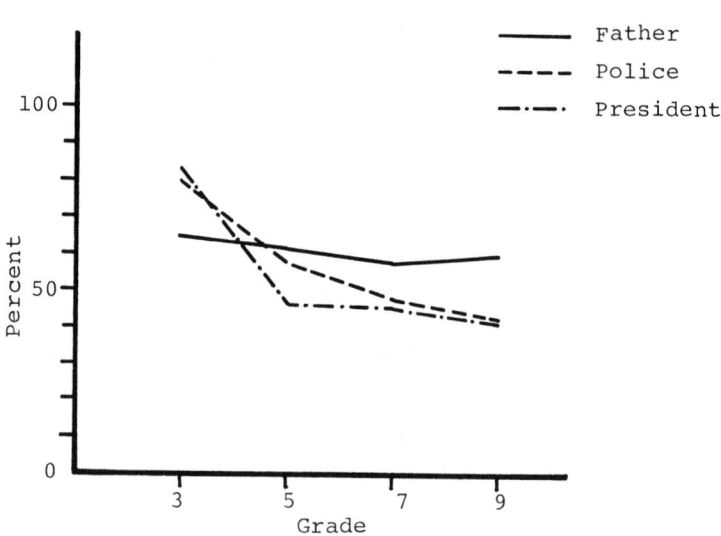

the President as more helpful than their fathers, with the policeman the top-rated helper. The President's rating quickly drops below the father's, but the policeman continues to receive a higher rating until the middle grades. Even more of an initial distinction is made on the diligence item (see Figure 6.27). Although the President and policeman are evaluated as working harder than the third-graders' fathers, by the fifth grade both public authorities receive lower ratings while the father's shows only a slight decline over the years.

The initial rating gap widens between public and private authorities on the dimension of knowledge (see Figure 6.28). The President is seen as having the most knowledge by third-graders. His rating subsequently declines rather sharply, parallel to that of the policeman, until by the ninth grade they are only slightly above the father's rating, which has declined at a lesser pace. An overall similarity occurs in the power graph, but with some interesting variations (see Figure 6.29). The policeman initially is rated even above the highly idealized President in his ability to make people do what he wants. One reason may be that the President is not actually seen exercising his coercive capacity, while the policeman often is viewed performing this role--both over the media and in actual experience. At the early adolescent stage, this power becomes even more obvious to the children; and the rating of the policeman, along with that of the father, changes its course upward, while the President's decline continues.

The father's evaluations all remain relatively constant over the years, a phenomenon noted by Easton and Dennis in their study, even though the father's overall rating moves upward or downward with the affective content of the dimension. Public authorities usually exhibit a substantial decline over the years. Relative to the father, they were rated lower on the affective items by the youngest Chicanos, but this same group increased their rankings on each successively performance-laden item until the father was left at the bottom.

Correlations between each ethnic group's perceptions of their fathers' and the President's qualities provide very little support for the transference theory (see Table 6.6). While there is a slightly higher correspondence in the comparisons of father and President made by Mexican Americans on the affective dimensions, no relationships are strong enough to hypothesize a direct transference of feelings. All of these comparative ratings reveal that Mexican American children react differently to various

FIGURE 6.28

Relative Knowledge of Authority Figures as
Perceived by Mexican American Children

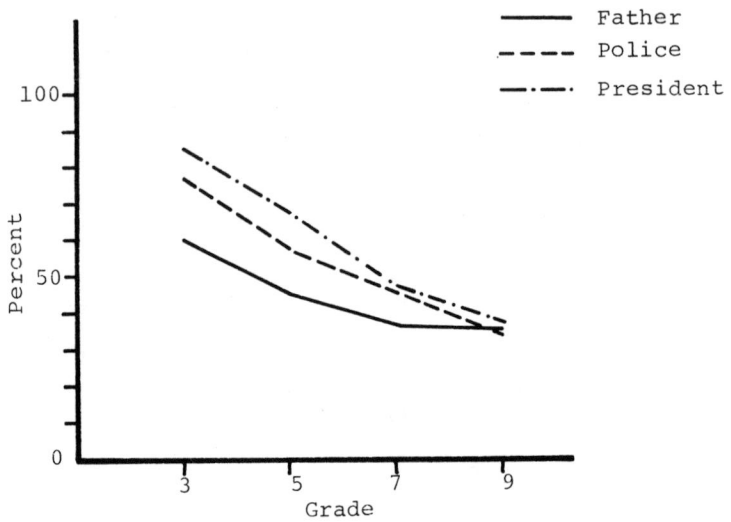

FIGURE 6.29

Relative Power of Authority Figures as
Perceived by Mexican American Children

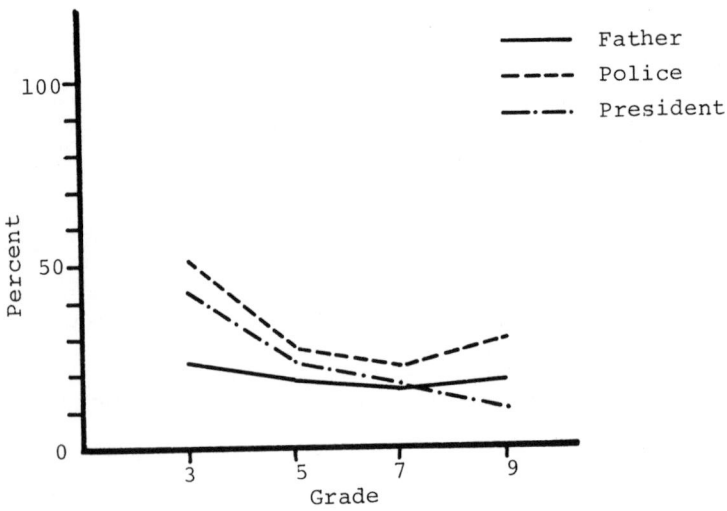

TABLE 6.6

Correlations (Gamma) of Father and Presidential Images

Characteristic of Images	Correlation for Mexican Americans	Correlation for Anglos
Likeableness	0.23	0.32
Friendliness	0.23	0.08
Fear	0.16	0.16
Helpfulness	0.19	0.16
Diligence	0.02	0.22
Knowledge	0.19	0.38
Power	0.09	0.11

figures of authority in a manner quite similar to Anglo Americans in this and previous studies. They are able to discriminate between private and political authorities quite well very early in their lives, and this ability increases with age. Thus "politicization" among Chicano children takes place quite early as children are able to differentiate political from familial authority.

SUMMARY AND CONCLUSIONS

It would seem that the earliest orientations of Mexican American children toward public authorities in the United States bodes fairly well for the legitimacy and resultant stability of the political system. In general the responses toward public figures by the youngest Chicanos are quite positive. On measures of affect the third-graders rate the President quite favorably; they feel the chief executive, and to a lesser extent the policeman, is almost as likeable and friendly as their own fathers. This high degree of idealization occurs mainly among working-class Chicano children and could be due to greater feelings of anxiety and vulnerability--as has been postulated for black children, especially those of the lower class.[31] However the small differences in fear illustrated in Table 6.7 weaken this hypothesis. Additionally, the transference of highly positive feelings toward the father to political authorities also seem unlikely.

If the vulnerability and anxiety feelings do not adequately explain the higher affect toward political authori-

TABLE 6.7

Percentage of Third-Grade Children Expressing Fear of the Government, The President And the Policeman, By Ethnicity and Social Class

	Mexican Americans			Anglos		
	Total	Working Class	Middle Class	Total	Working Class	Middle Class
"I'm often afraid of government"	17.1	17.4	15.0	15.2	16.7	16.9
"I'm afraid of the President"	14.3	14.3	15.0	7.2	11.1	3.3
"I'm afraid of the policeman"	8.6	8.7	10.0	16.8	16.7	18.2

ties exhibited by young Chicanos, we can only speculate as to its cause and await further investigation. It is possible that Mexican American children are taught by their families to respect the public officials of this nation, and the children enter school with a ready-made high evaluation. Parents, in general, tend to protect their children from overly harsh or critical comments regarding the outside world, and minority parents are at least as likely to react in this manner. The child having no personal experience demonstrating that these officials are not benign probably would rate them positively. Or perhaps the laudatory remarks of teachers or very favorable presentations in school materials of the first and second grades indoctrinate the youngest Chicano accordingly.

Whatever the reasons, this idealization carries over to the Chicanos' evaluation of the role performance of both the President and policeman, rating them generally higher than do the third-grade Anglos. The policeman receives slightly higher rankings on these dimensions than does the President (who rates slightly higher in affect), but the differences are irregular and slight.

Thus from a systemic perspective, the potential for feelings of political legitimacy among Mexican Americans receives a very favorable initial impetus as measured by the orientations of the youngest Chicano children.

However, as Mexican Americans mature they exhibit increasingly negative and divergent (from Anglos) orientations toward political authorities. On most of these evaluations, there emerges a cross pattern: the Anglo rating declines more slowly and levels off while that of the Chicanos plunges downward, often from initially higher levels. Social class differences among the older Mexican Americans usually are of minor significance, while area of residence or use of the Spanish language usually has a greater effect.

Later socialization experience, along with improved mental ability, seems to depress the ratings of affective dimensions more than performance factors, although both drop considerably. The President emerges as a not very well-liked and not especially competent or salient figure. The policeman also is a disappointment to teenage Chicanos, who on the average rate him about the same as the President, most similar in affect and varying on the more cognitive dimensions, probably depending on the youths' experiences with each official.

The overall support among Chicanos for the public authority component of the political system will be determined by the relative differential in the importance of early positive orientation versus a very serious erosion of respect for public authorities. However, a general acceptance of public authority by Chicanos in the future seems on shaky ground if it rests primarily on socialization to political authorities.[32]

7

SUMMARY AND
CONCULSION

Our intention in this study has been to explore the political orientations of Chicano and Anglo children in order to determine if there are any significant differences in attitudinal attachments to the political system. Recent militant political activities and civil disturbances in Mexican American communities give dramatic testimony that La Raza is not satisfied with some aspects of the American system. Our efforts have focused on socialization toward basic components of the political system--the political community, regime, and authorities--in order to understand better whether these manifestations of system stress are rooted in fundamental differences in political perceptions.

We do not mean to imply here that instability or system stress are necessarily undesirable phenomena. Indeed, stress often is necessary to overcome the overwhelming inertia of the American political system. While some feel that stability--the preservation of the status quo, or in system terms, the maintenance of accepted methods for allocating resources in a society--is the greatest good, this writer is not in agreement. Other values, such as justice, or the proportionate sharing of the values of a society, plus the basic tenets of the democratic creed-- liberty and equality--are at least of equal import.

Nor need the discovery of subgroup variations in political orientation be regarded as evidence of "incomplete" or in any other manner inferior socialization patterns. Almost all children growing up in different cultural environments are bound to be socialized adequately to their own surroundings. A pattern of socialization considered dysfunctional by the core culture may very well be entirely appropriate for thriving in an American subculture.[1] Mex-

179

ican Americans living in the barrios of east Los Angeles or the campos of Northern California are exposed to a very different reality than are Anglo children. Even though they may attend the same schools, much of their extra-academic socialization is the result of contact with culturally distinct experiences. The resultant attitudes may then reinforce differences among various cultural groups, thus contributing to the continuation of a society composed of heterogeneous social groupings. Such a culturally pluralistic society is a desirable situation and is preferred by this writer to a society in which cultural variations are eschewed and every effort is made to melt them down in the core culture crucible of the melting pot.

Different perspectives, customs, and life-styles are welcome seasonings in an all too conformist and bland society. There certainly is room for a multitude of values and opinions in the American polity. All values need not be shared in order that a society persist. Yet disagreement by significant numbers of people over very basic and fundamental political values, such as the nature and worth of the political order, does make political system stability less likely. Other things being equal, a polity in which major groups disagree over the very nature of the political order will be more unstable than a polity where no such cleavages exist. The sharing of certain minimal but basic orientations contributes to system persistence and makes reliance on other devices, such as coercion, less necessary.

Therefore, an investigation into the basic orientations of various major social groupings in the United States can provide insights into this system's potential for conflict and instability. Sharp distinctions in the perceptions of these groups might preclude any resolution of group-based political conflicts. Although studies of adult political attitudes are important in this regard, research into their origins and development also are necessary. A study of children's socialization patterns allows us to understand the patterns of attitude acquisition within these groups, thus providing a deeper and more sophisticated understanding of adult political orientations. In addition, investigations of childhood attitudes provide us with some insight into the possible future behavior of American citizens.

A study of the roots of Mexican American political attitudes is particularly important at a time when ethnic-based politics in America is assuming renewed importance. While the new Chicano political movement has been gaining

momentum and new adherents, very little research has focused on the political behavior of Mexican Americans.
This study, although necessarily exploratory and descriptive in nature, should help fill the gap in knowledge about
both the political behavior of Mexican Americans and the
socialization patterns of children from ethnic minority
backgrounds.

In this concluding chapter, we shall briefly review
the major findings and speculate on their political impli-
cations--including the possible impact of Mexican-American
socialization on the American political system.

REVIEW OF FINDINGS

The Political Community

We first examined the orientations of Mexican-American
and Anglo students toward the American political community
and discovered slight differences in the perceptions of
each group. Mexican American children, especially of the
working class, lag behind their Anglo classmates in ability
to verbalize symbols of the United States. They are most
familiar with the name of the local community, then with
the state, and least with the nation, confirming congruence
with the concentric circle theory of expanding geographical
awareness. The Chicanos' ability to recognize pictorial
representations of the national political community, e.g.,
the flag, was substantially greater. The Chicanos' "closeness" to Mexico, as measured by use of the Spanish language
and length of residence in this country, was associated
with cognition of American symbols.

Slightly less affect toward the American political
community was displayed by Chicano than by Anglo youngsters.
Actually, Chicanos' initial liking is greater than that of
Anglos, but with maturity an increased disaffection with
America, and a rise in feeling for the ancestral home, was
noted. Yet a fairly high degree of U.S. ethnocentrism also
was discovered through items comparing Chicano orientations
toward the United States with those toward other countries.
In any case, a serious erosion of affect occurs as Chicanos
mature. Growing up in America weakens the attachment of
Mexican Americans to this country, and some transfer their
affection toward Mexico. While social class was seen to
have some effect on this lessening of affect, the degree
of acculturation to the core American culture was understandably more significant.

Although both cognition of and affection for the American political community by Mexican American children generally are below the levels of the Anglos, these differences were not as large as might be expected on the basis of previous findings. The deterioration of support for the political community apparently is not as severe as that among black children in the United States, for example.[2] The divergence between the two ethnic groups of this study also may have been reduced because the orientations of Anglo children were less positive than those discovered in earlier studies.

The Regime: Images of Government

Young Mexican Americans, like Anglos, first perceive government in personalized terms as evidenced by their selection of President Nixon and George Washington as the best representatives of government. As Chicanos mature, personalization gives way to institutionalization and the Congress becomes highly equated with government. While Chicanos continue to perceive Congress as government, their Anglo age-mates move on to select a process--voting. The reluctance of Chicanos to select voting is largely a working-class phenomenon, reflecting the combined effect of low socioeconomic status and membership in a suppressed minority, both of which correlate with a lower rate of electoral participation.

Since most Anglo Americans select the Congress as the best representation of government while very young, this study does not support earlier findings of the tremendous importance of the thesis of President as a link to the system. Even the Chicanos' rate of selection of persons is at a lower rate than one would expect. The reason for this lesser identification may very well turn upon the particular presidential incumbent's popularity, or lack thereof.

In addition, Chicanos see the primary output of the government--laws--as stable but unfortunately unjust. This obstinate injustice of the laws conceivably could lead to a reaction against them that, especially if the government is equated with the law, could portend possible instability.

Chicano adolescents feel quite estranged from government, although lower-class students begin increasingly to appreciate the impact of the national government on their lives as they enter adulthood. State government is per-

ceived as less important and that of the city as nearly
irrelevant.

However, young Chicanos, especially those of the middle class, see government in highly favorable terms--very
nurturant, helpful, and friendly. But working-class, rural,
Spanish-speaking children are less taken with government
and become increasingly disaffected as they mature. The
government also is recognized by Chicanos as quite powerful, less knowledgeable than as perceived by the Anglos,
and prone to make mistakes.

Overall the picture is one of initial high affect for
the national government, usually higher than that of Anglos,
but also of a great deterioration in evaluation, perhaps
because Mexican Americans come to realize that the American
government has not been particularly responsive to their
situation. The governments of the state of California and
the city of residence also feature this change in evaluation from favorable to unfavorable, but at lower levels.

Regime Values

Democracy is accepted by young Chicanos as a primary
value of the American regime, although their interpretation
of it is more subject- than participant-oriented, similar
to that of some Anglo working-class children.[3] However,
as Mexican Americans mature, they reveal a great deal of
uncertainty as to whether or not the United States can
validly proclaim itself democratic. Freedom of expression,
one of the basic democratic liberties, is strongly supported
by Chicanos, but if speech is in the form of governmental
criticism the attitude, at least in the early grades, is
less supportive. Equality of opportunity for the advancement of all is strongly supported throughout the years,
at a slightly higher level by Chicanos than Anglos, especially than lower-class Anglos. Violations of the civil
rights of Chicanos are perceived more often by Chicanos
than by Anglos, a divergence that is especially strong at
the highest age levels--a perceptions that in turn seems
to have significant effects on other attitudes.

On measures of support for maximizing the individual
citizen's participation in governmental decision-making,
the third-grade Chicanos are most hesitant. It is hypothesized that this attitude is primarily a reflection of
parental socialization. Those Chicanos who are most Mexican tend to be least in favor of open participation in
decision-making, and some studies have presented evidence

that the Mexican family is one of restrictive decision-making procedures.[4] However, by the time they are teenagers Chicano students support expanding the arena of public decision-making at least as much as do their Anglo peers.

Regime Norms

Mexican American children are socialized to support system norms at a very early age. Their conception of the ideal citizen certainly conforms to the standard norms of American democratic theory. The law-abiding citizen is held in the highest esteem by Chicano third-graders, while political interest is seen by older students as the prime characteristic of a good democratic citizen.

Although one might expect young Chicanos to exhibit a great deal more cynicism than Anglos because of the past experiences of their parents with the U.S. government, this is not the case. Young children of all sociological categories are very trusting of government, although Chicanos of the working class and a more Mexican orientation are slightly more cynical. However, political distrust increases with maturity until most Chicanos become quite distrustful of government.

Chicano children's sense of citizen duty (electoral obligation) is relatively weaker. In all grades, Mexican Americans, especially those of low socioeconomic standing and Spanish language background, see less utility in casting a ballot than do their Anglo peers.

Perhaps mainly because of the fact that adult Mexican Americans in reality are less politically effective than most other groups, Chicano children feel less politically efficacious than do Anglos. While Anglo feelings of political efficacy rise substantially through the school years, those of Raza children increase very slightly, and among the middle class actually begin to decline in the later years.

In their attitudes toward other regime norms, such as majority rule, the candidacy and election of public officials, and constituency influence in decision-making, Mexican American children are very similar to their non-Chicano schoolmates. A few differences are apparent in the earliest years among the most culturally traditional Chicanos; all are hypothesized to be congruent with the values of Mexican society.

184

Perceptions of Political Authorities

The general pattern of Chicano children's orientations toward components of the political system is best typified by their reactions to public authorities. Idealization initially is quite high, but compared to Anglo feelings a tremendous erosion of affect takes place as Mexican-American youths mature. The President draws highly favorable responses from Chicano third-graders on measures of likeableness, friendliness, and helpfulness. Evaluations of the President's role performance also are highly positive. Early favorable attitudes toward the President would have to be very deeply ingrained in order to have the effect of adding to diffuse system support, because over the next few years Chicanos show dramatic deterioration in attachment to the chief executive. By adolescence the President is rated very low on all traits.

Police authorities rate slightly lower than the President but still very high in measures of affect among primary school Mexican Americans; however, erosion of these sentiments with age is at least as drastic. Older Chicanos rate the policeman's performance higher than that of the President but still much lower than do Anglos. Policemen are perceived as failing to carry out their primary functions of public assistance and instead concerned with discriminatory application of law enforcement. The Chicanos most critical of the police are those whose cultural characteristics expose them to more unfavorable contacts--those closest to the Mexican culture. Lower-class Chicanos usually are the most ardent supporters of the police when very young and become the strongest critics as teenagers.

Theories of transference or the generalization and projection of children's feelings for their fathers toward public authorities seem to have some applicability on early feelings of attachment but much less on the more cognitive evaluations.

Overall the early, very favorable orientations of Mexican American children seem to be more than neutralized by attitudes resulting from secondary socialization experiences with public authorities.

MEXICAN AMERICAN POLITICAL SOCIALIZATION

A fairly clear picture of the general patterns of political socialization of Chicano children in California has emerged. First of all, like other children, their initial diffuse, undifferentiated image of the political system becomes clearer with age. On the cognitive level, they proceed through the processes of idealization, personalization, institutionalization, and politicization at a pace quite similar to that of the Anglo children, although perhaps slightly slower. They are able to distinguish the political from the nonpolitical at a very early age. Their earliest view of the political situation, although relatively indistinct, is marked by a high degree of idealization; for lower-class Chicanos it often is higher than for any other group. With age, ability to evaluate independently each of the components of the system increases.

Affectively, Mexican American children generally begin with highly favorable orientations to the political system. On many dimensions their perceptions are even more supportive than those of Anglos. These may result from compensatory socialization by the Mexican American family eager to secure full membership in the system, or they may reflect the severity of early school efforts at socialization. If, as many students of the learning process contend, early attitudes are the most influential in the later formulation of opinion, then one might expect a relatively high level of positive orientation among older Chicanos. However, this is not the case. The initial attachment deteriorates severely as Mexican Americans increasingly contact hostile reality. Secondary socialization experiences appear at least as potent as primary ones, ostensibly overriding the early positive evaluations.

Easton and Dennis have stated that "the early adult years may reflect some tension between childhood affect and later disenchantment, with the net outcome dependent on the particular situational events."[5] In the case of Mexican American children, who are situated in a society with a history of prejudice and discrimination against their kind, events during adolescence must render the net outcome negative. Compared to Anglos, Mexican Americans come to possess orientations that provide a weaker foundation for diffuse system support.

It must be noted that several sociological variables produced significant intra-cultural variations in orientation. All Americans of Mexican ancestry are not socialized similarly. Middle-class Mexican Americans, for example, exhibit attitudes that in several instances are similar to those of Anglos, particularly in the later years when students have a better comprehension of their social position. On the other hand, working- or lower-class Chicanos often have the extreme opinions at each end of the grade scale. Their idealization often is greater than that in any other group, perhaps due to greater feelings of vulnerability, and as they mature the disillusionment often is the most drastic. Unfortunately, the combined effects of being at a societal disadvantage both ethnically and economically usually socialize lower-class Chicanos to be least supportive toward the American system.

Perhaps even more significant than socioeconomic status in its effect upon Chicano political socialization is the child's degree of assimilation. Coming from a household in which Spanish is the primary language or a household that recently arrived from Mexico almost always results in a more negative evaluation of the components of the American polity. Not that allegiance is to a foreign country, for this factor is least significant in attitudes toward the political community. But the "more Mexican" American reveals the results of a family socialization experience seemingly tied to the familial patterns of Mexican society. For one who is less acculturated to the American core culture, and thus undeniably distinct, later experiences with extrafamilial socializing forces are considerably more abrasive.

Although there is some disagreement on the matter, several social scientists hold that some Mexican values--passivity, dependency, a philosophy of acceptance and resignation, authoritarian family relationships--are antithetical to the ethic of Protestant-American core culture.[6] If these observations are accurate, it is likely they would be manifested in the young child's political orientations. This would be in accord with the hypothesis that "subgroups" that maintain or represent significant subcultural variations . . . are the ones most likely to impress their differences in childhood."[7] Yet it must be recalled that only on selective measures could a relationship be deduced between purported Mexican familial values and the children's earliest political attitudes, and the differences usually were not large. It was during secondary socialization that the opinions of less assimilated Mexican Americans diverged significantly. One can only conclude that any distinctiveness of Mexican American cultural values as manifested in the family has much less effect on the political socialization of Chicanos than do their experiences with American society as they mature.

Additionally, when the attitudes of Chicanos who perceive ethnic discrimination in America differ from those of their co-ethnics who do not detect discriminatory treatment, inevitably the difference is also in the direction of lower system support.

What we have, then, is a great transformation in the political orientations of Mexican Americans due mainly to negative socialization experiences as they mature. The overall pattern of socialization with regard to system support would be closest to Type III of three possible ideal developmental patterns suggested in Chapter 1 (see Figure 1.1 in Chapter 1). In only a few instances Chicano children begin at a greatly different level of perception and subsequently maintain this parallel difference throughout maturation (Type I). And seldom, usually in substantially less affect-laden opinions, do they follow the same pattern of socialization as Anglos, lagging somewhat behind (Type II). The typical configuration shows surprisingly similar orientations early in life, but maturity brings about increasingly divergent orientations (Type III).

SOME POLITICAL IMPLICATIONS

For those who attach the highest value to political stability per se, the results of this study, especially when combined with those concerning the socialization of American blacks, are not sanguine. Chicano adolescents are members of yet another ethnic minority whose diffuse support for the American political system is minimal. If the reservoir of goodwill has been drained empty by the time a Chicano reaches adulthood, the system must find other means of gathering support for itself. Coercion and the imposition of forced compliance, although often used against minority groups, would only add to the injustices perpetuated against Chicanos, and from the rulers' viewpoint is too costly to be used on a large scale over a long period of time. Hopefully, the government can and will act to bring Mexican Americans closer to the system by ensuring and encouraging their participation in political activities, thus enabling them to have a voice in the formulation of public policies. In addition to these "input" actions, the political decision-makers could produce and implement outputs (public policies) that are highly favorable to those dissatisfied with the system. It then would be possible that satisfaction with governmental programs plus increased input activities could produce specific support to bolster the feelings of legitimacy otherwise weakened by the low of diffuse support.[8] At present there is little evidence that the U.S. government is inclined to embark on the substantially different course of action designed to gain the goodwill of the Mexican-American people.

This is not meant to imply that the American political system is in danger of perishing because of the low level of support among its largest ethnic minorities; its resources for ridding itself of stress are too substantial for this to occur, short of a similar depletion of system support among massive numbers in the rest of the population. (It is thought-provoking to note that as political socialization studies of white American children become more contemporary, a progressively lower level of diffuse system support has become evident.)

However, these findings may have significant implications for system maintenance or stability. Many observers have noted that a lack of attitudinal system support among substantial groupings within the population provides an ideal condition for system stress. If these groups are of sufficient numbers and are strategically concentrated, if they have adequate resources including leadership, and if provocative circumstances and/or issues arise, a transformation of the political system probably will take place.[9] Currently these requisites are being fulfilled by Chicano political movements in the Southwest. Like blacks before them, Chicanos are becoming conscious of themselves and their ascribed inferior position in this country's sociopolitical structure and are proceeding to make demands upon the larger society. Increasingly militant voices of Chicano political activists are being heard. Although largely nonviolent in nature, protests against the system occasionally have erupted into violence throughout the Southwest.[10]

When similar low levels of system support are found among the nation's two largest ethnic groups, one may wonder about the prognosis for the future health of the American polity. This author is optimistic in that he hypothesizes the long-range effect of ethnic dissatisfaction with the system to be beneficial. The capacity of the system to operate need not be destroyed because of the differential socialization of its ethnic groups, such as the Mexican Americans. However, it must pay attention to these stresses and strains and respond by output policies that meet their needs and demands and, more importantly, by adapting its structural elements to be more in accord with the culturally pluralistic composition of the citizenry.

From this perspective, the divergent patterns of Mexican American political socialization actually may result in a more viable, and certainly a more democratic, political system. As Easton and Dennis have hypothesized:

> What may be "inadequate" socialization for main-
> taining existing political structures may be
> highly "appropriate" for bringing into being new
> structures based upon new ideals and new kinds of
> political accommodations among the members of a
> system.[11]

Hopefully this will be the situation, and both the American political system and its people of Mexican descent will be mutually benefited by the political socialization of Chicanos.

METHODOLOGICAL CONSIDERATIONS

Conducting empirical survey research often involves major methodological problems. The particular focus of this study made certain aspects easier to handle and at the same time magnified the difficulties of other parts of the project. The overall design and operation for this study is similar to most other political socialization research carried out by political scientists. It closely resembles the most extensive of all such studies carried out by the University of Chicago research team using a nationwide sample of 12,000 schoolchildren.[1] As in all scientific research, the explanation of social phenomena requires a cumulation of related data, the replication of experiments with varied controls, and the comparison of similar research. In this manner basic concepts are tested, modified, and refined in the light of ever-accumulating evidence. As discussed in Chapter 1, the earliest studies were conducted among urban, middle-class, white schoolchildren; later research projects widened their scope to include members of "subcultures" such as blacks and the poor. This study attempts to extend the research area by including children whose ancestry is Mexican-Spanish--the Chicanos.

Problems and Strategies

All previous studies have used children in the classroom as their sample. Gathering data on the relatively large number of young subjects needed for an adequate survey sample would be impossible without resorting to the school enclaves. Yet this in itself presents certain difficulties. Because the subjects are a captive audience, and not legally self-responsible, and because of the purported political sterility of the classroom, extra precautions must be taken when one seeks to use schoolchildren as respondents in political research.

Securing access to schoolchildren for "political" research is fast becoming impossible in this era of political tensions. In fact, the state in which this project was conducted, California, two years earlier had passed legislation prohibiting any

> test, questionnaire, survey, or examination containing any questions about the pupil's personal beliefs or practices in sex, family life, morality and religion, or any questions about his parents' or guardians' beliefs and practices in sex, family life, morality and religion—unless the parent or guardian of the pupil is notified in writing that such test, questionnaire, survey or examination is to be administered and the parent or guardian of the pupil gives written permission for the pupil to take such a test, questionnaire, survey or examination.[2]

Fortunately, an explicit prohibition against _political_ items was not included, but information on important sociological correlates might be precluded. The generality of the code's language allows administrators to interpret the code according to their own whims; generally the restriction was used as a reason for withholding permission for this study. Even when the law was not in question, district administrators were extremely wary of this kind of research. It certainly was not possible, then, to use any kind of strict random sampling technique for selection of a representative subset of Mexican American schoolchildren; securing even an "availability sample" was difficult.[3]

Following a strategy suggested by researchers experienced in school survey research,[4] letters first were sent to the principals of schools with grades three through nine located in districts containing large populations of Mexican-American children.[5] The particular range of grades (three to nine) was selected for several reasons. Foremost was the inclusion of the greatest range of political development possible within the limited resources of the project. Earlier studies have shown that by grade two or three children are able to respond meaningfully to the kinds of measurement devices used in this study and that the origins of system support are most appropriately tapped at these ages. The ninth grade was selected as the upper limit because by this age the political orientations of the young have been shown to be very similar to those of adult Americans.[6] With the range of ages (grades) established, alternate years were selected for reasons of economy.

It was felt that a sampling of both urban and rural areas, as well as a split between Northern and Southern California, might be of theoretical significance.

For the urban sampling, several schools in the east Los Angeles area were contacted. This area contains the third largest concentration of persons of Mexican ancestry outside of Mexico City and Guadalajara, Mexico; its barrios have seen several recent demonstrations and civil disturbances. It was felt that the concentrations of Mexican Americans, the nearness to Mexico, and the political salience of the area would provide a sample most significant for the purposes of this study. Several of the area's schools were contacted, and a majority of the principals expressed interest in the study. However, most gave their permission conditionally, dependent on securing approval from their superintendent's office. The administrative hierarchy proved the highest hurdle to surmount, and most of the principals' cooperation was negated by the refusal of central office bureaucrats. After much bargaining and negotiation, two elementary schools and two junior highs were included in the east Los Angeles area sample. Their ethnic composition was over 90 percent Mexican American.

The four schools are located in three small communities (average 1970 population of 40,000) located in east-central Los Angeles County, contiguous with the "heart" of the Mexican American barrios. Although sections of the communities are predominantly middle- and lower-middle class, the lower-class barrios extend into these areas. Median family income in 1969 was approximately $9,300, and the median number of school years completed was 11.7. Mexican Americans comprised about 45 percent of the population in 1969. Four-fifths of the Chicano population is native-born. Almost all the rest of the residents are white (Anglo); less than 2 percent are black or Oriental.

Since much recent Mexican American political awareness in California received its major stimulus from the activities of Cesar Chavez and the United Farm Workers Organizing Committee,[7] it was felt that a sample of children from a rural area in the Central Valley of California might disclose some interesting comparisons. After several refusals, permission was granted to conduct the study in a small rural community of approximately 4,500 inhabitants near Sacramento. The town is typical of the many small agricultural communities in this region of California. Although precise census data is unavailable, it is estimated that at least one-third of the residents are of Mexican ancestry. The responses of 496 students from this area and 731 from Southern California (total N = 1,227) were

included in the final sample.* Of the total, 55.6 percent
were students of Mexican-Spanish ancestry.

Parents also are an important factor to consider in
attempting this line of research. After one complained
strenuously of not being notified in advance of the project, forms were sent to the parents of all children in
the participating classes explaining the nature of the testing and allowing the parent to exclude their children from
participation if they so desired. Fewer than one percent
of the adults withheld their permission.

The measuring device was a 76-item printed questionnaire. It was felt that the major effort of the study
should be the collection, analysis, and interpretation of
data on a heretofore neglected ethnic group, rather than
the development of new measures and indexes of political
orientations. Therefore, most of the items included had
been previously developed, employed, and validated by social science researchers. The Chicago team's questionnaire, Citizen Attitudes No. 9 (CA-9), was the main source
of items, along with the questionnaire employed by Greenberg in his study of black socialization, itself highly
dependent upon the former effort.[8] Other items were added
from related studies or created especially for this project.
Items were selected using the criteria of whether or not
they contributed to the measurement of the dependent varia-
ble--diffuse system support--and important independent
variables, mainly relating to ethnicity and socioeconomic
status. Various single items and three indexes were included to measure perceptions of each of the three major
components of the "support" input in Easton's theoretical
conceptualization of the political system: the political
community, the regime, and the political authorities.

Independent Variables

When surveying attitudes, the selection of independent
variables involves several choices. The investigator may
choose to select from various classes of assumed antece-
dents to the attitudes he uses as dependent variables.
Particular kinds of behavior, such basic psychological
characteristics as personality or attitudinal states, or

_____

*Questionnaires were excluded if only a few responses
were indicated or if they were filled out by Mexican nationals, Oriental, or black children.

194

sociological-demographic variables may be considered.[9] This study primarily involves the correlation of traditional sociological variables--such as age, sex, status, and ethnicity--with orientations likely to be at least minimally affected by them.

Among the independent variables, the most theoretically significant one--ethnicity--also was the most difficult to operationalize. With respect to the particular group that is the subject of this study, even the label of identification is a topic of much controversy. Mexican American, Latin-American, Hispano, Hispanic-American, American of Mexican or Spanish ancestry, Chicano, La Raza, Mexicano --all are among the more acceptable names used to describe this group. With the increasingly adamant use of "Chicano" by the more vocal and active in the present sociopolitical movement, the debate over the most suitable term has been given new life.[10] To avoid this problem, all or any of these terms are used interchangeably to refer to those children, the subjects of this study, whose ancestors mainly came to the United States from Mexico, although the author's preference is for Chicano, Mexican American, Raza.

If the selection of a group label causes problems, the identification of individual members of the group is even more difficult. Since Mexican Americans can be considered a "partial minority"[11] less visible than, for example, black Americans, visual identification is tricky. Census Bureau identifications in the past have been based on "Spanish" surnames, but the inclusion of a name on this kind of a questionnaire seriously impairs the respondent's belief in its confidentiality. In addition, marriage with members of other cultural groups diminishes the discriminatory power of this measure. Directly asking a person to write down his ethnicity is in some cases illegal, and when asked of children is subject to much misunderstanding. Therefore, for this study a combination of identification devices were used. An attempt at visual identification was made by the interviewer, and his judgment was compared with that of the classroom teacher. In addition, the child was asked to "guess" from what part of the world most of his ancestors had come to the United States. Also, a question on the use of the Spanish language in the home was included. It is felt that with all these checking devices, very close to 100 percent reliability in identification was attained.

Socioeconomic status is a variable that is used in a great deal of attitudinal research, as it has been found to be significantly correlated with an individual's orien-

tations. Although various measures of socioeconomic standing, such as education, life-style, and self-identification, have been employed, the determination in this project was based primarily upon the occupation of the child's
father (and/or mother, where applicable). Sociologists
have indicated that occupation is the single best objective
indicator of economic standing. Parents' education and
home furnishings originally were included as additional
items in an index of socioeconomic status, but pre-testing
among 50 elementary schoolchildren pointed out serious
shortcomings in their use.

The sample was divided into two socioeconomic categories, middle class and working (or lower) class. Since
the occupational range of Mexican Americans is relatively
restricted, it was felt that a dichotomization of occupational categories would serve best to measure the effects
of socioeconomic status.[12] The socioeconomic composition
of each ethnic group is presented in Table A.1.

Consequently, ethnicity and socioeconomic status are
the two major variables considered in this study. Therefore, their association with almost every dependent variable is analyzed. Although such other sociological factors
as age (grade), sex, native or foreign-born parentage,
length of U.S. residence, Spanish language usage, and geographical location (Northern rural or Southern urban California) also are employed, these are discussed only when
they are found to be of special significance for any particular attitude.

TABLE A.1

Socioeconomic Classification of Mexican American
and Anglo Children
(in percentages; number of responses in parentheses)

Socioeconomic Class	Mexican American		Anglo		Total	
Middle	21.9	(150)	56.3	(306)	37.2	(456)
Lower	73.2	(500)	41.4	(225)	59.1	(725)
Not ascertain-able	4.9	(33)	2.3	(13)	3.7	(46)
Total	100.0	(683)	100.0	(544)	100.0	(1,227)

Gamma = −0.64.

196

Since a developmental or quasi-longitudinal assumption underlies this study (i.e., it is assumed that a third-grader will, as he matures, come to resemble in turn the fifth-, seventh-, and ninth-graders in the sample), it is necessary to demonstrate that cross-grade demographic differences are minimal. Otherwise, one could as validly attribute differences in the orientations of third- and ninth-graders not to hypothesized developmental patterns but to dissimilar experiential milieus. A comparison of demographic characteristics across the four grades reveals very few differences (see Table A.2). Since the age groups are very similar in all respects but maturity and education, we can more confidently postulate that the older children were themselves like the younger students a few years back. Moreover, these similarities increase the probability that the younger children will encounter many of the same socializing experiences during their maturation as did the older students. Of course, the third-graders will mature at a time that is objectively distinct from that of their older counterparts, and societal events of major significance conceivably might result in serious discontinuities in their socialization patterns. Yet the highly comparable sociological characteristics of age groups, plus the limitations on resources for a true longitudinal study, must render tenable the developmental assumption of this study.

Interviewing Technique

Obviously one of the major problems in working with children of La Raza is that of communication--more specifically, language. Consequently a Spanish language questionnaire was devised and used when necessary. Moreover, all the interviewers were bilingual, fluent in both Spanish and English. Those children who were more at ease communicating in Spanish rather than English were administered the questionnaire in Spanish.

The data was collected during the spring of 1970 and the month of January 1971. The interviewers all were college students residing in the area of testing, bilingual and experienced in working with Mexican American children. They distributed the schedules to the regular mixed classrooms of Anglos (non-Chicanos) and Mexican Americans and read the items to the class, as the children followed along and marked their responses on their own copies. In some seventh-grade classes, and in all ninth grades, the

Selected Demographic Characteristics of Total Sample, By Grade
(in percentages; number of responses in parentheses)

	Third		Fifth		Seventh		Ninth		Total	
Sex										
Male	48.7	(129)	51.2	(151)	55.5	(183)	52.5	(177)	52.2	(640)
Female	50.9	(135)	48.5	(143)	43.9	(145)	46.9	(158)	47.4	(581)
Don't know/no answer	1	(1)	0.3	(1)	0.6	(1)	0.6	(2)	0.5	(6)

(Gamma = 0.05)

	Third		Fifth		Seventh		Ninth		Total	
Socioeconomic Status										
Middle	33.2	(88)	39.0	(115)	37.3	(123)	38.6	(130)	37.2	(456)
Lower	64.2	(170)	58.0	(171)	58.2	(192)	57.0	(192)	59.1	(725)
Don't know/no answer	2.6	(7)	3.1	(9)	4.5	(15)	4.5	(15)	3.7	(46)

(Gamma = 0.03)

	Third		Fifth		Seventh		Ninth		Total	
Language Usage										
Mainly English	75.5	(200)	71.5	(211)	72.1	(238)	75.1	(253)	73.5	(902)
Mainly Spanish	24.2	(64)	28.5	(84)	25.4	(84)	23.2	(78)	25.2	(310)
Don't know/no answer	0.4	(1)	0.0	(0)	2.4	(8)	1.8	(6)	1.2	(15)

(Gamma = 0.02)

	Third		Fifth		Seventh		Ninth		Total	
Length of U.S. Residence										
Under 1 year	3.8	(10)	3.7	(11)	3.0	(10)	1.5	(5)	2.9	(36)
1-5 years	9.8	(26)	5.8	(17)	5.5	(18)	3.3	(11)	5.9	(72)
Over 5 years, foreign-born	12.8	(34)	6.8	(20)	6.4	(21)	7.4	(25)	8.1	(100)
Over 5 years, U.S.-born	63.0	(167)	74.6	(220)	82.4	(272)	86.4	(290)	77.3	(949)
Don't know/no answer	10.6	(28)	9.2	(27)	2.7	(9)	1.8	(6)	5.7	(70)

(Gamma = 0.05)

	Third		Fifth		Seventh		Ninth		Total	
Both Parents Born in United States										
Yes	50.6	(134)	60.0	(177)	63.9	(211)	67.7	(228)	61.1	(750)
No	45.7	(121)	35.6	(105)	28.8	(95)	28.5	(96)	34.0	(417)
Don't know/no answer	3.8	(10)	4.4	(13)	7.3	(24)	3.9	(13)	4.9	(60)

(Gamma = -0.17)

	Third		Fifth		Seventh		Ninth		Total	
Geographical Location										
Northern rural	49.8	(132)	43.4	(128)	30.0	(99)	40.7	(137)	40.0	(496)
Southern urban	50.2	(133)	56.6	(167)	70.0	(231)	59.3	(203)	59.6	(731)
Don't know/no answer	0.0	(0)	0.0	(0)	0.0	(0)	0.0	(0)	0.0	(0)

(Gamma = 0.12)

tests were self-administered. Completion time ranged from 30 minutes in upper classes to one and a half hours in some third-grade rooms. Although over 1,500 questionnaires were collected, a total of 1,227 (683 Chicanos and 544 Anglos) were suitable for inclusion in the final analysis.

Analysis Procedures

Tabulation and statistical analysis of the data was accomplished by the OSIRIS data management and analysis computer programs constructed by the Survey Research Center at the University of Michigan and processed at the University of New Mexico Computing Center. The basic form of analysis involved cross-tabulation of sociological variables and item responses. Statistical analyses of these bivariate frequency distributions included Goodman and Kruskals' gamma, a measure of association with an intrinsic meaning. Since several independent variables were introduced, a form of multivariate analysis was necessary and the Multiple Classification Analysis Program (MCA) in the OSIRIS package was selected.[13] This program examines the relationships between several categorical variables and a single dependent variable and determines the effects of each predictor before (eta coefficient) and after adjustment for its intercorrelation with other predictors (partial beta coefficients). It assumes additive effects and combines some features of both multiple regressions and analysis of variance techniques. Unlike conventional regression procedures, it allows predictor variables in the form of nominal as well as higher order scales, and it does not require nor assume linearity of regression.

When a stepwise regression was deemed appropriate, the Automatic Interaction Detector Program (AID)[14] was employed. This variety of multivariate analysis attempts to determine an optimal set of predictors through the ordering of independent variables by the relative capacity of each to account for variance in the dependent variable, and also provides an assessment of how much variance is accounted for by each independent variable.

QUESTIONNAIRE

This survey is designed to find out what boys and girls
your age know about government and politics, and how you
feel about them. This is not a test. There is no "right"
or "wrong" answer to many of the questions. Your answers
are confidential. . . . No names will be used in the study.

(1) How old are you? Circle your age.

   7   8   9   10   11   12   13   14   15   16   17

(2) What grade are you in? Circle your grade.

   3   4   5   6   7   8   9   10   11

(3) What is the name of this country (nation)?_____

   _____

(4) What is the name of this state?_____

(5) What is the name of this city?_____

(6) Are you a boy or a girl? Check one.

   _____ Boy   _____ Girl

(7) When we say the pledge of allegiance, we say it

   _____ To the country   _____ To the President

   _____ To God   _____ To the flag

          _____ I don't know

(8) Which of these people work for the government? Put a
     check mark beside every person who works for the gov-
     ernment.

   _____ Milkman   _____ Judge

   _____ Policeman   _____ Mailman

   _____ Soldier   _____ Teacher

200

(9) So many other people vote in the national elections that it doesn't matter much whether or not any one person votes.

_____ True

_____ False

_____ I don't know

(10) Which <u>one</u> of these pictures shows best what our <u>government</u> is? Check one.

_____ 1. Policeman

_____ 2. George Washington

_____ 3. Voting

_____ 4. Supreme Court

_____ 5. Capitol

_____ 6. Congress

_____ 7. Flag

_____ 8. Statue of Liberty

_____ 9. President

_____ 10. I don't know

201

(11) I think that just about everybody in this world would like to live in the United States of America. Do you think that this statement is true or false?

_____ True

_____ I don't know

_____ False

(12) I think that people who live in England are just as proud of their country as we are of ours. Do you think that this statement is true or false?

_____ True

_____ I don't know

_____ False

(13) Anyone should be able to say what he feels like saying even if it makes other people angry. Do you agree or disagree?

_____ Agree

_____ I don't know

_____ Disagree

(14) Which of the following sentences do you think is correct? Check one.

_____ The United States is in California.

_____ The United States is in Mexico.

_____ California is in the United States.

_____ California is in Mexico.

_____ I don't know

(15) The government in Washington can be trusted. Do you think this statement is true or false?

_____ True

_____ I don't know

_____ False

(16) Do you think the United States government

_____ Makes things better for most people

_____ Makes things worse for most people

_____ Makes no difference

_____ I don't know

(17) Which is the flag of this country? Circle the number
      of the flag of this country.

(1)   (2)   (3)

                       (4)

(18) Which of the following items best shows what this
      country is? Circle the number of one item.

(1)   (2)   (3)   (4)

(19) Which of the following flags is the best flag? Cir-
      cle the number of the best flag.

(1)   (2)   (3)

                       (4)

            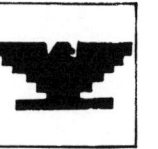

(20) What makes you most proud to be an American? Check one.

_____ Americans are the most generous people in the world.

_____ America has beautiful parks and highways.

_____ Americans can vote for their own leaders.

_____ Americans have freedom.

_____ Our President.

(21) I think that people who live in Mexico are just as proud of their country as we are of the United States of America. Do you think this statement is true or false?

_____ True

_____ I don't know

_____ False

(22) What happens in the government will happen no matter what people do. It is like the weather, there is nothing people can do about it.

_____ Yes, this is true.

_____ I don't know

_____ No, this is false.

(23) Every person should have the same right as any other person to get ahead. Do you agree or disagree?

_____ Agree

_____ I don't know

_____ Disagree

(24) Do you think the United States government is very important in what happens to you and your family?

_____ Yes

_____ I don't know

_____ No

(25) Sometimes I'm not very proud to be an American. Is this the way you sometimes feel? Check one.

_____ Yes

_____ I don't know

_____ No

(26) People in other countries think their country is the best in the world. Do they?

_____ Yes   _____ No

_____ Probably so   _____ Probably not

       _____ I don't know

(27) A lot of elections are not important enough for a person to bother with.

_____ True

_____ False   _____ I don't know

(28) The United States of America is the best country in the world.

_____ Yes   _____ No

_____ Probably so   _____ Probably not

       _____ I don't know

(29) Do you think that the government of California

_____ Makes things better for most people

_____ Makes things worse for most people

_____ Makes no difference

_____ I don't know

(30) Many people would like to be President, a senator, or a governor. Why do you think these people would like to have these jobs?

_____ They want to change things that are not good in government.

_____ They want to make a lot of money or be important.

_____ They want to keep things just as good as they are in our country.

_____ I don't know

(31) My family doesn't have any say about what the government does. Is this true or false?

_____ True

_____ False   _____ I don't know

(32) Do you think that the government of <u>California</u> is very important in what happens to you and your family?

_____ Yes

_____ No

_____ I don't know

(33) I think that whatever goes on in government is all for the best.

_____ Yes

_____ No

_____ I don't know

(34) Some kinds of grown-ups should <u>not</u> have a say in what government does. Do you agree with this statement?

_____ Agree

_____ Disagree

_____ I don't know

(35) If most people agree to do something, everyone should go along with it. True or false?

_____ True

_____ False

_____ I don't know

(36) Do you think that the government of this city

_____ Makes things worse for most people

_____ Makes things better for most people

_____ Makes no difference

_____ I don't know

(37) Even if some people do not agree with what the government does, they should go along and should not criticize or complain. True or false?

_____ True

_____ False

_____ I don't know

(38) Do you think that the government of this city is very important in what happens to you and your family?

_____ Yes

_____ No

_____ I don't know

(39) Anglos (whites) and Mexican Americans (Chicanos) are not treated the same. Is this statement true or false?

_____ True, they are not

_____ False, they are

_____ I don't know

(40) Some grown-ups should not be allowed to vote for the leaders of government. Is this statement true or false?

_____ True

_____ False

_____ I don't know

(41) In your opinion, which of these sentences best tells what democracy is?

_____ Where leaders do what they think is best for the people.

_____ Where leaders do what most people want.

_____ Where people can do what they want.

_____ Where people have lots of things, like cars and television sets.

_____ I don't know

(42) Would you like to work for the government someday?

_____ Yes   _____ No

_____ Probably so   _____ Probably not

_____ I don't know

(43) What do you think of the government? Circle the letter of the statement in each line that best describes the government.

(A)	(B)	(C)
(1) The government is very powerful.	The government is not very powerful.	I don't know

(A)	(B)	(C)
(2) The government knows a lot.	The government does not know much.	I don't know

	(A)	(B)	(C)
(3)	The government is very helpful.	The government is not very helpful.	I don't know

	(A)	(B)	(C)
(4)	I'm often afraid of the government.	I'm hardly ever afraid of the government.	I don't know

	(A)	(B)	(C)
(5)	The government is very friendly.	The government is not very friendly.	I don't know

	(A)	(B)	(C)
(6)	The government almost never makes mistakes.	The government makes lots of mistakes.	I don't know

	(A)	(B)	(C)
(7)	The government cares about us.	The government does not care about us.	I don't know

(44) By the time you are grown up

_____ All laws will change   _____ Just a few laws

_____ Most laws will change   will change

_____ No laws will change   _____ I don't know

(45) All laws are fair. Is this statement true or false?

_____ True
                                      _____ I don't know
_____ False

(46) I don't think that people in government care much about what people like my family think.

_____ True
                                      _____ I don't know
_____ False

(47) Who does the most to run the country?

_____ Congress   _____ Supreme Court

_____ President   _____ I don't know

(48) It isn't so important to vote when you know the people you vote for don't have a chance to win. Is this statement true or false?

_____ True

_____ False   _____ I don't know

(49) If the President came to your town to give prizes to the two grown-ups who were the best citizens, which grown-ups would you choose as the best citizens? Choose two.

_____ Someone who works hard.

_____ Someone who goes to church.

_____ Someone who everybody likes.

_____ Someone who helps others.

_____ Someone who votes and gets others to vote.

_____ Someone who always obeys the laws.

_____ Someone who is interested in the way our country is run.

(50) There are some big powerful men in the government who are running the whole thing and they do not care about us ordinary people.

_____ True

_____ False   _____ I don't know

(51) Who do you think should be picked as leaders in this country?

_____ Whoever is strongest.   _____ Whoever the most

_____ Whoever is smartest   people want.

_____ Whoever is oldest.   _____ I don't know

(52) Who is the top leader in this country today?

_____ President Washington   _____ President Diaz

_____ President Nixon   _____ President Johnson

_____ President Kennedy   _____ I don't know

(53) Which do you think is the most true?

_____ If you write to the President he cares <u>a lot</u> what you think.

_____ If you write to the President he cares <u>some</u> what you think.

_____ If you write to the President he cares <u>a little</u> what you think.

_____ If you write to the President he does <u>not</u> care.

(54) What do you think of the <u>President</u>? Circle the letter of the statement in each line that best describes the President.

(A)	(B)	(C)
(1) The President is friendlier than most people.	The President is not as friendly as most people.	I don't know

(A)	(B)	(C)
(2) The President is more helpful than most people.	The President is not as helpful as most people.	I don't know

(A)	(B)	(C)
(3) The President knows more than most people.	The President does not know as much as most people.	I don't know

(A)	(B)	(C)
(4) I'm afraid of the President.	I'm not afraid of the President.	I don't know

(A)	(B)	(C)
(5) The President can make everybody do what he wants them to do.	The President cannot make everybody do what he wants them to do.	I don't know

(A)	(B)	(C)
(6) The President works harder than most people.	The President does not work as hard as most people.	I don't know

	(A)	(B)	(C)
(7)	I like the President very much.	I don't like the President very much.	I don't know

(55) Here are some things that boys and girls have said about what the President's job is. What do you think the President's job is? Choose <u>two</u>.

_____ His job is to keep us out of war.

_____ His job is to make friends with other countries.

_____ His job is to help people in our country.

_____ His job is to stand for our country.

_____ His job is to make people obey the laws.

_____ His job is to make sure our country is run well.

(56) What do you think of the <u>policeman</u>? Circle the letter of the statement in each line that best describes the policeman.

	(A)	(B)	(C)
(1)	The policeman is friendlier than most people.	The policeman is not as friendly as most people.	I don't know

	(A)	(B)	(C)
(2)	The policeman is more helpful than most people.	The policeman is not as helpful as most people.	I don't know

	(A)	(B)	(C)
(3)	He knows more than most people.	He knows less than most people.	I don't know

	(A)	(B)	(C)
(4)	I'm afraid of the policeman.	I'm not afraid of the policeman.	I don't know

	(A)	(B)	(C)
(5)	He can make people do what he wants.	He cannot make people do what he wants.	I don't know

(A)	(B)	(C)

(6) The policeman   The policeman does   I don't know
works harder than   not work as hard
most people.   as most people.

(A)	(B)	(C)

(7) I like him very   I don't like him   I don't know
much.   very much.

(57) What is most important for the policeman to do?
Check one.

_____ Help people who are in trouble.

_____ Make people obey the law.

_____ Catch people who break the law.

_____ I don't know

(58) If you think a policeman is wrong in what he tells
you to do, what would you do?

_____ Do what he tells you and forget about it.

_____ Do what he tells you but tell your father about
it.

_____ Do what he tells you but ask the policeman why.

_____ Do what he tells you but tell the policeman
he is wrong.

_____ Not do what the policeman said.

(59) The police are harder on people like me and my family
than on other people. Is this statement true or
false?

_____ True

_____ False   _____ I don't know

(60) Who has the most to do with making laws?

_____ The President   _____ Congress

_____ The Supreme Court   _____ I don't know

(61) <u>Disobey</u> means to not do what you are told. Which <u>one</u> of these is most wrong?

_____ To disobey your mother.

_____ To disobey the President.

_____ To disobey your teacher.

_____ To disobey your father.

_____ To disobey a policeman.

_____ I don't know

(62) We live in a democratic country. Is this true or false?

_____ True

_____ False

_____ I don't know

(63) Citizens don't have a chance to say what they think about running this country.

_____ True

_____ False

_____ I don't know

(64) If the President came to your school to give a prize to two students who were the <u>best citizens,</u> which two students would he pick? Choose <u>two</u>.

_____ A student who helps others.

_____ A student who does what he is told.

_____ A student who gets good grades.

_____ A student who is interested in the way our country is run.

_____ A student who everybody likes.

_____ A student who works hard.

_____ A student who goes to church.

(65) What do you think of your <u>father</u>? Circle the letter of the statement in each line that best describes your father.

	(A)	(B)	(C)
(1)	My father is friendlier than most people.	My father is not as friendly as most people.	I don't know

	(A)	(B)	(C)
(2)	He is more help-ful than most people.	He is not as help-ful as most people.	I don't know

	(A)	(B)	(C)
(3)	He knows more than most people.	He does not know as much as most people.	I don't know

	(A)	(B)	(C)
(4)	I'm often afraid of my father.	I'm not very afraid of my father.	I don't know

	(A)	(B)	(C)
(5)	He can make most people do what he wants them to do.	He cannot make most people do what he wants them to do.	I don't know

	(A)	(B)	(C)
(6)	My father works harder than most people.	My father does not work as hard as most people.	I don't know

	(A)	(B)	(C)
(7)	I like my father very much.	I don't like my father very much.	I don't know

(66) Who helps your family the most?

_____ The policeman   _____ Your teacher

_____ The soldier   _____ The President

_____ Your father   _____ The governor

(67) There are other countries in the world that are more democratic than the United States. Is this true or false?

_____ True

_____ False   _____ I don't know

(68) My father and mother were **both** born in the United States. Circle one.

Yes   No

(69) How long have you lived in the, United States?

_____ Less than one year, I was **not** born in the United States.

_____ Between 1 year and 5 years, I was **not** born in the United States.

214

_____ More than 5 years, but I was <u>not</u> born in the United States.

_____ More than 5 years, I <u>was</u> born here in the United States.

(70) Who does your father work for?_____

_____

(71) What kind of work does he do?_____

_____

(72) If your mother has a job outside your home, who does she work for?_____

(73) If your mother has a job outside your home, what kind of work does she do?_____

(74) Can your mother speak

_____ English only, no Spanish

_____ Spanish only

_____ Mostly English, with some Spanish

_____ Mostly Spanish, with some English

_____ Both Spanish and English, about half and half

(76) Although you are probably an American, your ancestors (parents, grandparents, or great-grandparents) may have moved to the United States from another country. Where do you think most of your ancestors were born before coming to the United States?

_____ England or Europe   _____ Japan or China

_____ Mexico   _____ Africa

_____ Other country:_____

Thank you! (Muchas gracias!)

NOTES

CHAPTER 1
1. The concept "political system" can be defined broadly as consisting of those interactions through which resources and values are authoritatively allocated for American society. This idea is elaborated extensively in David Easton, A Systems Analysis of Political Life (New York: John Wiley & Sons, 1965). Easton's preliminary expositions of this are found in "An Approach to the Analysis of Political Systems," World Politics, IX (1957), 383-400; and A Framework for Political Analysis (New York: Prentice-Hall, 1965).
2. Political culture in general and that of the United States in particular is elaborated in Gabriel Almond and Sidney Verba, The Civic Culture (Boston: Little, Brown, 1965); Donald J. Devine, The Political Culture of the United States: The Influence of Member Values on Regime Maintenance (Boston: Little, Brown, 1972).
3. Gunnar Myrdal, An American Dilemma (New York: Harper, 1944).

4. See, for example, Raymond Wolfinger, "The Development and Persistence of Ethnic Voting," American Political Science Review, LIX (December 1965), 896-908; Michael J. Parenti, "Ethnic Politics and the Persistence of Ethnic Identification," American Political Science Review, LXI (September 1967), 717-26; Edgar Litt, Ethnic Politics in America (Glenview, Ill.: Scott, Foresman, 1970).
5. For the impact of social group membership on political perspectives, see Angus Campbell et al., The American Voter: An Abridgement (New York: John Wiley & Sons, 1964), pp. 161-83.
6. A synthesis of the various kinds of "accommodation politics" is presented in Litt, Ethnic Politics in America, pp. 60-74.
7. For a graphic illustration of such occurrences, see Chuck Stone, Black Political Power in America (New York: Dell, 1970), pp. 105-54.
8. Ibid., pp. 3-81, 165-288.
9. For example, see Lewis Coser, The Function of Social Conflict (Glencoe, Ill.: The Free Press, 1956).

10. Devine, Political Culture of the United States.
11. The most complete elaboration is in Easton, A Systems Analysis of Political Life.
12. David Easton and Jack Dennis, Children in the Political System: Origins of Political Legitimacy (New York: McGraw-Hill, 1969), p. 57.
13. Ibid., p. 58.
14. Ibid., p. 59.
15. Ibid., p. 60.
16. William A. Gamson, among others, has suggested that generalization of discontent occurs according to a hierarchical process from policy dissatisfaction through disaffection for authorities, then institutions and ideologies (regime), and finally to the political community, with increasingly serious consequences. See William A. Gamson, Power and Discontent (Homewood, Ill.: Dorsey, 1968), especially pp. 51-52.
17. Easton and Dennis, Children in the Political System, pp. 62-63.
18. Richard E. Dawson and Kenneth Prewitt, Political Socialization (Boston: Little, Brown, 1969), p. 212.
19. Easton and Dennis, Children in the Political System, p. 238.
20. Richard M. Merelman, "Learning and Legitimacy," American Political Science Review, LX, 3 (September 1966), 552.
21. Dawson and Prewitt, Political Socialization, p. 48.
22. For example, Orville G. Brim and Stanton Wheeler define socialization as "the acquisition of habits, beliefs, attitudes, and motivations which enable a person to perform satisfactorily the roles expected of him in society," in Socialization After Childhood (New York: John Wiley & Sons, 1966), p. 5; Donald R. Young defines socialization as "the process which enables individuals to participate effectively as members of interest groups, local communities and the larger society," in "The Socialization of Minority Peoples," in David A. Goslin, ed., Handbook of Socialization Theory and Research (Chicago: Rand, McNally, 1970); Frederick Elkin defines socialization as "the process by which someone learns the ways of a society or social group so that he can function within it," in The Child and Society (New York: Random House, 1960), p. 3.
23. Gerald Bender, "Political Socialization and Political Change," Western Political Quarterly, XX (June 1967), 390-407.

24. Fred I. Greenstein, "Political Socialization,"
in David Sills, ed., International Encyclopedia of the
Social Sciences, Vol. XIV (New York: Macmillan and The
Free Press, 1968), p. 1.
25. Fred I. Greenstein, "A Note on the Ambiguity
of 'Political Socialization': Definitions, Criticisms,
and Strategies of Inquiry," Journal of Politics, XXXII,
4 (November 1970), 969-78.
26. Easton and Dennis, Children in the Political
System, p. 7.
27. Studies of socialization in general, as compared
to explicitly political literature, are very numerous.
A review of this literature is beyond the scope of this
work. Discussions of this literature are presented in
Irwin L. Child, "Socialization," in Garner Lindzey, ed.,
Handbook of Social Psychology, Vol. II (Cambridge, Mass.:
Harvard University Press, 1954), pp. 655-92; William H.
Sewell, "Some Recent Developments in Socialization Theory
and Research," The Annals of the American Academy of Po-
litical and Social Science, CCCXLIX (June 1963), 163-81.
For an excellent collection of much of the important work
in this field, see Goslin, ed., Handbook of Socialization
Theory and Research.
28. Greenstein, "Note on the Ambiguity of 'Political
Socialization,'" p. 969.
29. Herbert Hyman, Political Socialization (Glencoe,
Ill.: The Free Press, 1959).
30. Fred I. Greenstein, Children and Politics (New
Haven, Conn.: Yale University Press, 1965). A useful
chronological listing of the major empirical research
projects in political socialization has been compiled by
Judith Torney in the appendix of a collection edited
by Norman Adler and Charles Harrington, The Learning of
Political Behavior (Glenview, Ill.: Scott, Foresman,
1970), pp. 193-96.
The works mentioned here are included for the following reasons: (1) they are perhaps the most influential and widely known major studies and have served as
bench marks for related research and (2) their methods,
theories, and data are most comparable to our study.
For a comprehensive listing of current political socialization research, see John S. Jackson, "A Political Socialization Bibliography and Survey of Projects in Progress" (mimeo.), prepared for the Committee on Pre-Collegiate Education, American Political Science Association,
September 1972.

31.   Robert D. Hess and Judith V. Torney, The Development of Political Attitudes in Children (Chicago:
Aldine, 1967).
32.   Kenneth P. Langton, Political Socialization
(New York: Oxford University Press, 1969).
33.   Dawson and Prewitt, Political Socialization, p.
viii.
34.   Easton and Dennis, Children in the Political
System.
35.   The need for socialization research dealing
with cultural and group variations is included as a
major problem area in Jack Dennis, "Major Problems of
Political Socialization Research," Midwest Journal of
Political Science, XII, 1 (February 1968), 85-114.   Other
assessments are by John J. Patrick, Political Socialization of American Youth: Implications for Secondary
School Social Studies--A Review of Research, Research
Bulletin No. 3 (Washington, D.C.:   National Council for
the Social Studies, 1967); Greenstein, "Note on the Ambi-
guity of 'Political Socialization'"; William R. Schonfeld,
"The Forms of Political Socialization Research: An
Evaluation," World Politics, XXIII, 3 (April 1971),
544ff.; Donald S. Baker, "Political Socialization:
Parameters and Predispositions," Polity, III, 4 (Summer
1971), 586-600; Richard M. Merelman, "The Adolescence
of Political Socialization," Sociology of Education,
XLV, 2 (Spring 1972), 134-66; Thomas Cook and Frank
Scioli, Jr., "Political Socialization Research in the
United States: A Review," in Dan Nimmo and Charles Bonjean, eds., Political Attitudes and Public Opinion (New
York: David McKay, 1972), pp. 154-74.
36.   Greenstein, Children and Politics, p. 185.
37.   See especially Kenneth P. Langton and M. Kent
Jennings, "Political Socialization and the High School
Civics Curriculum," The American Political Science Review,
LXII, 3 (September 1968), 832-68; Langton, Political Socialization, pp. 84-119.
38.   Dawson and Prewitt, Political Socialization, p.
33.
39.   Ibid., p. 216.
40.   Hess and Torney, Development of Political Attitudes, p. 229.
41.   Ibid., p. 230, n. 4.
42.   Easton and Dennis, Children in the Political
System, p. 335, n. 11.
43.   Ibid., p. 335, n. 12.
44.   Ibid., p. 401.

45. _Ibid._, p. 422.

46. Works dealing with the formation of political attitudes of African Americans include Lee H. Ehman, "An Analysis of the Relationships of Selected Educational Variables with the Political Socialization of High School Students," American Educational Research Journal, VI, 4 (November 1969), 559-80; Richard L. Engstrom, "Race and Compliance: Differential Political Socialization," Polity, III (Fall 1970), 100-11; Dean Jaros, "Children's Orientations Toward the President: Some Additional Theoretical Considerations and Data," Journal of Politics, XXIX, 2 (May 1967), 368-87; Joan E. Laurence, "White Socialization: Black Reality," Psychiatry, XXIII, 2 (May 1970), 174-94; Schley Lyons, "The Political Socialization of Ghetto Children: Efficacy and Cynicism," Journal of Politics, XXXII, 2 (May 1970), 288-304; Dwaine Marvick, "The Political Socialization of the American Negro," The Annals of the American Academy of Political and Social Sciences, CCCLXI (September 1965), 112-27; John Orbell, "Protest Activity Among Southern Negro College Students," American Political Science Review, XLI, 2 (June 1967), 446-56; Harrell R. Rodgers, Jr. and George Taylor, "The Policeman as an Agent of Regime Legitimation," Midwest Journal of Political Science, XV, 1 (February 1971), 72-86; "Pre-Adult Attitudes Toward Legal Compliance: Notes Toward a Theory," Social Science Quarterly, LI, 3 (December 1970), 539-51.

Edward S. Greenberg has done the most extensive research: "Black Children and the Political System," Public Opinion Quarterly, XXXIV, 3 (Fall 1970), 333-45; "Black Children, Self-Esteem and the Liberation Movement," Politics and Society, II, 3 (Spring 1972), 293-307; "Children and the Political Community: A Comparison Across Racial Lines," Canadian Journal of Political Science, II (December 1969), 471-92; and "Orientations of Black and White Children to Political Authority Figures," Social Science Quarterly, LI, 3 (December 1970), 561-71.

Other studies include David O. Sears, "Black Attitudes Toward the Political System in the Aftermath of the Watts Insurrection," Midwest Journal of Political Science, XIII (November 1969), 515-44; David Sears and J. B. McConkay, "Racial Socialization, Comparison Levels, and the Watts Riots," Journal of Social Issues, XXVI, 1 (Winter 1970), 121-40; Bradbury Seasholes, "Political Socialization of Negroes: Image Development of Self and Polity," in William C. Kvaraceus, ed., Negro Self-Concept:

Implications for School and Citizenship (New York: Mc-
Graw-Hill, 1965), pp. 52-90. Also Roberta S.
Sigel, "An Exploration into Some
Aspects of Political Socialization: School Children's
Reactions to the Death of a President," in Martha Wolfenstern and Gilbert Kliman, eds., Children and the Death
of a President: Multidisciplinary Studies (Garden City,
N.Y.: Doubleday, 1965), pp. 30-59; "Image of a President: Some Insights into the Political Views of Children," American Political Science Review, LXII, 1 (March
1968), 216-44; "Television and the Reactions of School
Children to the Assassination," in Bradley S. Greenberg
and Edwin B. Parker, eds., The Kennedy Assassination and
the American Public (Stanford, Calif.: Stanford University Press, 1965); Alden Jay Stevens, "Children's Acquisitions of Regime Norms in Subcultures of Race and Social
Class: The Problem of System Maintenance" (unpublished
Ph.D. thesis, University of Maryland, 1969); Joel D.
Aberbach and Jack Walker, "Political Trust and Racial
Ideology," American Political Science Review, LXIV (December 1970), 1199-1219.

47. The exploitation of Mexican Americans as a labor
resource in California is described as "economic colonialism" in Joan Moore, "Colonialism: The Case of the Mexican American," Social Problems, XVII (Spring 1970), 463-
72.

48. Data are from the U.S. Bureau of the Census,
Census of Population: 1970, General Social and Economic
Characteristics, Final Report, PC(1)-C6, California
(Washington, D.C.: The Bureau, 1972).

49. The imputation of certain cultural traits by
(mostly Anglo) social scientists to the Mexican and
Mexican American peoples currently is under severe attack
from Chicano scholars as derogatory stereotyping. Some
of the researchers often taken to task are Margaret
Clark, Health in the Mexican-American Culture (Berkeley:
University of California Press, 1959); Celia S. Heller,
Mexican American Youth: Forgotten Youth at the Cross-
roads (New York: Random House, 1968); Florence R.
Kluckhohn and Fred L. Strodtbeck, Variations in Value
Orientations (Evanston, Ill.: Row, Peterson, 1961);
William H. Madsden, Mexican Americans of South Texas
(New York: Holt, Rinehart and Winston, 1964); and Ruth
D. Tuck, Not with the Fist: Mexican-Americans in a
Southwest City (New York: Harcourt, Brace, 1956).
Some well-written examples of criticism of such
works are E. J. Casavantes, A New Look at the Attributes

of the Mexican American (Albuquerque, N.M.: Southwest
Cooperative Educational Laboratory, 1969); Octavio I.
Romano, "The Anthropology and Sociology of the Mexican
Americans: The Distortion of Mexican American History,"
El Grito, II, 1 (Fall 1968); 13-26; Deluvina Hernandez,
Mexican American Challenge to a Sacred Cow (Los Angeles:
Mexican American Cultural Center, University of Cali-
fornia, 1970), Nick C. Vaca, "The Mexican American in
the Social Sciences: 1912-1970," El Grito, III (Spring
1970), 3-24, and IV (Fall 1970), 17-52.

Leo Grebler, Joan W. Moore, and Ralph C. Guzman
have warned that many of the earlier studies are very
time- and place-bounded and should not be used as bases
for the formulation of generalizations about cultural
traits of all, or even most, Mexican Americans. They
note that several of the studies focused on rural areas,
the poorest urban barrios, and other geographically
atypical localities, in addition to being based on the
Mexican Americans of a generation or more ago. The
UCLA group found that a wide range of beliefs, attitudes,
and values exists among Mexican Americans today. Many
of these orientations are generally within the range of
American core cultural values while few aspects of traditional Mexican culture have been preserved but adapted
to the American experience. See Leo Grebler, Joan W.
Moore, and Ralph C. Guzman, The Mexican American People:
The Nation's Second Largest Minority (New York: The
Free Press, 1970).

50. An excellent discussion of these and related
points may be found in Ralph C. Guzman, "The Political
Socialization of the Mexican American People" (unpublished Ph.D. thesis, University of California, Los
Angeles, 1969). Although not in the mold of empirical
survey research on children most often considered as
"political socialization" studies, this thesis is the
most comprehensive analysis with the greatest insight
on the politically relevant contacts between Mexican
Americans and the American core culture yet produced.

51. However, contrary to popular assumption that
Mexican Americans have been politically apathetic and
slow to develop community action organizations, Miguel
D. Tirado has reported a history of viable, multifunc-
tional organizations in the Mexican American community.
See his "Mexican American Community Organization--The
Key to Chicano Political Power," Aztlan, I (Spring 1970),
53-78.

52. The colonial analogy is advanced as an appropriate paradigm for understanding Chicano status in Mario Barerra, Carlos Muñoz, and Charles Ornelas, "The Barrio as an Internal Colony," in Harlan Hahn, ed., Urban Politics and People (Beverly Hills, Calif.: Sage Publications, 1972); Tomas Almaguer, "Toward the Study of Chicano Colonialism," Aztlan, II, 1 (Spring 1970), 7-20; Moore, "Colonialism: The Case of the Mexican American."

53. The factors contributing to the exclusion of Mexican Americans from political participation in the state of California were documented by the California State Advisory Committee to the U.S. Commission on Civil Rights in Political Participation of Mexican Americans in California, A Report (Washington, D.C., August 1971).

54. Several books have examined this phenomenon. Perhaps the best is John Gregory Dunne, Delano (New York: Farrar, Straus and Giroux, 1967). Others include George Horowitz, La Causa: The California Grape Strike (New York: Macmillan, 1970); George Ballis, et al., Basta! La Historia de Nuestra Lucha (The Tale of Our Struggle) (Delano, Calif.: Farm Workers Press, 1966); Ernesto Galarza, Spiders in the House and Workers in the Field (Notre Dame, Ind.: Notre Dame University Press, 1970); Peter Matthiessen, Sal Si Puedes: Cesar Chavez and the New American Revolution (New York: Random House, 1969); Eugene Nelson, Huelga: The First Hundred Days of the Great Delano Grape Strike (Delano, Calif.: Farm Workers Press, 1966); Mark Day, Forty Acres: Cesar Chavez and the Farm Workers (New York: Praeger Publishers, 1971).

55. See Peter Nabokov, Tijerina and the Courthouse Raid (Albuquerque: University of New Mexico Press, 1966); Richard M. Gardner, Grito! Reies Tijerina and the New Mexico Land Grant War of 1967 (Indianapolis: Bobbs-Merrill, 1970).

56. Works surveying the major political movements of the Mexican Americans include Patty Newman, Do It Up Brown! (San Diego: Viewpoint, 1971); Armando Rendon, Chicano Manifesto (New York: Macmillan, 1971); Stan Steiner, La Raza: The Mexican Americans (New York: Harper and Row, 1969).

57. Many of the criticisms by Chicanos of what they consider to be social scientists' negative stereotyping of cultural traits are based on the opinion that attitudinal and behavioral attributes of Mexican Americans actually are those of any depressed economic class. See, for example, Hernandez, Mexican American Challenge.

CHAPTER 2

1. Parallel findings are reported by Jean Piaget and Anne-Marie Weil, "The Development in Children of the Idea of the Homeland and of Relations with Other Countries," International Social Science Bulletin, III (1951), 561-78; Gustav Jahoda, "The Development of Children's Ideas About Country and Nationality," Parts I, II, British Journal of Educational Psychology, XXXIII (June 1963), 47-60, 143-53; Leonard W. Doob, Patriotism and Nationalism (New Haven, Conn.: Yale University Press, 1964).

2. For example, David Easton and Jack Dennis, Children in the Political System: Origins of Political Legitimacy (New York: McGraw-Hill, 1969); Fred Greenstein, Children and Politics (New Haven, Conn.: Yale University Press, 1965); Robert Hess and Judith V. Torney, The Development of Political Attitudes in Children (Chicago: Aldine, 1967).

3. Hess and Torney, Development of Political Attitudes, p. 213.

4. Edward S. Greenberg, "Children and the Political Community: A Comparison Across Racial Lines," Canadian Journal of Political Science, II (December 1969), 471-92.

5. For a comprehensive discussion of population patterns among Americans of Mexican-Spanish ancestry, see Leo Grebler, Joan W. Moore, and Ralph C. Guzman, The Mexican American People: The Nation's Second Largest Minority (New York: The Free Press, 1970). This volume is a major contribution to social-scientific writings on Mexican Americans. Although criticized for its omissions and (Anglo) perspective--see, for example, the review symposium in the Social Science Quarterly, LII (June 1971), 8-38--this cumulative result of the UCLA Mexican American Study Project stands out as the most comprehensive investigation to date of this overlooked minority.

6. U.S. Bureau of the Census, Census of Population: 1970, General Social and Economic Characteristics, Final Report, PC(1)-C6, California (Washington, D.C.: The Bureau, 1972).

7. Leonard W. Doob, Patriotism and Nationalism, p. 34.

8. Greenberg, "Children and the Political Community," pp. 481-82.

9. Eugene L. Horowitz, "Some Aspects of the Development of Patriotism in Children," Sociometry, III, 4 (October 1940), pp. 329-41.

10. Edwin D. Lawson, "Development of Patriotism in Children: A Second Look," Journal of Psychology, LV (April 1963), 279-86.

11. Greenberg, "Children and the Political Community," p. 484.

12. David Easton and Robert D. Hess, "The Child's Political World," Midwest Journal of Political Science, VI (August 1962), 229-46; Greenberg, "Children and the Political Community," p. 484.

13. Grebler, Moore, and Guzman, The Mexican American People, pp. 428-32.

14. Although mention of all the studies on this subject is impossible, a concise discussion with special reference to Los Angeles schools is found in Grebler, Moore, and Guzman, The Mexican American People, pp. 142-79. The footnotes on Chapter VII, "The Education Gap," contain an excellent discussion of related references.

15. Although adult attitudes are the result of more than childhood socialization, most experts would agree that "the child is father to the man" in the sense that the child contains the basic outlines that will play a substantial role in the formation of adult orientations. That the range of alternative behaviors open to the adult is a function of his experiences as a child is best stated in Easton and Hess, "The Child's Political World," pp. 229-46.

16. Lawson, in "Development of Patriotism in Children," also found a steadily increasing appreciation for the UN flag until it was more popular in grades 10 and 11 than that of the United States.

17. Doob, Patriotism and Nationalism, discusses several elements of nationalism in Chapters 4-9.

18. A related work, employing a cross-national sample, is Wallace E. Lambert and Otto Klineberg, Children's Views of Foreign Peoples: A Cross-National Study (New York: Appleton-Century-Crofts, 1967). A recent study by Harry R. Targ, "Children's Developing Orientations to International Politics," Journal of Peace Research, VII, 2 (1970), 79-98, demonstrates that by fifth or sixth grade American children begin to develop clear-cut preferences for this country and disdain for certain others.

19. Many instances are cited in Ralph C. Guzman, "The Political Socialization of the Mexican American People" (unpublished Ph.D. thesis, University of California, Los Angeles, 1969).

20. Greenberg, "Children and the Political Community."

225

CHAPTER 3
1. David Easton, <u>A Systems Analysis of Political</u>
<u>Life</u> (New York: John Wiley & Sons, 1965), p. 206.
2. David Easton and Jack Dennis, <u>Children in the</u>
<u>Political System: Origins of Political Legitimacy</u> (New
York: McGraw-Hill, 1969), pp. 69-100.
3. <u>Ibid</u>., p. 100. For another analysis of the
importance of socialization to political legitimacy,
see Richard M. Merelman, "Learning and Legitimacy,"
<u>American Political Science Review</u>, LX, 3 (September 1966),
548-61.
4. Easton and Dennis, <u>Children in the Political</u>
<u>System</u>, p. 100.
5. <u>Ibid</u>., p. 113.
6. These are the findings of most investigators,
including David Easton and Jack Dennis, "The Child's
Image of Government," <u>The Annals of the American Academy</u>
<u>of Political and Social Science</u>, CCCLXI (September 1965),
40-57; Fred Greenstein, <u>Children and Politics</u> (New Haven,
Conn.: Yale University Press, 1965); Robert Hess and
Judith V. Torney, <u>The Development of Political Attitudes</u>
<u>in Children</u> (Chicago: Aldine, 1967).
7. Edward S. Greenberg, "Political Socialization
to Support of the System: A Comparison of Black and
White Children" (unpublished Ph.D. thesis, University of
Wisconsin, 1969), pp. 137-38.
8. Such as the research by Easton and Dennis,
<u>Children in the Political System</u>; Greenberg, "Political
Socialization to Support"; Greenstein, <u>Children and Poli-</u>
<u>tics</u>; Hess and Torney, <u>Development of Political Attitudes</u>.
9. California State Advisory Committee to the U.S.
Commission on Civil Rights, <u>Political Participation of</u>
<u>Mexican Americans in California: A Report</u> (Washington,
D.C.: The Commission, 1971), pp. 35-44.
10. Easton and Dennis, <u>Children in the Political</u>
<u>System</u>, pp. 118-21; Hess and Torney, <u>Development of</u>
<u>Political Attitudes</u>, pp. 50-52.
11. Robert E. Lane, <u>Political Ideology</u> (New York:
The Free Press, 1962), pp. 146-48.
12. This is a phenomenon related to developmental
psychology theory by Hess and Torney, <u>Development of</u>
<u>Political Attitudes</u>, pp. 51-52.
13. Not many childhood socialization studies have
researched orientations toward different levels of government. Two that have are M. Kent Jennings, "Pre-Adult
Orientations to Multiple Systems of Government," <u>Midwest</u>
<u>Journal of Politics</u>, II, 3 (1967), 291-317; Edward S.

Greenberg, "Children and Government: A Comparison Across Racial Lines," Midwest Journal of Political Science, XIV, 2 (February 1970), 249-75.
14. The peculiar sociopsychological characteristics of the economically disadvantaged, white, American child and their effects on political socialization are most thoroughly examined in the works of Dean Jaros and Herbert Hirsch. See, for example, Herbert Hirsch, Poverty and Politicization: Political Socialization in an American Sub-Culture (New York: The Free Press, 1971); Dean Jaros, Herbert Hirsch, and Frederic Fleron, Jr., "The Malevolent Leader: Political Socialization in an American Sub-Culture," American Political Science Review, LXII, 2 (June 1968), 564-75.
15. Greenberg, "Children and Government," pp. 263-67.
16. Ibid.
17. Julian Samora, ed., La Raza: Forgotten Americans (South Bend, Ind.: University of Notre Dame Press, 1966); Goerge Sanchez, Forgotten People (Albuquerque: University of New Mexico Press, 1940).

CHAPTER 4
1. These and the following points relating system values to members' support for that system are elaborated upon in David Easton, A Systems Analysis of Political Life (New York: John Wiley & Sons, 1965), pp. 194-200.
2. Much of the literature dealing with the school's role in political socialization is summed up in Richard Dawson and Kenneth Prewitt, Political Socialization (Boston: Little, Brown, 1969), pp. 143-80.
3. The hypothesis that adult political orientations are greatly influenced by attitudes acquired as children is fairly well established and serves as a basic assumption for much of the political socialization literature. See, for example, Richard E. Dawson, "Political Socialization," in James Robinson, ed., Political Science Annual: An International Review, Vol. I (Indianapolis and New York: Bobbs-Merrill, 1966), pp. 29-35; Dawson and Prewitt, Political Socialization; Fred Greenstein, Children and Politics (New Haven, Conn.: Yale University Press, 1965); David Easton and Jack Dennis, Children in the Political System: Origins of Political Legitimacy (New York: McGraw-Hill, 1969); Robert D. Hess and Judith V. Torney, The Development of Political Attitudes in Children (Chicago: Aldine, 1967).

4. For example, an investigation involving a cross-national sample of children found that American children outranked those of Italy, Germany, and the United Kingdom in their preferences for democratic options. Of American fifth-graders, 46 percent considered democracy to be the best form of government, and this proportion increased to 74 percent by the eleventh grade. See Jack Dennis, et al., "Political Socialization to Democratic Orientations in Four Western Systems," Comparative Political Studies, I, 1 (April 1968), 71-101.

5. Robert E. Scott, "Mexico," in Sidney Verba and Lucian W. Pye, eds., Political Culture and Political Development (Princeton, N.J.: Princeton University Press, 1965).

6. See, for example, Frederick Elkin, The Child and Society: The Process of Socialization (New York: Random House, 1960); James C. Davies, "The Family's Role in Political Socialization," The Annals of the American Academy of Political and Social Science, Vol. CCCLXI (September 1965); Dawson and Prewitt, Political Socialization, pp. 105-26.

7. Other parts of this study indicate that lower-class Chicano youngsters are most disposed to idealize various political authorities and institutions. Such idealization has been thought to be a psychologically compensating mechanism among young children whose dependent, vulnerable status evokes the attribution of benevolent characteristics to objects of superior status. This theory is advanced by David Easton and Robert D. Hess in "The Child's Political World," Midwest Journal of Political Science, VI (August 1962), 229-46 and continued in Hess and Torney, Development of Political Attitudes, pp. 38-40; Easton and Dennis, Children in the Political System, pp. 189-90, 356-58.

8. See the discussion on Mexico in Gabriel A. Almond and Sidney Verba, The Civic Culture (Boston: Little, Brown, 1965).

9. High percentages of agreement with abstract statements of regime norms have been reported in several studies, for example: Samuel A. Stouffer, Communism, Conformity and Civil Liberties (New York: Doubleday, 1955); Herbert McCloskey, "Consensus and Ideology in American Politics," American Political Science Review, LVIII (June 1964), 361-82; James Prothro and Charles M. Grigg, "Fundamental Principles of Democracy: Bases of Agreement and Disagreement," Journal of Politics, XXII (Spring 1960), pp. 276-94.

10. <u>Ibid.</u> See also V. O. Key, <u>Public Opinion and American Democracy</u> (New York: Alfred A. Knopf, 1961), p. 558. Research with children of high socioeconomic status conducted by Joan E. Laurence and Harry M. Scoble revealed that these children were exceedingly pro-democratic and supportive of the democratic creed long before they cast their first votes. See Joan E. Laurence and Harry M. Scoble, "Ideology and Consensus Among Children of the Socioeconomic Elite," <u>Western Political Quarterly</u>, XXII, 1 (March 1969), 151-62.

11. This theory is advanced, for example, in Gordon Allport, <u>The Nature of Prejudice</u> (Garden City, N.Y.: Doubleday, 1958); Bruno Bettelheim and M. Janowitz, <u>Dynamics of Prejudice</u> (New York: Harper and Row, 1950); R. M. Williams, <u>Strangers Next Door</u> (Englewood Cliffs, N.J.: Prentice-Hall, 1964).

12. That "racism" is a major characteristic of American society is officially recognized in <u>Report of the National Advisory Commission on Civil Disorders</u> (Washington, D.C., 1968). See also Louis Knowles and Kenneth Prewitt, eds., <u>Institutional Racism in America</u> (Englewood Cliffs, N.J.: Prentice-Hall, 1969).

13. The individual versus system perspectives on the consequences of individual participation are exemplified, respectively, in Bernard R. Berelson, Paul Lazarsfeld, and William N. McPhee, <u>Voting</u> (Chicago: University of Chicago Press, 1954), Chapter 4, and Jack L. Walker, "A Critique of the Elitist Theory of Democracy," <u>American Political Science Review</u>, LX (June 1966), pp. 285-95.

14. There is some evidence that Mexican children participate less frequently in familial decision-making than do American children. See, for example, Almond and Verba, <u>The Civic Culture</u>, p. 275. The pattern of familial decision-making among Mexican Americans is unclear. A recent survey work speaks of the patriarchial decision-making model as the cultural ideal if not the behavioral norm. See Leo Grebler, Joan W. Moore, and Ralph C. Guzman, <u>The Mexican American People: The Nation's Second Largest Minority</u> (New York: The Free Press, 1970), pp. 359-64.

15. Hess and Torney, <u>Development of Political Attitudes</u>, p. 20.

16. Almond and Verba, <u>The Civic Culture</u>; Gabriel A. Almond, "A Functional Approach to Comparative Politics," in Gabriel A. Almond and James S. Coleman, eds., <u>The Politics of the Developing Areas</u> (Princeton, N.J.: Princeton University Press, 1960).

17. Much of the research on the effect of family characteristics on the political socialization of children has been done by Kenneth P. Langton. See, for example, his Political Socialization (New York: Oxford University Press, 1969), especially Chapters 2 and 3. However, the transmission of certain political values from parent to child is seriously questioned in M. Kent Jennings and Richard G. Niemi, "The Transmission of Political Values from Parent to Child," American Political Science Review, LXII, 1 (March 1968), 169-84.

CHAPTER 5

1. David Easton and Jack Dennis, Children in the Political System: Origins of Political Legitimacy (New York: McGraw-Hill, 1969), p. 59.

2. As posited by David Easton, A Systems Analysis of Political Life (New York: John Wiley & Sons, 1965), pp. 200-4.

3. Ralph C. Guzman, "The Political Socialization of the Mexican American People" (unpublished Ph.D. thesis, University of California, Los Angeles, 1970); California State Advisory Committee to the U.S. Commission on Civil Rights, Political Participation of Mexican Americans in California: A Report (Washington, D.C.: The Commission, 1971).

4. Michael Lipsky, "Protest as a Political Resource," American Political Science Review, LXII (December 1968), p. 1158.

5. Guzman, "Political Socialization of the Mexican American People," pp. 302-5, 347-55.

6. This point is elaborated in David Easton and Jack Dennis, "The Child's Acquisition of Regime Norms: Political Efficacy," American Political Science Review, LXI (March 1967), 25-38.

7. The more "passive" role qualities of a citizen also were the most popular choices of the national sample researched by Robert D. Hess and Judith V. Torney, The Development of Political Attitudes in Children (Chicago: Aldine, 1967), pp. 37-39.

8. A similar trend with maturity toward a more participative and political role of the ideal citizen also is noted in M. Kent Jennings and Richard G. Niemi, "Patterns of Political Learning," Harvard Educational Review, XXXVIII (Summer 1968), 443-67.

9. The ability to distinguish the political from essentially private spheres--"politicization"--is one of the developmental processes examined by Easton and Dennis in Children in the Political System.

230

10. For example, Leo Grebler, Joan W. Moore, and Ralph C. Guzman, The Mexican American People: The Nation's Second Largest Minority (New York: The Free Press, 1970), pp. 556-72.

11. The subject of fatalism as a cultural trait of Mexican Americans is an extremely controversial topic of debate among Mexican American scholars. Many Chicanos reject this trait as a derogatory stereotype created by a racist Anglo society. Those admitting the possibility of its existence hold that this is not an attitude peculiar to Mexican Americans but rather is found among any group that is economically depressed or subject to racial discrimination. Evidence has been mustered to support all positions and much of it is presented by David Lopez Lee, along with his own ideas, in "Mexican-American Fatalism--An Analysis and Some Speculations," Journal of Mexican American Studies, I, 1 (Fall 1970), pp. 44-53.

12. Although the literature on this subject is vast, a summary of much of it is found in Lester Milbrath, Political Participation (Chicago: Rand, McNally, 1965), and Robert E. Lane, Political Life (New York: The Free Press, 1959).

13. Robert E. Agger, Marshall N. Goldstein, and Stanley A. Pearl, "Political Cynicism: Meaning and Measurement," Journal of Politics, XXIII (August 1961), 477-506; Edgar Litt, "Political Cynicism and Political Futility," Journal of Politics, XXV (May 1963), 312-23.

14. These are recounted in Guzman, "Political Socialization of the Mexican American People," pp. 106-70.

15. Grebler, Moore, and Guzman, The Mexican American People, pp. 567-69.

16. However, some research has shown that a particular norm, such as political cynicism, may not be a value passed from parent to child. See, for example, M. Kent Jennings and Richard G. Niemi, "The Transmission of Political Values from Parent to Child," American Political Science Review, LXII, 1 (March 1968), 169-84.

However, others have held that trust in the political system is greatly dependent on familial socialization. Allman, for example, contends that political trust is more dependent upon primary socialization than on secondary experiences: see Joseph M. Allman, "Socialization, Personality and the Orientation Toward Change (unpublished Ph.D. thesis, Michigan State University, 1968), p. 142. And a study of Appalachian children also added evidence that political cynicism is transmitted from parents to their children: see Dean Jaros, Herbert Hirsch, and Frederic Fleron, Jr., "The Malevolent Leader: Political Socialization in an American Sub-Culture," American Political Science Review, LXII, 2 (June 1968), 564-75.

17. Jennings and Niemi, "Transmission of Political Values," p. 179.

18. Ibid., p. 178.

19. Ibid. See also Jennings and Niemi, "Patterns of Political Learning," p. 456.

20. According to the developmental profile theory formulated in Richard E. Dawson and Kenneth Prewitt, Political Socialization (Boston: Little, Brown, 1969).

21. Catherine Cornbleth, "Political Socialization and the Social Studies: Political Beliefs of Mexican-American Youth" (mimeo., University of Texas, Austin, 1970).

Findings that black children possess higher levels of cynicism than Anglos are reported in Lee H. Ehman, "An Analysis of the Relationships of Selected Educational Variables with the Political Socialization of High School Students," American Educational Research Journal, VI (November 1969), 559-80; Schley Lyons, "The Political Socialization of Ghetto Children: Efficacy and Cynicism," Journal of Politics, XXXII, 2 (May 1970), 288-304.

22. Cornbleth, "Political Socialization and the Social Studies," p. 8.

23. As do, for example, the rural, lower-class, Anglo children of Appalachia. See Jaros, Hirsch, and Fleron, "The Malevolent Leader."

24. Research on the levels of political cynicism among black and white children residing in slums indicates that their high school years are an important period of political socialization with respect to this norm. While ghetto children of both races lead their suburban counterparts in the development of distrustful attitudes, the trend is particularly pronounced among black children, regardless of their milieu. See Lyons, "The Political Socialization of Ghetto Children," and also the study of black and white high school students in Detroit by Ehman, "An Analysis of the Relationships of Selected Educational Variables."

25. Milbrath ranks voting as a "spectator" activity rated only above "exposing oneself to political stimuli" on a scale of increasing levels of participation. See Milbrath, Political Participation, pp. 16-22.

26. As thoroughly documented in Bernard R. Berelson, Paul Lazarsfeld, and William N. McPhee, Voting (Chicago:

University of Chicago Press, 1954); Angus Campbell, Gerald Gurin, and Warren Miller, The Voter Decides (Evanston, Ill.: Row, Peterson, 1954); Angus Campbell, et al., The American Voter: An Abridgement (New York: John Wiley & Sons, 1964).

27. Guzman, "Political Socialization of the Mexican American People," pp. 145-281.

28. For example, Ehman, "An Analysis of the Relationships of Selected Educational Variables"; Kenneth P. Langton and M. Kent Jennings, "Political Socialization and the High School Civics Curriculum in the United States," The American Political Science Review, LXII, 3 (September 1968), 852-67; Alden Jay Stevens, "Children's Acquisitions of Regime Norms in Subcultures of Race and Social Class: The Problem of System Maintenance" (unpublished Ph.D. thesis, University of Maryland, 1969).

29. Stevens, "Children's Acquisitions of Regime Norms," pp. 56-65.

30. Robert Hess maintains that civics teachers dangerously exaggerate the importance of the individual vote as a method of influencing government. See Robert D. Hess, "Political Attitudes in Children," Psychology Today, II (January 1969), 24-28, and "Political Socialization in the Schools," Harvard Educational Review, XXXVIII (Summer 1968), 528-36.

31. Castro v. California, 1970.

32. Easton and Dennis, in a footnote to an article on the subject, list 12 books and 17 articles dealing with political efficacy. See Easton and Dennis, "The Child's Acquisition of Regime Norms, p. 27, n. 4.

33. Campbell, Gurin, and Miller, The Voter Decides.

34. Easton and Dennis, "The Child's Acquisition of Regime Norms," pp. 25-38.

35. Ibid., p. 31.

36. Ibid., p. 32.

37. Ibid. Also reported in Hess and Torney, Development of Political Attitudes, pp. 68-69.

38. As reported in Easton and Dennis, Children in the Political System; Hess and Torney, Development of Political Attitudes; Herbert Hirsch, Poverty and Politicization: Political Socialization in an American Sub-Culture (New York: The Free Press, 1971).

39. Ehman, "An Analysis of the Relationships of Selected Educational Variables"; Langton and Jennings, "Political Socialization and the High School Civics Curriculum"; Joan E. Laurence, "White Socialization: Black Reality," Psychiatry, XXXIII (May 1970), 174-94; Lyons,

"The Political Socialization of Ghetto Children"; Stevens, "Children's Acquisitions of Regime Norms."

40. Cornbleth, "Political Socialization and the Social Studies."

41. Grebler, Moore, and Guzman, The Mexican American People, pp. 557-72.

42. Florence R. Kluckhohn and Fred L. Strodtbeck, Variations in Value Orientations (Evanston, Ill.: Row, Peterson, 1961); William H. Madsden, Mexican Americans of South Texas (New York: Holt, Rinehart and Winston, 1964).

43. Ibid. See also M. S. Edmondson, Los Manitos: A Study of Institutional Values (New Orleans: Tulane University Press, 1957); Celia S. Heller, Mexican American Youth: Forgotten Youth at the Crossroads (New York: Random House, 1966).

44. The importance of the family to the general socialization of the child is reviewed in Richard E. Dawson and Kenneth Prewitt, Political Socialization (Boston: Little, Brown, 1969), pp. 105-26.

45. A study of learning models suggests that political efficacy necessarily will decline from grade nine onward. See T. G. Harvey, "Models of the Adolescent Socialization Process" (unpublished Ph.D. thesis, University of Hawaii, 1968).

46. Elliott S. White has argued that social class is not a significant predictor of feelings of political efficacy among school-age children in his "Intelligence and Sense of Political Efficacy in Children," Journal of Politics, XXX, 30 (August 1968), pp. 710-31. But this contention is criticized as being the result of faulty methodology in Robert A. Jackman, "A Note on Intelligence, Social Class and Political Efficacy in Children," Journal of Politics, XXXII (November 1970), 984-88.

47. Such is the hypothesis of Kenneth P. Langton and David A. Karns, "The Relative Influence of the Family, Peer Group and School in the Development of Political Efficacy," Western Political Science Quarterly, XXII (December 1969), 813-26. The effect of teaching methods on the political attitudes (including efficacy) of biracial classes has been investigated by Ehman, "An Analysis of the Relationships of Selected Educational Variables."

48. Allman, "Socialization, Personality and Orientation," p. 142, hypothesizes that feelings of efficacy are almost entirely the products of secondary, rather than primary, socialization.

49. In fact, one author has defined democracy solely in terms of majority rule. See Bernard Crick, In Defence of Politics (Baltimore: Penguin Books, 1964).
50. Constituency influence on decision-making is the subject of much empirical research. Some of the best includes Warren Miller and Donald Stokes, "Constituency Influence in Congress," American Political Science Review, LVII (March 1963), 45-56; Charles F. Cnudde and Donald J. McCrone, "The Linkage Between Constituency Attitudes and Congressional Voting Behavior: A Casual Model," American Political Science Review, LX (March 1966), pp. 66-72; Walter Wilcox, "The Congressional Poll and Non-Poll," in Edward C. Dreyer and Walter A. Rosenbaum, eds., Political Opinion and Electoral Behavior (Belmont, Calif.: Wadsworth, 1966), pp. 390-400.
51. However, the decline with age in the perceived responsiveness of the President is much more drastic than that discovered by Hess and Torney in their national sample ten years earlier. See Hess and Torney, The Development of Political Attitudes, pp. 38-40.

CHAPTER 6
1. David Easton and Jack Dennis, Children in the Political System: Origins of Political Legitimacy (New York: McGraw-Hill, 1969).
2. Fred I. Greenstein, Children and Politics (New Haven, Conn.: Yale University Press, 1965).
3. See, for example, Robert D. Hess and Judith V. Torney, The Development of Political Attitudes in Children (Chicago: Aldine, 1967).
4. Dean Jaros, "Children's Orientations Toward the President: Some Additional Theoretical Considerations and Data," Journal of Politics, XXIX, 2 (May 1967), 368-87.
5. Dean Jaros, Herbert Hirsch, and Frederic Fleron, Jr., "The Malevolent Leader: Political Socialization in an American Sub-Culture," American Political Science Review, LXII, 2 (June 1968), 564-75.
6. Easton and Dennis, Children in the Political System, p. 204. Some psychologists contend that children's introduction to the political system is through the more salient political topics of the day rather than through the person of the President. See Freda Rebelsky, Cheryl Conover, and Patricia Chafetz, "The Development of Political Attitudes in Young Children," Journal of Psychology, LXXII (November 1969), pp. 141-46.

7. Richard E. Dawson and Kenneth Prewitt, _Political Socialization_ (Boston: Little, Brown, 1969), pp. 201-15.

8. William H. Madsden, _The Mexican Americans of South Texas_ (New York: Holt, Rinehart and Winston, 1964).

9. Easton and Dennis, _Children in the Political System_, p. 168.

10. The effect of children's sex on their political orientations is explored in Fred I. Greenstein, "Sex-Related Political Differences in Childhood," _Journal of Politics_, XXIII, 2 (May 1961), 353-71.

11. According to Madsden, _Mexican Americans of South Texas_.

12. For example, Edward S. Greenberg, "Political Socialization to Support of the System: A Comparison of Black and White Children" (unpublished Ph.D. thesis, University of Wisconsin, 1969).

13. Mary Ellen Goodman, "Emergent Citizenship: A Study of Relevant Values in Four-Year Olds," _Childhood Education_, XXXV (1958-59), 248-51.

14. Easton and Dennis, _Children in the Political System_, pp. 208-42.

15. Edward S. Greenberg, "Orientations of Black and White Children to Political Authority Figures," _Social Science Quarterly_, LI, 3 (December 1970), 561-71.

16. For documented examples, see the U.S. Commission on Civil Rights, _Mexican Americans and the Administration of Justice in the Southwest_ (Washington, D.C.: The Commission, 1970), especially pp. 1-13. See also Armando Morales, _Ando Sangrando (I Am Bleeding): A Study of Mexican American-Police Conflict_ (La Puente, Calif.: Perspectiva Publications, 1972), especially pp. 20-32.

17. Only three decades ago, the Los Angeles Police Department endorsed a report concluding that Mexican Americans were biologically inclined to criminality. For details, see Ralph C. Guzman, "The Political Socialization of the Mexican American People" (unpublished Ph.D. thesis, University of California, Los Angeles, 1969), pp. 122-24; also Morales, _Ando Sangrando_, pp. 33-46.

18. A somewhat similar conclusion is reached in a study of black children by Harrell R. Rodgers, Jr., and George Taylor, "The Policeman as an Agent of Regime Legitimation," _Midwest Journal of Political Science_, XV, 1 (February 1971), 72-86.

19. The importance of children's images of local public officials, especially the governor and mayor,

also is presented in Fred I. Greenstein, "More on Children's Images of the President," Public Opinion Quarterly, XXV, 4 (Winter 1961), 648-54.

20. U.S. Bureau of the Census, Census of Population: 1970, General Social and Economic Characteristics, Final Report, PC(1)-C6, California (Washington, D.C.: The Bureau, 1972).

21. See, for example, Greenstein, Children and Politics, pp. 46-52.

22. Easton and Dennis, Children in the Political System, p. 250.

23. Ibid., pp. 254-71.

24. Ibid., p. 365.

25. Ibid., p. 366.

26. Ibid., p. 371.

27. Ibid.

28. Robert D. Hess, "The Socialization of Attitudes Toward Political Authority: Some Cross-National Comparisons," International Social Science Journal, XV (1963), 542-59.

29. Robert Levine, "Political Socialization and Cultural Change," in Clifford Goertz, ed., Old Societies and New States (Glencoe, Ill.: The Free Press, 1963), p. 283.

30. Kenneth P. Langton, Political Socialization (New York: Oxford University Press, 1969), pp. 21-83.

31. Greenberg, "Political Socialization to Support," pp. 215-17.

32. In a recent article, two students of socialization suggest that, although children's attitudes toward police are important correlates of authority acceptance for white students, such is not the case for blacks. Rodgers and Taylor, "The Policeman as an Agent of Regime Legitimation."

CHAPTER 7

1. Joan E. Laurence makes this point well with regard to American blacks in her article, "White Socialization: Black Reality," Psychiatry, XXXIII (May 1970), 174-94.

2. As posited in Edward S. Greenberg, "Children and the Political Community: A Comparison Across Racial Lines," Canadian Journal of Political Science, II (December 1969), 471-92.

3. That these varying political roles are reinforced in the schools is suggested in Edgar Litt, "Civic Education, Community Norms, and Political Indoctrination,"

American Sociological Review, XXVIII, 1 (February 1963), 69-75.

4. Chilicott, for one, has stated that the child has little status in the Mexican family and that decisions are arrived at in an authoritarian manner. See "Some Perspectives for Teaching First Generation Mexican-Americans," in John H. Chilicott, Norman Greenberg, and Herbert B. Wilson, eds., Readings in the Socio-Cultural Foundations of Education (Belmont, Calif.: Wadsworth, 1968).

5. David Easton and Jack Dennis, Children in the Political System: Origins of Political Legitimacy (New York: McGraw-Hill, 1969), p. 310.

6. For example, William H. Madsden, Mexican Americans of South Texas (New York: Holt, Rinehart and Winston, 1964); Chilicott, "Teaching First Generation Mexican-Americans"; Robert L. Derbyshire, "The Adaption of Adolescent Mexican Americans to United States Society," American Behavioral Scientist, XIII, 1 (September-October, 1969), 88-103. However, a warning as to the appropriateness of equating traditional Mexican familial values with those of contemporary Mexican Americans is contained in Leo Grebler, Joan W. Moore, and Ralph Guzman, The Mexican American People: The Nation's Second Largest Minority (New York: The Free Press, 1970).

7. Easton and Dennis, Children in the Political System, p. 328.

8. It has been suggested that this is largely the case in West Germany. The German citizenry displays no particular support for the current regime but is so satisfied with governmental performance and policies (mainly along economic lines) that adequate system support to maintain the system is generated. See Gabriel A. Almond and Sidney Verba, The Civic Culture (Boston: Little, Brown, 1965), p. 313.

9. Some of the conditions mentioned by Easton and Dennis, Children in the Political System, pp. 308-9.

10. Armando Morales reports that since 1970 at least 30 "riots" have occurred in Spanish-speaking communities. See Armando Morales, Ando Sangrando (I Am Bleeding): A Study of Mexican American-Police Conflict (La Puente, Calif.: Perspectiva Publications, 1972), p. v.

11. Easton and Dennis, Children in the Political System, p. 42.

APPENDIX A

1. As reported in David Easton and Jack Dennis, _Children in the Political System: Origins of Political Legitimacy_ (New York: McGraw-Hill, 1969); Robert D. Hess and Judith V. Torney, _The Development of Political Attitudes in Children_ (Chicago: Aldine, 1967).

2. _California Educational Code_, 1968, Article 9, Paragraph 10901, p. 185.

3. G. David Garson, _Handbook of Political Science Methods_ (Boston: Holbrook Press, 1971), p. 91.

4. M. Kent Jennings and L. F. Fox, "The Conduct of Socio-Political Research in Schools: Strategies and Problems of Access," _School Review_, LXXVI (December 1968), 428-44.

5. The California State Department of Education makes a yearly survey of the ethnic composition of its public schools. See, for example, California State Department of Education, Bureau of Intergroup Relations, Division of Compensatory Education, _Racial and Ethnic Survey of California Public Schools: Fall 1967_ (California State Department of Education, 1969). The Bureau of Intergroup Relations kindly made available computer printouts of the latest information. On the basis of these statistics, inquiries were initially sent to schools having over 50 percent Chicano population.

6. Developmental psychologists Adelson and O'Neil find only a slight difference between the cognitive development of 15- and 18-year-olds (political adults) in their sample: Joseph Adelson and Robert P. O'Neil, "The Growth of Political Ideas in Adolescence: The Sense of Community," _Journal of Personality and Social Psychology_, IV, 3 (September 1966), 295-306. Moreover, the University of Chicago researchers found very slight differences between the political orientations of their eighth-graders and those of their teachers: Easton and Dennis, _Children in the Political System_; Hess and Torney, _Development of Political Attitudes_. Although developmental research, i.e., studies involving patterns of personal changes over a period of years, ideally would be conducted by examining the maturation of a group of subjects through the years, such a study requires abundant time and money. This study is "quasi-longitudinal" in design: the assumption is that the older students in the sample possess characteristics similar to those the younger ones would have at a similar stage of development.

7. Cesar Chavez and the UFWOC are the subject of several works. See, for example, John Gregory Dunne,

Delano (New York: Farrar, Straus and Giroux, 1967);
George Horowitz, La Causa: The California Grape Strike
(New York: Macmillan, 1970); George Ballis, et al.,
Basta! La Historia de Nuestra Lucha (The Tale of Our
Struggle) (Delano, Calif.: Farm Workers Press, 1966);
Ernesto Galarza, Spiders in the House and Workers in the
Field (Notre Dame, Ind.: Notre Dame University Press,
1970); Peter Matthiessen, Sal Si Puedes: Cesar Chavez
and the New American Revolution (New York: Random House,
1969); Eugene Nelson, Huelga: The First Hundred Days of
the Great Delano Grape Strike (Delano, Calif.: Farm
Workers Press, 1966); Mark Day, Forty Acres: Cesar
Chavez and the Farm Workers (New York: Praeger Publishers, 1971).

    8. Edward S. Greenberg, "Political Socialization
to Support of the System: A Comparison of Black and
White Children" (unpublished Ph.D. thesis, University
of Wisconsin, 1969).

    9. These are elaborated in, for example, Lewis A.
Froman, "Personality and Political Socialization," Jour-
nal of Politics, XXIII, 2 (May 1967), 341-52; Fred I.
Greenstein, "The Standing of Social and Psychological
Variables: An Addendum to Jackman's Critique," Journal
of Politics, XXXII (November 1970), 989-92.

    10. For a discussion of the importance of labels
applied to this group, see Tom Pino and Daniel T. Valdes,
"Ethnic Labels in Majority-Minority Relations," Journal
of Mexican-American Studies, I, 1 (Fall 1970), 16-30.

    11. The term has been used by a sociologist to de-
scribe ethnic minority groups that are "less unequal,"
less identifiable visually, and more geographically concentrated than American blacks. See John R. Howard, ed.,
Awakening Minorities (Chicago: Aldine, 1970), pp. 3-9.

    12. Warner, Meeker, and Eell's Revised Scale for
Rating Occupation as found in Delbert C. Miller, Handbook of Research Design and Social Measurement (New York:
David McKay, 1964), pp. 103-5, was used. Their seven-
classification scale was dichotomized into middle (1-5)
and lower (6-7) classes for this study. Middle-class
occupations included the following: (1) high executives,
proprietors of large concerns, and major professionals;
(2) business managers, proprietors of medium-sized businesses, and lesser professionals; (3) administrative personnel, small independent business owners, and semipro-
fessionals; (4) clerical and sales workers, technicians,
and owners of small businesses; and (5) skilled manual
employees. Some of the last class were included in the

working-class category, which was primarily composed of
(6) machine operators and semiskilled employees and (7)
unskilled workers (plus the unemployed).

13. Frank Andrews, James Morgan, and John Sonquist,
Multiple Classification Analysis (Ann Arbor: Institute
for Social Research, University of Michigan, 1967).

14. Described in John A. Sonquist and James N. Morgan, The Detection of Interaction Effects: A Report on
a Computer Program for the Selection of Optimal Combinations of Explanatory Variables, Monograph No. 35, Survey
Research Center, Institute for Social Research (Ann
Arbor: University of Michigan Press, 1964).

BIBLIOGRAPHY

Adelson, Joseph, and Robert P. O'Neil. "The Growth of
    Political Ideas in Adolescence: The Sense of Commu-
    nity," Journal of Personality and Social Psychology,
    IV, 3 (September 1966), 295-306.

Adler, Norman, and Charles Harrington, eds. The Learning
    of Political Behavior. Glenview, Ill.: Scott, Fores-
    man, 1970.

Agger, Robert E., Marshall N. Goldstein, and Stanley A.
    Pearl. "Political Cynicism: Meaning and Measure-
    ments," Journal of Politics, XXIII (August 1961), 477-
    506.

Almaguer, Tomas. "Toward the Study of Chicano Colonialism,"
    Aztlan, II, 1 (Spring 1970), 7-20.

Almond, Gabriel A. "A Functional Approach to Comparative
    Politics." In Gabriel A. Almond and James S. Coleman,
    eds., The Politics of the Developing Areas. Prince-
    ton, N.J.: Princeton University Press, 1960.

_____, and Sidney Verba. The Civic Culture. Boston:
    Little, Brown, 1965.

Andrews, Frank, James Morgan, and John Sonquist. Multiple
    Classification Analysis. Ann Arbor: Institute for
    Social Research, University of Michigan, 1967.

Baker, Donald S. "Political Socialization: Parameters
    and Predispositions," Polity, III, 4 (Summer 1971),
    586-600.

Ballis, George, et al. Basta! La Historia de Nuestra
    Lucha (The Tale of Our Struggle). Delano, Calif.:
    Farm Workers Press, 1966.

Barrera, Mario, Carlos Muñoz, and Charles Ornelas. "The
    Barrio as an Internal Colony." In Harlan Hahn, ed.,
    Urban Politics and People. Beverly Hills, Calif.:
    Sage Publications, 1972.

Bender, Gerald. "Political Socialization and Political Change," Western Political Quarterly, XX (June 1967), 390-407.

Berelson, Bernard R., Paul Lazarsfeld, and William N. Mc-Phee. Voting. Chicago: University of Chicago Press, 1954.

Brim, Orville G., and Stanton Wheeler. Socialization After Childhood. New York: John Wiley & Sons, 1966.

California State Advisory Committee to the U.S. Commission on Civil Rights. Political Participation of Mexican Americans in California: A Report. Washington, D.C.: The Commission, 1971.

California State Department of Education, Bureau of Intergroup Relations, Division of Compensatory Education. Racial and Ethnic Survey of California Public Schools: Fall 1967. California State Department of Education, 1969.

Campbell, Angus, et al. The American Voter: An Abridgement. New York: John Wiley & Sons, 1964.

_____, Gerald Gurin, and Warren Miller. The Voter Decides. Evanston, Ill.: Row, Peterson, 1954.

Casavantes, E. J. A New Look at the Attributes of the Mexican American. Albuquerque, N.M.: Southwest Cooperative Educational Laboratory, 1969.

Child, Irwin L. "Socialization." In Gardner Lindzey, ed., Handbook of Social Psychology. Vol. II. Cambridge, Mass.: Harvard University Press, 1954.

Chilicott, John H. "Some Perspectives for Teaching First Generation Mexican-Americans." In John H. Chilicott, Norman Greenberg, and Herbert B. Wilson, eds., Readings in the Socio-Cultural Foundations of Education. Belmont, Calif.: Wadsworth, 1968.

Clark, Margaret. Health in the Mexican-American Culture. Berkeley: University of California Press, 1959.

Cnudde, Charles F., and Donald J. McCrone. "The Linkage Between Constituency Attitudes and Congressional Voting

Behavior: A Causal Model," _American Political Science Review_, LX (March 1966), 66-72.

Cook, Thomas, and Frank Scioli, Jr. "Political Socialization Research in the United States: A Review." In Dan Nimmo and Charles Bonjean, eds., _Political Attitudes and Public Opinion_. New York: David McKay, 1972.

Cornbleth, Catherine. "Political Socialization and the Social Studies: Political Beliefs of Mexican-American Youth." Mimeo., University of Texas, Austin, 1971.

Coser, Lewis. _The Function of Social Conflict_. Glencoe, Ill.: The Free Press, 1956.

Crick, Bernard. _In Defence of Politics_. Baltimore: Penguin Books, 1964.

Dawson, Richard E. "Political Socialization." In James Robinson, ed., _Political Science Annual: An International Review_. Vol. I. Indianapolis and New York: Bobbs-Merrill, 1966.

_____, and Kenneth Prewitt. _Political Socialization_. Boston: Little, Brown, 1969.

Day, Mark. _Forty Acres: Cesar Chavez and the Farm Workers_. New York: Praeger Publishers, 1971.

Dennis, Jack. "Major Problems of Political Socialization Research," _Midwest Journal of Political Science_, XII, 1 (February 1968), 85-114.

_____, et al. "Political Socialization to Democratic Orientations in Four Western Systems," _Comparative Political Studies_, I, 1 (April 1968), 71-101.

Derbyshire, Robert L. "The Adaptation of Adolescent Mexican Americans to United States Society," _American Behavioral Scientist_, XIII, 1 (September-October 1969), 88-103.

DiPalma, Giuseppe, and Herbert McCloskey. "Personality and Conformity: The Learning of Political Attitudes," _American Political Science Review_, LXIV, 4 (December 1970), 1054-74.

Doob, Leonard W. Patriotism and Nationalism. New Haven, Conn.: Yale University Press, 1964.

Dunne, John Gregory. Delano. New York: Farrar, Straus and Giroux, 1967.

Easton, David. A Framework for Political Analysis. New York: Prentice-Hall, 1965.

_____. "An Approach to the Analysis of Political Systems," World Politics, IX (1957), 383-400.

_____. A Systems Analysis of Political Life. New York: John Wiley & Sons, 1965.

_____, and Jack Dennis. Children in the Political System: Origins of Political Legitimacy. New York: McGraw-Hill, 1969.

_____. "The Child's Acquisition of Regime Norms: Political Efficacy," American Political Science Review, LXI (March 1967), 25-38.

_____. "The Child's Image of Government," The Annals of the American Academy of Political and Social Science, CCCLXI (September 1965), 40-57.

Easton, David, and Robert D. Hess. "The Child's Political World," Midwest Journal of Political Science, VI (August 1962), 229-46.

_____. "Youth and the Political System." In S. M. Lipset and L. Lowenthal, eds., Culture and Social Character. New York: The Free Press, 1961.

Ehman, Lee H. "An Analysis of the Relationships of Selected Educational Variables with the Political Socialization of High School Students," American Educational Research Journal, VI (November 1969), 559-80.

Elkin, Frederick. The Child and Society: The Process of Socialization. New York: Random House, 1960.

Engstrom, Richard L. "Race and Compliance: Differential Political Socialization," Polity, III (Fall 1970), 100-11.

245

Froman, Lewis A. "Personality and Political Socialization," Journal of Politics, XXIII, 2 (May 1967), 341-52.

Galarza, Ernesto. Spiders in the House and Workers in the Field. Notre Dame, Ind.: Notre Dame University Press, 1970.

Gamson, William A. Power and Discontent. Homewood, Ill.: Dorsey, 1968.

Gardner, Richard M. Grito! Reies Tijerina and the New Mexico Land Grant War of 1967. Indianapolis: Bobbs-Merrill, 1970.

Garson, G. David. Handbook of Political Science Methods. Boston: Holbrook Press, 1971.

Goodman, Mary Ellen. "Emergent Citizenship: A Study of Relevant Values in Four-Year Olds," Childhood Education, XXXV (1958-59), 248-51.

Goslin, David A., ed. Handbook of Socialization Theory and Research. Chicago: Rand McNally, 1968.

Grebler, Leo, Joan W. Moore, and Ralph C. Guzman. The Mexican American People: The Nation's Second Largest Minority. New York: The Free Press, 1970.

Greenberg, Edward S. "Black Children and the Political System," Public Opinion Quarterly, XXXIV, 3 (Fall 1970), 333-45.

_____. "Black Children, Self-Esteem and the Liberation Movement," Politics and Society, II, 3 (Spring 1972), 293-307.

_____. "Children and Government: A Comparison Across Racial Lines," Midwest Journal of Political Science, XIV, 1 (February 1970), 249-75.

_____. "Children and the Political Community: A Comparison Across Racial Lines," Canadian Journal of Political Science, II (December 1969), 471-92.

_____. "Orientations of Black and White Children to Political Authority Figures," Social Science Quarterly, LI 3 (December 1970), 561-71.

_____. "Political Socialization to Support of the System: A Comparison of Black and White Children." Unpublished Ph.D. thesis, University of Wisconsin, 1969.

Greenstein, Fred I. "A Note on the Ambiguity of 'Political Socialization': Definitions, Criticisms, and Strategies of Inquiry," Journal of Politics, XXXII, 4 (November 1970), 969-78.

_____. Children and Politics. New Haven, Conn.: Yale University Press, 1965.

_____. "More on Children's Images of the President," Public Opinion Quarterly, XXV, 4 (Winter 1961), 648-54.

_____. "Political Socialization." In David Sills, ed., International Encyclopedia of the Social Sciences. Vol. XIV. New York: Macmillan and The Free Press, 1968.

_____. "Sex-Related Political Differences in Childhood," Journal of Politics, XXIII, 2 (May 1961), 353-71.

_____. "The Benevolent Leader: Children's Images of Political Authority," American Political Science Review, LIV, 4 (December 1960), 934-43.

_____. "The Standing of Social and Psychological Variables: An Addendum to Jackman's Critique," Journal of Politics, XXXII (November 1970), 989-92.

Guzman, Ralph C. "The Political Socialization of the Mexican American People." Unpublished Ph.D. thesis, University of California, Los Angeles, 1970.

Heller, Celia S. Mexican American Youth: Forgotten Youth at the Crossroads. New York: Random House, 1968.

Hernandez, Deluvina. Mexican American Challenge to a Sacred Cow. Los Angeles: Mexican American Cultural Center, University of California, 1970.

Hess, Robert D. "Political Socialization in the Schools," Harvard Educational Review, XXXVII (Summer 1968), 528-36.

_____, and David Easton. "The Child's Changing Image of the President," Public Opinion Quarterly, XXIV (1960), 632-44.

_____, and Judith V. Torney. The Development of Political Attitudes in Children. Chicago: Aldine, 1967.

Hirsch, Herbert. Poverty and Politicization: Political Socialization in an American Sub-Culture. New York: The Free Press, 1971.

Horowitz, Eugene L. "Some Aspects of the Development of Patriotism in Children," Sociometry, III, 4 (October 1940), 329-41.

Horowitz, George. La Causa: The California Grape Strike. New York: Macmillan, 1970.

Howard, John R., ed. Awakening Minorities. Chicago: Aldine, 1970.

Hyman, Herbert. Political Socialization. Glencoe, Ill.: The Free Press, 1959.

Jackson, John S. "A Political Socialization Bibliography and Survey of Projects in Progress," Mimeo. prepared for the Committee on Pre-Collegiate Education, American Political Science Association, September 1972.

Jahoda, Gustav. "The Development of Children's Ideas About Country and Nationality," Parts I, II, British Journal of Educational Psychology, XXXIII (June 1963), 47-60, 143-53.

Jaros, Dean. "Children's Orientations Toward the President: Some Additional Theoretical Considerations and Data," Journal of Politics, XXIX, 2 (May 1967), 368-87.

_____, Herbert Hirsch, and Frederic Fleron, Jr. "The Malevolent Leader: Political Socialization in an American Sub-Culture," American Political Science Review, LXII, 2 (June 1968), 564-75.

Jennings, M. Kent. "Pre-Adult Orientations to Multiple Systems of Government," Midwest Journal of Politics, II, 3 (1967), 291-317.

_____, and L. F. Fox. "The Conduct of Socio-Political Research in Schools: Strategies and Problems of Access," School Review, LXXVI (December 1968), 428-44.

_____, and Kenneth P. Langton. "Mothers Versus Fathers: The Formation of Political Orientations Among Young Americans," Journal of Politics, XXXI, 2 (May 1969), 329-58.

_____, and Richard G. Niemi. "The Division of Political Labor Between Mother and Father," American Political Science Review, LXV, 1 (March 1971), 69-83.

_____. "Patterns of Political Learning," Harvard Educational Review, XXXVIII (Summer 1968), 443-67.

_____. "The Transmission of Political Values from Parent to Child," American Political Science Review, LXII, 1 (March 1968), 169-84.

Key, V. O. Public Opinion and American Democracy. New York: Alfred A. Knopf, 1961.

Kluckhohn, Florence R., and Fred L. Strodtbeck. Variations in Value Orientations. Evanston, Ill.: Row, Peterson, 1961.

Knowles, Louis, and Kenneth Prewitt, eds. Institutional Racism in America. Englewood Cliffs, N.J.: Prentice-Hall, 1969.

Lambert, Wallace E., and Otto Klineberg. Children's Views of Foreign Peoples: A Cross-National Study. New York: Appleton-Century-Crofts, 1967.

Langton, Kenneth P. "Peer Group and School and the Political Socialization Process," American Political Science Review, LXI (1967), 751-58.

_____. Political Socialization. New York: Oxford University Press, 1969.

_____, and M. Kent Jennings. "Political Socialization and the High School Civics Curriculum in the United States," The American Political Science Review, LXII, 3 (September 1968), 852-67.

_____, and David A. Karns. "The Relative Influence of the Family, Peer Group and School in the Development of Political Efficacy," Western Political Science Quarterly, XXII (December 1969), 813-26.

Laurence, Joan E. "White Socialization: Black Reality," Psychiatry, XXXIII (May 1970), 174-94.

_____, and Harry M. Scoble. "Ideology and Consensus Among Children of the Socioeconomic Elite," Western Political Quarterly, XXII, 1 (March 1969), 151-62.

Lawson, Edwin D. "Development of Patriotism in Children: A Second Look," Journal of Psychology, LV, 2 (April 1963), 279-86.

Lee, David Lopez. "Mexican-American Fatalism--An Analysis and Some Speculations," Journal of Mexican American Studies, I, 1 (Fall 1970), 44-53.

Levine, Robert. "Political Socialization and Cultural Change." In Clifford Goertz, ed., Old Societies and New States. Glencoe, Ill.: The Free Press, 1963.

Litt, Edgar. "Civic Education, Community Norms, and Political Indoctrination," American Sociological Review, XXVIII, 1 (February 1963), 69-75.

_____. Ethnic Politics in America. Glenview, Ill.: Scott, Foresman, 1970.

_____. "Political Cynicism and Political Futility," Journal of Politics, XXV (May 1963), 312-23.

Lyons, Schley. "The Political Socialization of Ghetto Children: Efficacy and Cynicism," Journal of Politics, XXXII, 2 (May 1970), 288-304.

Madsden, William H. Mexican Americans of South Texas. New York: Holt, Rinehart and Winston, 1964.

Marvick, Dwaine. "The Political Socialization of the American Negro," The Annals of the American Academy of Political and Social Sciences, CCCLXI (September 1965), 112-27.

Matthiessen, Peter. Sal Si Puedes: Cesar Chavez and the New American Revolution. New York: Random House, 1969.

McCloskey, Herbert. "Consensus and Ideology in American Politics," _American Political Science Review_, LVIII (June 1964), 361-82.

Merelman, Richard M. "Learning and Legitimacy," _American Political Science Review_, LX, 3 (September 1966), 548-61.

_____. "The Adolescence of Political Socialization," _Sociology of Education_, XLV, 2 (Spring 1972), 134-66.

Milbrath, Lester. _Political Participation_. Chicago: Rand, McNally, 1965.

Miller, Delbert C. _Handbook of Research Design and Social Measurement_. New York: David McKay, 1964.

Miller, Warren, and Donald Stokes. "Constituency Influence in Congress," _American Political Science Review_, LVII (March 1963), 45-56.

Morales, Armando. _Ando Sangrando (I Am Bleeding): A Study of Mexican American-Police Conflict_. La Puente, Calif.: Perspectiva Publications, 1972.

Mussen, Paul. _The Psychological Development of the Child_. Englewood Cliffs, N.J.: Prentice-Hall, 1963.

Myrdal, Gunnar. _An American Dilemma_. New York: Harper, 1944.

Nabokov, Peter. _Tijerina and the Courthouse Raid_. Albuquerque: University of New Mexico Press, 1966.

Nelson, Eugene. _Huelga: The First Hundred Days of the Great Delano Grape Strike_. Delano, Calif.: Farm Workers Press, 1966.

Orbell, John. "Protest Activity Among Southern Negro College Students," _American Political Science Review_, LXI, 2 (June 1967), 446-56.

Parenti, Michael J. "Ethnic Politics and the Persistence of Ethnic Identification," _American Political Science Review_, LXI (September 1967), 717-26.

Patrick, John J. Political Socialization of American
    Youth: Implications for Secondary School Social
    Studies--A Review of Research, Research Bulletin No.
    3. Washington, D.C.: National Council for the Social
    Studies, 1967.

Piaget, Jean, and Anne-Marie Weil. "The Development in
    Children of the Idea of the Homeland and of Relations
    with Other Countries," International Social Science
    Bulletin, III (1951), 561-78.

Pino, Tom, and Daniel T. Valdes. "Ethnic Labels in Major-
    ity-Minority Relations," Journal of Mexican-American
    Studies, I, 1 (Fall 1970), 16-30.

Rebelsky, Freda, Cheryl Conover, and Patricia Chafetz.
    "The Development of Political Attitudes in Young
    Children," Journal of Psychology, LXXIII (November
    1969), 141-46.

Rendon, Armando. Chicano Manifesto. New York: Macmillan,
    1971.

Rodgers, Harrell R., and George Taylor. "Pre-Adult Atti-
    tudes Toward Legal Compliance: Notes Toward a Theory,"
    Social Science Quarterly, LI, 3 (December 1970), 539-
    51.

_____. "The Policeman as an Agent of Regime Legitima-
    tion," Midwest Journal of Political Science, XV, 1
    (February 1971), 72-86.

Romano, Octavio I. "The Anthropology and Sociology of the
    Mexican Americans: The Distortion of Mexican American
    History," El Grito, II, 1 (Fall 1968), 13-16.

Sanchez, George. Forgotten People. Albuquerque: Univer-
    sity of New Mexico Press, 1940.

Schonfeld, William R. "The Forms of Political Socializa-
    tion Research: An Evaluation," World Politics, XXIII,
    3 (April 1971), 544ff.

Schwartz, A. J. "Comparative Study of Values and Achieve-
    ments: Mexican American and Anglo Youth," Sociology
    of Education, XLIV (Fall 1971), 438-62.

Scott, Robert E. "Mexico." In Sidney Verba and Lucien W.
Pye, eds., Political Culture and Political Development. Princeton, N.J.: Princeton University Press,
1965.

Sears, David O. "Black Attitudes Toward the Political System in the Aftermath of the Watts Insurrection," Midwest Journal of Political Science, XIII (November
1969), 515-44.

_____, and J. B. McConkay. "Racial Socialization, Com-
parison Levels, and the Watts Riots," Journal of Social
Issues, XXVI, 1 (Winter 1970), 121-40.

Seasholes, Bradbury. "Political Socialization of Negroes:
Image Development of Self and Polity." In William C.
Kvaraceus, ed., Negro Self-Concept: Implications for
School and Citizenship. New York: McGraw-Hill, 1965.

Sewell, William H. "Some Recent Developments in Socializa-
tion Theory and Research," The Annals of the American
Academy of Political and Social Science, CCCXLIX
(June 1963), 163-81.

Sigel, Roberta S. "An Exploration into Some Aspects of
Political Socialization: School Children's Reactions
to the Death of a President." In Martha Wolfenstern
and Gilbert Kliman, eds., Children and the Death of
a President: Multidisciplinary Studies. Garden City,
N.Y.: Doubleday, 1965.

_____. "Assumptions About the Learning of Political
Values," The Annals of the American Academy of Political and Social Science, CCCLXI (September 1965), 1-10.

_____. "Image of a President: Some Insights into the
Political Views of School Children," American Political Science Review, XLII (March 1968), 216-24.

_____. "Television and the Reactions of School Children
to the Assassination." In Bradley S. Greenberg and
Edwin B. Parker, eds., The Kennedy Assassination and
the American Public. Stanford, Calif.: Stanford University Press, 1965.

Sonquist, John A., and James N. Morgan. The Detection of
Interaction Effects: A Report on a Computer Program

for the Selection of Optimal Combinations of Explana-
tory Variables. Monograph No. 35, Survey Research
Center, Institute for Social Research. Ann Arbor:
University of Michigan Press, 1964.

Steiner, Stan. La Raza: The Mexican Americans. New York:
Harper and Row, 1969.

Stevens, Alden Jay. "Children's Acquisitions of Regime
Norms in Subcultures of Race and Social Class: The
Problem of System Maintenance." Unpublished Ph.D.
thesis, University of Maryland, 1969.

Stone, Chuck. Black Political Power in America. New
York: Dell, 1970.

Stouffer, Samuel A. Communism, Conformity and Civil Liberties. New York: Doubleday, 1955.

Targ, Harry R. "Children's Developing Orientations to International Politics," Journal of Peace Research, VII,
2 (1970), 79-98.

Tirado, Miguel D. "Mexican American Community Organiza-
tion--The Key to Chicano Political Power," Aztlan,
I (Spring 1970), 53-78.

Tuck, Ruth D. Not with the Fist: Mexican-Americans in a
Southwest City. New York: Harcourt, Brace, 1956.

U.S. Bureau of the Census. Census of Population: 1970,
General Social and Economic Characteristics, Final
Report, PC(1)-C6, California. Washington, D.C.: The
Bureau, 1972.

U.S. Commission on Civil Rights. Mexican Americans and the
Administration of Justice in the Southwest. Washington, D.C.: The Commission, 1970.

U.S. National Advisory Commission on Civil Disorders. Report of the National Advisory Commission on Civil
Disorders. Washington, D.C.: The Commission, 1968.

Vaca, Nick C. "The Mexican American in the Social Sciences:
1912-1970," El Grito, III (Spring 1970), 3-24, and IV
(Fall 1970), 17-52.

Walker, Jack L. "A Critique of the Elitist Theory of
Democracy," American Political Science Review, LX
(June 1966), 285-95.

Wilcox, Walter. "The Congressional Poll and Non-Poll."
In Edward C. Dreyer and Walter A. Rosenbaum, eds.,
Political Opinion and Electoral Behavior. Belmont,
Calif.: Wadsworth, 1966.

Wolfinger, Raymond. "The Development and Persistence of
Ethnic Voting," American Political Science Review,
LIX (December 1965), 896-908.

Young, Donald R. "The Socialization of Minority Peoples."
In David A. Goslin, ed., Handbook of Socialization
Theory and Research. Chicago: Rand, McNally, 1968.

F. CHRIS GARCIA is Assistant Professor of Political Science at the University of New Mexico in Albuquerque. His professional interests center on political education and ethnic politics, particularly with regard to Mexican Americans, and he is the author of several articles and papers on these topics. Currently, he is a member of the Pre-Collegiate Education Committee and the Committee on the Status of Chicanos of the American Political Science Association.

Dr. Garcia, a native Albuquerquean, spent his early years in New Mexico and the Los Angeles area of California. He received his bachelor's degree from the University of New Mexico and his doctorate degree in political science from the University of California at Davis.

Professor Garcia's teaching experience includes positions at the high school and junior college level, as well as faculty appointments at universities in California, Indiana, and New Mexico.

BLACK COMMUNITY CONTROL
A Study of Transition in a Texas Ghetto

Joyce E. Williams

BLACK STUDENTS AT WHITE COLLEGES

Charles V. Willie and Arline Sakuma McCord

CHILDREN AND THE URBAN ENVIRONMENT: A LEARNING EXPERIENCE
Evaluation of the WGBH-TV Educational Project

Marshall Kaplan, Gans, and Kahn

DEADLOCK IN SCHOOL DESEGREGATION
A Case Study of Inglewood, California

Edna Bonacich and Robert F. Goodman